PAUL ELMER MORE
AND AMERICAN CRITICISM

Other Books by the Same Author

CHRISTIANITY AND NATURALISM
PROGRESS AND SCIENCE

PAUL ELMER MORE

AND

AMERICAN CRITICISM

BY

ROBERT SHAFER

NEW HAVEN · YALE UNIVERSITY PRESS
LONDON · HUMPHREY MILFORD · OXFORD UNIVERSITY PRESS
MDCCCCXXXV

TO

MARTHA

PREFACE

THE writing of this book has extended over a considerable period, in part because of a rather long interruption, arising from circumstances outside of my control. The first and second chapters were written during the winter of 1932–1933. Chapter III was written in the following spring and summer, and Chapter IV was then immediately begun. It had to be laid aside, however, for about six months, and was not completed until last spring. The concluding chapter was written during the summer. I mention this because the question "When?" always has some bearing upon a discussion of contemporaries. Had my first chapter, for example, been written more recently, I should doubtless have referred to Miss Gertrude Stein's latest deviation into sense, and perhaps to several other books by other writers. Yet nothing has appeared during the last year and a half which suggests the desirability of altering the argument or any of the conclusions of this chapter, so that it has seemed best to me to allow it to stand as it was originally written, without factitious additions.

I should like to thank the publishers named below for permission to quote from the following books and articles: *The Great Refusal, A Century of Indian Epigrams*, and *Shelburne Essays*, First, Second, Third, Fifth, Sixth, Seventh, Eighth, and Ninth Series, by P. E. More (all published by Houghton Mifflin Company, with whom special arrangement has been made); *The Demon of the Absolute, Platonism, The Religion of Plato, Hellenistic Philosophies, The Christ of the New Testament, Christ the Word*, and *The Catholic Faith*, by P. E. More (Princeton University Press); *Expression in America*, by Ludwig Lewisohn (Harper & Brothers); *The Creative Life*, by Ludwig Lewisohn

(Liveright Publishing Corporation); Ludwig Lewisohn's "Introduction" to *A Modern Book of Criticism* (The Modern Library, Inc.); *The Life and Letters of Stuart P. Sherman,* by Jacob Zeitlin and Homer Woodbridge (Farrar & Rinehart, Inc.); Van Wyck Brooks's "Letters and Leadership" in *Three Essays on America* (published and copyrighted by E. P. Dutton & Company); *The New History and Social Studies,* by Harry Elmer Barnes (D. Appleton-Century Company); *Notes of a Son and Brother,* by Henry James (Charles Scribner's Sons); *Axel's Castle,* by Edmund Wilson (Charles Scribner's Sons); "Notes on Babbitt and More," by Edmund Wilson (*The New Republic*); *Selected Essays,* by T. S. Eliot (copyrighted, 1932, by Harcourt, Brace & Company, Inc.); "As an Irishman Sees It," by Ernest Boyd, in *Civilization in the United States,* edited by Harold E. Stearns (Harcourt, Brace & Company, Inc.); Francis Hackett's review of *A New England Group and Others, Shelburne Essays,* Eleventh Series (*The New Republic*); "Humanism as Dogma," by Walter Lippmann (*The Saturday Review of Literature*); Clifton Fadiman's review of the *Collected Plays* of Noel Coward (*The New Yorker*); *The Great Tradition,* by Granville Hicks (The Macmillan Company); and J. E. Spingarn's "The New Criticism," in *Criticism in America* (Harcourt, Brace & Company, Inc.). I have also gratefully received Dr Spingarn's personal permission to quote from "The New Criticism," and the permission of Mr Bernard Bandler, II, to quote from "Paul Elmer More and the External World," in *The Critique of Humanism,* edited by C. Hartley Grattan. (The publishers of this book are no longer in business, and I have been unable to learn whether or not the copyright has been taken over by any other house.) Finally, by special arrangement with Alfred A. Knopf, Inc., I have received permission to quote from *Prejudices,* Second, Third, and Fourth Series, and *Treatise on the Gods,* by H. L. Mencken.

I owe hearty thanks to Dean Louis T. More of the University of Cincinnati for the loan of several scarce books and for much other kindness; and I am specially indebted to Mr Paul Elmer More, who has patiently answered many questions. It is possible that other questions which have been the subject of friendly debate between us, concerning for the most part Mr More's interpretation of Plato, may be answered in his forthcoming volume of "New Shelburne Essays," *The Sceptical Approach to Religion*. To that, at any rate, we must look for his final word on Plato and for a systematic explanation of his own religious position.

R. S.

Graduate School,
University of Cincinnati,
2 October, 1934.

CONTENTS

Which is the wiser part d'ye think,
T'approve, and smile, and eat, and drink;
Or sourly criticisms mutter,
And quarrel with your bread and butter?

RICHARD OWEN CAMBRIDGE

PAUL ELMER MORE AND
AMERICAN CRITICISM

I. CRITICISM

I

"CRITICISM," Mr T. S. Eliot has remarked, "is as inevitable as breathing." This is scarcely self-evident; and indeed the comparison at once suggests certain obvious dissimilarities. There have been no important quarrels over the nature, purpose, or right method of breathing. It takes care of itself; is uniform; is universal; has not changed its character since long before the appearance of the first man; and will not change while the human race lasts. Notoriously, none of these things can be said of criticism.

Nevertheless, Mr Eliot is right; and only those who have been misled—possibly by this critic himself—can disagree with his pronouncement; though he might truly have added that criticism is also scarcely less important than breathing. For criticism is inseparable from intelligence. It is the food upon which intelligence is nourished, without which the development of civilized societies would be inconceivable. Most of us, however, take our civilization for granted, the basest sort even fancying they can safely play fast and loose with it, almost none realizing how hazardous and extraordinary an achievement it is, resting at every point upon the exercise of critical intelligence. This grave failure of the understanding should not be regarded as a cause for profound astonishment. Most of us are, after all, most of the time, stupid and thoughtless creatures; and in this particular case there is a definite further reason for our blindness; because, paradoxically enough, our very triumphs of critical discrimination foster the blindness I speak of—actually foster it, in a direct, positive manner which can be, as we shall see, very easily explained. Civilization, even when less complex than our modern overgrown societies, is a most intricate social structure, depending upon co-operative but highly differen-

tiated labour. Hence, as the work of men is divided and subdivided, criticism tends inevitably to become the particular
concern, and responsibility, of a small number devoted primarily to that one activity. More than this, at the same time
criticism itself is divided and subdivided. Exact science becomes an established and continuing factor in life in proportion as it achieves adequate critical standards and methods.
History becomes something more than mere legend as it
achieves its own appropriate critical standards and methods.
And so it is with every activity in which men are employed,
including, of course, literature.

The gains of specialization are so obvious, so irresistible,
that it is idle to talk of renouncing them. Yet this renunciation is advocated, even passionately advocated, from time to
time, because losses of the most serious kind also are in-
curred. The mere specialist is always something less than a
man, sometimes a great deal less, and is often a source of
deep injury to society. In general, he can be tolerated only
in so far as he can be humanized, or in so far as society can
otherwise protect itself against the combined bigotry and
wrongheadedness normally accompanying extreme specialization. Lopsidedness, however, may go very far without protest or check—with, on the contrary, a general feeling of
satisfaction, and conviction that thus men have become splen-
didly progressive—when a society happens to be cut off
partially from its own past, when it inclines towards individualism and equalitarianism, when it enjoys great and widespread material prosperity, and when it is evident that its
prosperity has arisen largely from the work of scientific
specialists.

This has been, in brief, our situation in America. The
necessity of criticism has been adequately recognized only
within certain special and clearly defined fields. Within them,
genuine, vigorous, and fruitful criticism has flourished. But,
though it has been indispensable, its pertinence has been
strictly limited—has been special, not general. And the consequence is that most of us, when the subject of criticism is
broached, do not think of these fields at all. We think only
of the fine arts, and chiefly of literature. For this there is a

reason which presently will be mentioned; but first it is to be noticed that literature, like everything else, tends to follow the line of least resistance. In an age of specialization it also tends to become something special, to mark off a little field for itself where it may remain unchallenged. There are, because of the nature of literature, peculiar difficulties in the attempt, and, one must add, peculiar absurdities in the results—but this has only made it the more necessary for our "creators" to busy themselves in encouraging each other's efforts and in harshly warning off objectors. And they have thus brought into existence a considerable body of writing which attracts general attention and passes for criticism.

Concerning this ostensible criticism I shall have something to say. It is necessary, however, in order to understand and rightly to value either this or any other specialized development, to go back to the common source of all criticism. We cannot turn to philosophy, to which, in the division of labour, the task of general criticism is entrusted, because philosophy to-day has become—as fully as any of the exact sciences or any of the branches of history—a specialized activity. Its votaries have withdrawn into a corner of their own, where they can be seen talking to each other with evident interest, some even with evident excitement;—but what they are saying is interesting chiefly to themselves, and seems, when we overhear some part of the conversation, suspiciously like the subtle argument over questions at once insoluble and trifling which fatally attracted philosophers towards the close of the Middle Age. It may be retorted, of course, that our opinion would be different could we be forced into the metaphysical corner, and could we then understand everything we heard. But such a retort is really an acknowledgement that the situation described does exist, whatever the plausible or compelling reasons. There are, however, certainly exceptions, shining or other; and, in general, I hope it may be understood that I am summarily describing nothing absolute, but only a pronounced tendency.

In the direction of this tendency we have, nevertheless, gone a great distance; and this is, I believe, universally recognized. But in so far as we have become a nation of specialists

we have become not only uncritical—we have largely forgotten what criticism is—even though we are wholly dependent on it in varying rigidly limited spheres, and for varying
strictly defined purposes. We have learned the importance of
having pure water to drink. There are a few men who have
made it their business in life to know all about this particular
thing, who have devised methods of testing water and of
purifying it when it fails to satisfy their requirements, and
who also have devised means of storing it safely and of con-
veying it, still pure, to our homes. We entrust our lives to
these men without hesitation or question, relinquishing in
their favour this special problem and so freeing ourselves for
other tasks, because we know in a general way that their
methods are scrupulously careful and that in practice these
experts do succeed. Here is probably the simplest and most
familiar illustration that can be given of the nature and import of criticism, in one of its characteristic modern forms.
The uncritical attitude towards water is, in thickly popu-
lated areas, a standing invitation to disease. The adoption of
the critical attitude results in the elimination of danger. In
what does the difference consist? Only one answer is possible:
it consists fundamentally in scepticism, which in turn renders discrimination possible, and the creation of standards.
Doubt concerning that which hitherto has been accepted
without question prompts examination. Despite its harmless
appearance, water is scrutinized carefully. As a consequence,
standards are established; and water which conforms to these
standards can safely be drunk. "Purity" in this connexion
means simply this, and nothing more. We now take pure
water for granted. Our municipalities pay experts to keep
looking after the matter, and we ourselves think no more of
it. For a trifling monetary consideration we purchase the
privilege of remaining just as uncritical of the water we
drink as were our ancestors a hundred and fifty years ago.
Because of the specialized character of this achievement,
moreover, we describe it as a triumph of bacteriological science, and so blind ourselves to its real nature.

For this achievement is a triumph of criticism, and in it
we see criticism for what it essentially and really is. Upon

it, as was said, is built the whole fabric of our civilization. Without it even mere existence is unimaginable. It is the common element in countless triumphs which we think of as different only because their circumstances and applications differentiate them from each other. There is a popular saying which good Americans are fond of: The man who hesitates is lost. But in the case glanced at—and in how many others!—the man who does not hesitate is lost, and thousands with him. There is a time for hesitation as truly as there is a time for action; and perhaps the invariable characteristic of the stupid man is his inability to distinguish these times with any certainty. It is, in fact, the ability to discriminate successfully which is the very foundation of intelligence.

The importance of intelligence, fortunately, needs no emphasis. One gets the impression that some of our social scientists have sweet visions of themselves standing as supreme law-givers to communities of morons. But, however it may be with our children's imbecile children in some perfectly planned society, gyrating with the precision and monotony of the complex machines of to-day, we meanwhile need all the intelligence we have, and more. An uncritical intelligence, however, is an absurd contradiction; and in fact we are intelligent to precisely the extent that we are critical, and no further. This is the measure of criticism's importance. What we also have to realize is that fundamentally criticism consists in the effort to solve the problems given us by life—to solve them, not to shut our eyes to them and rush blindly through the years from birth to death. The example I have given exhibits the complete and exact solution of a problem in the sphere of "public health," as it is oddly called. I need not dwell upon the number or the variety of the problems every man is faced with. All of them, however, no matter how various in character they may be, have one common source. They are recognized as problems when, for whatever reason, we become sceptical—when doubt forces itself into the field of consciousness, and causes us to stop, and examine, and try to understand before we decide how to think or act.

This, then, is the basis of all that can be called criticism. And in every field the process of criticism—identical, really, with the emergence and development of intelligence—is fundamentally the same. Actuated by scepticism, the critic must first endeavour to take in, fully and fairly, the situation or thing before him. His effort of appreciation may require study or careful analysis. In any event it demands a sensitive receptiveness, and a firm refusal to conclude hastily. The critic's concern is not with superficial appearances, but with the realities, often—as in the case of bacterial growths in water—invisible to the unaided or careless eye. Such concern naturally prohibits the critic from paying heed to popular clamour or commonly received opinion—save as these may, at times, be real parts of the problem before him—and it equally compels him to be resolute, disinterested, and scrupulous. Nothing is to be taken for granted, and the case is not to be prejudged.

It is, however, to be judged, and this is the reason for painstaking examination of it. The water, it will be recalled, was to be judged "pure" or "impure." The standard by which it was to be measured was unmistakably present in the circumstances which brought about critical inquiry. In general, this is how judgement becomes possible; and we understand what the judgement means because it is a statement of the relation between the thing or situation judged and the standard employed—or, in other words, the circumstances which suggested critical scrutiny. "I can judge but poorly of anything while I measure it by no other standard than itself," wrote Burke, with a feeling for the truth of the matter, but with an imperfect grasp on it. For it is not only difficult, it is impossible to form a judgement save in relation to standards derived from some source other than the object judged. The erection of standards, consequently, is important—is a fundamental part of the process of criticism.

But when we reach the question of standards we have arrived at the point where criticism can no longer be discussed in general terms. Up to this point it not only can be so discussed, but must be, if we are ever to know what it is. We can now see it as an organic part of the life of man. It is by no means the whole of life; it is the deliberative part, pre-

liminary to the life of action. But, though only an instrument, it is indispensable if we are to live and act intelligently.
The standards, however, through which the critical process
is completed, are many, not few, and are of various kinds,
not reducible to unity; because they are derived from the
whole field of man's experience, and are perforce narrowed,
more closely defined, and increased in number as we divide
and subdivide that field in furtherance of human purposes.
If I may revert again to the example I have used, it is evident that the purpose here entertained was the preservation
of health. Doubt arose concerning the relation between this
purpose and drinking water. Thus a standard for water
came to be erected; and obviously the standard would be
useful in proportion as it could be exactly and completely
formulated;—but, at the same time and in the same proportion, it would also be useless for any other purpose, and for
any other substance than water. Hence it is that when we
once have seen how standards come to be erected, and what
part they play in criticism, no further generalizations concerning them are possible.

II

THE reason why most of us in the present age, when the subject of criticism is opened, think only, as I have said, of the
fine arts, and chiefly of literature, can now be made clear. I
must first observe, however, that though there is a certain
undeniable unity binding these arts together, I shall concern
myself in what follows only with literature. For while the
admitted, yet elusive, underlying unity of the arts has again
and again tempted men to elaborate abstract aesthetic theories, these theories have never satisfied anybody for long, and
have, indeed, always made thinking people extremely uncomfortable. There are, of course, discoverable reasons for
the "backwardness" of aesthetics, but this obviously is not
the place for a general discussion of the problem. Hence I
will merely say that at present, I am sure, nothing will be
lost, and much will be gained, if we confine our attention to
literature.

The written or spoken word, in truth, covers a field large

enough!—for literature reflects, in myriad ways, the whole range of man's life and experience. Thus its subject-matter is so intimate, varied, and indeterminate that it is not possible to erect clearly defined standards of judgement which are at all likely to be universally accepted as applicable and binding. This is the more true because literature has been immemorially composed, under constantly changing conditions. Furthermore, the processes of literary creation are in part mysterious. There have been a number of attempts to show that genius is really something else—a form of insanity, a capacity for taking infinite pains, and so on—but these cannot be regarded very seriously. If genius is only a form of insanity, it is a very special form of it—a form so unusual that we may call it, as the Greeks did, a *divine* madness. This definition, then, omits the very thing it was to account for, and so it is with the others;—and genius remains something really inexplicable, manifesting itself in ways which, also, cannot fully be explained. Works of genius are not, of course, independent of time or place; but attempts to reduce them to the terms of these and similar external circumstances always fail.

And hence it is that the relation of criticism to literature is necessarily very different from its relation to the sciences or to history. Criticism, as I have said, is an essential and inseparable part both of scientific discovery and of historical investigation; and precisely because of this it is taken for granted and, as criticism, is lost sight of. No impulse arises in these fields to question its character or value. It does its proper work to perfection, but does it, from the nature of the calls made on it, only for accurately defined purposes, within rigidly delimited special fields—with the result that we think of the differences between scientific achievements rather than of the process of discovery; and, even when we think of scientific method, tend to focus our attention on details—on techniques developed for special purposes—rather than on the common fundamental nature of all scientific inquiry.

But if we lose sight of the criticism implicated in science, partly because it is eminently successful criticism and partly,

too, because we have hitherto chiefly *used* science, without attempting to understand or to evaluate it, we remain familiar
with literary criticism because, in the first place, the critical
attitude is far less intimately and closely implicated in the
creation of literature. That this is a fact, simply to be accepted like all other given facts, history makes abundantly
clear; but the reason for it is no less evident. It is fully explained by what has just been said concerning genius. And
because the wind of inspiration bloweth where it listeth—a
truth, we observed, not in the least doubtful—it follows inevitably that "creation" is one thing, and judgement another. Confusion over precisely this distinction, we shall see,
is at the root of the whole "modernist" *débâcle*.[1] In addition,
as I have said, literature is so various in its forms, its subjects, and its implications, that it constitutes an inexhaustible mine for the study of humanity—but, for that very
reason, one which cannot be worked without skill and training. Indeed, in each generation, as conditions change and as
new material is added, the effort must constantly be renewed
to discriminate carefully literature's real bearings, relationships, and ordination; and the attempt must constantly be
made, even though it can never be wholly successful, to come
to the conclusions about man and his life which literature is
always *suggesting* in rich but chaotic variety, and which,
therefore, require comparison, analysis, combination, crys-
tallization. Hence the criticism of literature very early became established as a necessary *but independent* activity,
with a dual part to play. It took its place midway between

[1] This distinction exhibits a difference both striking and fundamental.
Nevertheless, it will be badly misunderstood if the difference is supposed to
be absolute. "Inspiration" has been important in science, as the biographies
of some of the greatest men of science clearly show. Criticism of the most
rigorous kind likewise may enter integrally into the creation of literature,
as Mr T. S. Eliot has correctly pointed out. He seems to have in mind, however, simply the "creator's" self-criticism in "sifting, combining, construct-
ing, expunging, correcting, testing" (*Selected Essays,* p. 30)—in other
words, strictly technical or aesthetic self-criticism—and even this, as far as
we know, has been deliberate and conscious only in the case of some writers,
at some times, in some places. It was with Horace; it was with Ben Jonson;
it was not with Shakespeare. The author of the treatise *On the Sublime* said
what still remains the last word on this subject.

writers and the public, aiming to serve the interests of each. This place it still keeps, and so has a recognized position of its own amongst us.

From ancient times, however, it has held its position with difficulty. Men have ever been more ready to believe and act than to pause for deliberation and reasoned decision, and the passage of years has not changed them in this respect. Many in our modern age, indeed, have suffered an access of barbaric wilfulness, induced, as we can now see, by the very triumphs of critical discrimination in specialized fields, which have encouraged the demi-intelligent to entertain fanciful notions concerning the security of civilization and concerning man's mastery over nature. On the one hand, consequently, the public has always tended to disregard the critics, and, on the other, creative writers have often tended not only to disregard critical judgements, but to regard critics themselves as natural enemies. In addition, as has been observed above, for approximately a century a growing number of writers have been trying to make of literature—or rather of the fine arts collectively—something highly specialized, with a field exclusively its own within which the creative artist might be completely free; and the view of criticism which has been spread abroad in support of this effort is really subversive of all critical activity, and is as confusing as it is itself confused.

III

THIS critical doctrine is more important than the creative literature which has necessitated it. The latter has small value except as a sign of the times; for its most characteristic pieces, in English, are the *Wasteland, Ulysses*, and the several productions of Miss Gertrude Stein. To Miss Stein, at least, we may be inclined to feel grateful; because she has made it impossible for any one who reads her, save Mr Edmund Wilson, to deceive himself concerning the results of encouraging artists—and others—to feel completely free. Miss Stein's precious volumes, however, have become rather notorious than familiar; and so have not hitherto been really useful from any point of view. And meanwhile the gospel of literary freedom is sedulously preached, and seems to be widely accepted as a desirable, "progressive" change, bringing criticism into line with other modern developments.

The doctrine may be stated briefly in the words of Mr T. S. Eliot and Dr J. E. Spingarn. When the critic goes seriously to work, says the former, he "must not coerce, and he must not make judgements of worse and better. He must simply elucidate: the reader will form the correct judgement for himself." Hence criticism, Mr Eliot adds, "is a development of sensibility." Sensibility is a gift, but it can be developed, through the development of pure or free intelligence. "And the free intelligence is that which is wholly devoted to inquiry." Its only motive-force is, of necessity, a boundless, impartial, disinterested curiosity, untainted by any constructive purpose. That which the critic's "elucidation" may make possible is the enjoyment of poetry; and "the end of the enjoyment of poetry is a pure contemplation from which all the accidents of personal emotion are removed."[2]

Dr Spingarn tells us that after many struggles, many mistakes, much misunderstanding, it has at length become clear that the critic's sole function is to answer, concerning any work of art, a single question: "What has it expressed, and how completely?" Dr Spingarn rings certain variations on this to show more fully his meaning:

What has the poet tried to do, and how has he fulfilled his intention? What is he striving to express and how has he expressed it? What vital and essential spirit animates his work, what central impression does it leave on the receptive mind, and how can I best express this impression? Is his work true to the laws of its own being rather than to laws formulated by others? These are the questions that modern critics have been taught to ask when face to face with the work of a poet. Only one *caveat* must be borne in mind when attempting to answer them; the poet's aim must be judged at the moment of the creative act,

[2] These passages are quoted from the essay entitled *The Perfect Critic,* in *The Sacred Wood.* The sentence quoted at the beginning of this chapter comes from *Tradition and the Individual Talent,* in the same volume.

that is to say, by the art of the poem itself, and not by the vague ambitions which he imagines to be his real intentions before or after the creative act is achieved.

Dr Spingarn further clarifies his meaning by pointing out the "dead lumber" and "weeds" disposed of by "the new criticism." "We," he says, have destroyed all "the old mechanical rules" or literary conventions; likewise "the *genres*, or literary kinds," and "the comic, the tragic, the sublime, and an army of vague abstractions of their kind"; also "the theory of style, with metaphor, simile, and all the paraphernalia of Graeco-Roman rhetoric." And in addition "we have done with all moral judgement of art as art," with "the confusion between the drama and the theatre," with "technique as separate from art," with "the history and criticism of poetic themes," with "the race, the time, the environment of a poet's work as an element in criticism," with "the 'evolution' of literature," and with "the old rupture between genius and taste."[3]

Dr Spingarn does not pretend that this doctrine is newer than it really is. It had its birth along with German romanticism, of which indeed it is an integral part, and was long ago presented to English readers by Carlyle. It was also presented to them by Coleridge; but both Carlyle's teacher, Goethe, and Coleridge gave it a form unacceptable to Dr Spingarn, so that, in speaking of Goethe, he suppresses part of the evidence, while he barely mentions Coleridge. It remained, in fact, for the Italian philosopher of our time, Benedetto Croce, to develop fully the theory that all art is simply "expression," and to conclude thence that all expression is art;—and it is as an ambassador or disciple of Senatore Croce that Dr Spingarn avowedly speaks.

The common element, obviously, binding together Mr Eliot and Dr Spingarn, is the contention that the critic's function is rigidly limited to "elucidation." And this is in truth the prevalent contemporary theory. It is held, for

[3] My quotations all come from a lecture entitled *The New Criticism* which was delivered at Columbia University on 9 March, 1910. Dr Spingarn has printed and reprinted this lecture a number of times in various volumes.

example, by Mr Edmund Wilson, who, in dedicating his
Axel's Castle to Dean Gauss of Princeton, writes: "It was
principally from you that I acquired my idea of what literary criticism ought to be—a history of man's ideas and imaginings in the setting of the conditions which have shaped
them." But this is an "idea" which Mr Wilson might have
acquired from almost any professor of literature almost anywhere in the United States at the time when he was an under-
graduate. There is a real difference, of course, which I should
not wish to minimize, between the professorial conception
and Dr Spingarn's conception of what is requisite for "elucidation." Indeed Mr Mencken, when he discovered—some
seven years after its first publication—the essay by Dr Spingarn from which I have quoted, accepted it with joy, chiefly
on the ground that it was "magnificently unprofessorial."[4]
Nevertheless, the resemblances between these gentlemen are
much more important than the differences. For in taking the
position that the critic can be concerned only with some kind
of "elucidation," they, and many more, have united simply
to betray criticism from within and to promote, as I have
said, endless confusion.

How have they done so? The effort already made to set
forth the real nature and place of criticism in human life
shows, I think conclusively, that the elimination of judgement, so vehemently demanded by those under discussion,
strikes at the heart of criticism, and thus opens the door to
chaos. What these gentlemen tell us is really that every contribution to literature must be uncritically accepted just as
it is. Every poem, every piece composed by a writer, is a
sacred organic structure, a pure gift to man from the system of things, and is consequently above or beyond judgement. Some of our contemporaries say in effect, with romanticists of a century and more ago, that the writer is a being
set apart from other men, animated by a Power which makes
him the mere medium of its revelations. The writer is thus
the "inspired" creator of pure beauty. Whatever he creates
is beauty. His creations are to be contemplated, studied, un-

---

[4] Subsequently, however, Mr Mencken repudiated Dr Spingarn.

derstood, enjoyed—but they are not to be questioned, or compared with the productions of other writers, or assessed in accordance with any notions of beauty hitherto prevalent, or considered as anything except embodiments of beauty. For not only is it true that whatever the writer creates *is* beauty, it is "pure" beauty and nothing else under the sun. Our new teachers are particularly insistent, as everybody knows, in asserting that beauty and goodness are wholly unrelated; but their argument, if it is accepted at all, perforce goes much further, and "proves" that beauty must be wholly unrelated to anything within our fields of experience.

Others amongst our contemporaries take a point of departure apparently quite different. They are converts to a philosophy of iron law, an unqualifiedly deterministic naturalism. This was thought, fifty years ago, to be the teaching of science. It is now chiefly held to, not by contemporary men of science, but by sociologists[5] and literary men who get their science at second-hand and long after the event. According to this view everything is necessarily just what it is. Every natural phenomenon, every creature, every act whether of man or of insect, is completely determined by the antecedent circumstances. The writer who composes a poem or a play is the helpless medium of the system of things. By no possible means can he do anything other than exactly what he does, as he does it, when he does it. It is as foolish to suppose that Mr Joyce could have avoided writing *Ulysses*, and writing it, alas, just as he wrote it, as it is to suppose that a moth can avoid flying towards a light. Every literary piece, consequently, must be accepted just as it is presented to us. It is the inevitable, necessary outcome, under the given conditions, at a particular time and place, of the whole congeries of forces making our world what we see it to be. Since literature is one of the fine arts, the literary compositions which make their appearance amongst us are beautiful. That is

5 For example, by Professor Harry Elmer Barnes. In his *Twilight of Christianity* (p. 282), he writes: "The modern scientific conception of human conduct . . . insists upon the complete determination of human behaviour through the joint influence of our original equipment and our social experience." What he means, he goes on to make clear: "In the light of this attitude the criminal is no more responsible for his acts than the philanthropist."

their nature. What they are, beauty is. It is futile and irrelevant to suggest that any literary piece should be something other than it is. And such pieces, moreover, cannot usefully be compared with each other, or classified, or otherwise be related to anything. For each is absolutely unique. All that we can do is to sit down before a piece of literature with perfect docility, just as men of science docilely accept other natural phenomena. Scientists never absurdly pretend that one phenomenon is *better* than another. Phenomena simply *are*, and are accepted unquestioningly as things purely given. They are merely studied, "explained" in terms of antecedent circumstances, analysed, "elucidated"—and precisely so it is and must be with literary compositions.

The two points of departure, one sees, make no difference in the end. In either case criticism is left equally helpless and irrelevant. In both cases "elucidation" is all that is possible or desirable. And in both cases the freedom of art is secured at the expense, not only of the critic's freedom, but also of the freedom of the artist, and at the expense of completely divorcing art from life. For this is precisely what is sought by our contemporaries in their effort to find an exclusive corner for literature, wherein it may remain unchallenged— an authentic speciality in an age of anarchic specialization. Dr Spingarn, in the lecture from which I have quoted, is positive, explicit, and almost gleeful in banishing literature from all connexion with reality:

To say that poetry, as poetry, is moral or immoral is as meaningless as to say that an equilateral triangle is moral and an isosceles triangle immoral, or to speak of the immorality of a musical chord or a Gothic arch. . . . We do not concern ourselves with morals when we test the engineer's bridge or the scientist's researches; indeed we go farther, and say that it is the moral duty of the scientist to disregard any theory of morals in his search for truth. Beauty's world is remote from both these standards; she aims neither at morals nor at truth. Her imaginary creations, by definition, make no pretence to reality, and cannot be judged by reality's tests.

This is the gospel of art for art's sake preached, in England, by Oscar Wilde and others, in the eighteen-nineties, and somewhat earlier in France.[6] I think it illustrates what was earlier said—that bigotry and wrongheadedness normally accompany extreme specialization. It is true that no one should deny freedom to the artist. It is a question whether any one really can do so,[7] but, certainly, strenuous attempts to shackle artists had been made, and protests were in order. This, however, was no reason why our new teachers, with a smart self-assurance amounting to bigotry, should have refused to be contented until they had carried protest over into an absurd and vicious extreme. Yet precisely this was done; for it is nothing less to pretend that literature has no relation to life. Literature has immemorially subsisted on the closeness and comprehensiveness of its relation to life. It has been the most important and significant of the fine arts because this relationship was incontestably real and vital. It has played a great part in the development and conservation of culture. It has exerted a profound influence by achieving, in its own appropriate way, a truth superior to that of history and more deeply felt than that of philosophy. This is a truism, and it should be axiomatic. It is suicidal to forget it. Literature remains what it has been, central in man's study of man; and to sacrifice its human significance for the sake of the artist's freedom is to strike a wanton blow at civilization—and, at the same time, to make the freedom thus achieved perfectly worthless.

In his brightly written essay, *The Genius of America*, Stuart Sherman put his finger on the truth of this matter,

6 Dr Spingarn, it should be said, in a later essay (*Criticism in the United States*, reprinted in revised form in *Criticism in America*, 1924) speaks of art for art's sake as a "distorted" theory. The distinction he seeks to make may seem more real to others than it does to me. In any event, he continues to assert that the poet creates and lives in a "world of fantasy," which must not be confused with reality nor be subjected "to the moods and tests of actual life."

7 To put the question in its extremest form, it is a fact, as Hobbes asserted, that even under the absolute tyranny which he advocated freedom was not taken from men, simply because, although you may place penalties on certain actions, and may thus even take life, you cannot take away freedom. The freedom to rebel is absolutely inalienable. It is only a question whether, in any given case, men think the cause worth the risk involved.

though the essay as a whole is superficial and its conclusions open to serious objection. Civilized man in America, Sherman said in effect, has become progressively more expert in feeding the belly, while growing less and less able to feed the head and the heart. Such character as he retains has become, like himself, lopsided, dehumanized, because his mind has been open only to economic and sociological problems. He regards the fine arts generally, and literature in particular, as "frills," as "the superfluous things" in life. But, Sherman correctly argued, life is going to be of small worth to future Americans, no matter how well they may be housed and clothed and fed, unless our "practical men" can be made to realize that literature is not one of "the superfluous things." Yet, he continued, what hope of that may we cherish?— when our writers and too many of our teachers are wholly engaged in proving, by both example and precept, that literature is *and should be* just what the "practical men" now think it—wholly superfluous. This accusation has been sneered at, but has not been, so far as I know, answered. It is in fact unanswerable, and damning. A literature divorced from reality *is* superfluous, and the freedom to create it worthless.

This divorce, however, is not the only price paid for a worthless freedom. As I have said, it has been purchased also at the expense of the artist as well as of criticism. For the artist emerges, after his supposed friends have done their best for him, a mere helpless puppet, as irresponsible as any insect, or rabbit, or monkey. Thus the argument for absolute freedom ends by proving entirely too much. It is self-defeating, self-destroying, like all similar arguments in a world where everything we experience is really relative and conditioned.

Self-defeat is so evident in this instance that it need not be dwelt on; but the case of criticism is somewhat different, and perhaps even more illuminating. For we have now to notice that the attempt to debar the critic from the exercise of judgement, and to confine him strictly to "elucidation," itself necessitates the most sweeping judgements, both of criticism and of literature. Judgement cannot possibly be eliminated. If you attempt to put it out by one door, it straightway enters by another. But there is bad judgement, unfortunately, as well as good; and if one deludes one's self into supposing that judgement can be got rid of, one merely condemns one's self to the exercise of bad judgement. Surely it is very close to the height of absurdity to write and cause to be published a dogmatic judgement that judgement is impossible. A dogmatic judgement is an unexamined judgement. It has its origin in emotion. A passionate desire to believe induces the conviction that the proposition entertained is self-evident. It has only to be announced loudly enough, it would appear, and positively enough, in a self-righteous and assured tone, in order to merit acceptance. In the present instance a whole series of dogmatic or unconscious judgements is involved—the judgement that only critics of "the poetical" can be critics, that critics cannot judge, that literature is that which cannot be judged, that literature is "creative poetry," that nothing else is literature, that every literary composition is unique, purely fanciful, and beautiful, and so on.[8] Obviously, by the time our new teachers are through, a very special and sharply exclusive definition has been made for literature, and another, similar one for criticism. If this is not setting up standards, and absolute standards, for the judgement of literature and criticism, what is it?

IV

ONLY one answer can be given to the above question. But, as far as one can tell from anything they write, these gentlemen, moving briskly about in a world unrealized, are not in

---

[8] In the one question which Dr Spingarn would permit the critic to ask— What has a poem expressed, and how completely?—there would seem to be a place for what might be called judgement of the second rank. I cannot believe, however, that Dr Spingarn very seriously considered this question in the context he provided for it, and I am not aware that he has ever tried to practise the criticism he has sought to impose on others. The practising critic will immediately discover, when he tries to obey Dr Spingarn's directions, that the second half of this question is entirely meaningless; for if the poet's expression is cloudy, it follows that what the poem expresses is cloudy; if the poet's expression is fragmentary, it follows that what the poem expresses is fragmentary; and, in general, the poem expresses simply whatever it expresses.

the least aware of it. And what have they accomplished, if they have not really freed the artist, but have instead bound him more tightly than ever?—and if, though they have done their utmost to stultify criticism, they have not after all evaded its necessities? The "new criticism" may be a convenient club with which to hit one's enemies, sometimes below the belt. It may be, and has been, potent in spreading confusion. Can much else be said of it?

When one turns from Mr Eliot's essays in theory to his discussions of books and writers, one is likely to feel surprise. A critic who has decided exactly what criticism is and what its field is, and who seems very sure that any decisions different from his own must be fatuous, or at least unintelligent, should be on the way to systematic practice. We look for "elucidation." Now I do not want to deny that we find it; on the contrary, I wish to emphasize the fact that we find a great deal of it, of a certain kind. But what first strikes a reader is the apparent absence of method in Mr Eliot's critical ventures. I say "ventures" because that really characterizes them. Each essay seems to be strictly occasional, and fragmentary. Mr Eliot, it would appear, reads a book, knowing he has to write a review of it, wondering what he can find to say about it. His review should be, if possible, distinguished from the general run of these things; and usually some isolated point or other does strike him as the significant thing to say—and he is off. But he is off, practically always, on his way to some definite, sweeping judgement, or to a whole series of them. And he is content to explain or defend his verdicts, apparently, by any readiest and shortest means that offers. It looks as if the significant thing he found to say framed itself in his mind as a judgement, and as if he then glanced around to discover something to base it on. His judgements, in other words, are likely to be comprehensive, and are announced with an air of finality, but are mysterious, in the sense that one fails to see how they could be reached after the fashion in which Mr Eliot ostensibly does reach them.

These judgements are mysterious in another sense, too, which reveals, seemingly, absence of method. For if Mr

Eliot's essays, in their organization, bear a resemblance to
the informal dogmatic talk of a critic in his sociable hours,
rather than to a critic's serious work, they resemble such
talk also in their substance. One would expect many good
things to be said, and they are said. Mr Eliot is widely read,
reflective, and acute. He is often a master of the telling
phrase; and we may suppose that his mastery has not been
won without toil. I do not mean at all to suggest that his
essays are casually or hastily written. "Easy writing is
damned hard reading"; and these essays, for the most part,
are deceptively easy in the reading. But this increases one's
wonder when one is informed that "honest criticism and sensitive appreciation is directed not upon the poet but upon
the poetry"; because elsewhere we read that "the great, the
perennial, task of criticism" is "to bring the poet back to
life."[9] Again, in the course of a single short essay, of less
than ten pages, one reads:

If we write about Middleton's plays we must write about
Middleton's plays and not about Middleton's personality. . . .
His greatest tragedies and his greatest comedies are as if written by two different men. . . . Between the tragedies and the
comedies of Shakespeare, and certainly between the tragedies
and the comedies of Jonson, we can establish a relation. . . .
But with Middleton we can establish no such relation. He remains merely a name, a voice, the author of certain plays, which
are all of them great plays. He has no point of view, is neither
sentimental nor cynical; he is neither resigned, nor disillusioned,
nor romantic; he has no message. He is merely the name which
associates six or seven great plays. . . . If Middleton understood woman in tragedy better than any of the Elizabethans
. . . he was also able, in his comedy, to present a finer woman
than any of them. . . . In his tragedies Middleton employs all
the Italianate horrors of his time, and obviously for the purpose
of pleasing the taste of his time; yet underneath we feel always
a quiet and undisturbed vision of things as they are and not

9 *Selected Essays* (1932), pp. 17 and 278. According to the publishers, this
volume contains "the author's choice among all the prose that he has
written." Subsequent passages here quoted all come from this book.

"another thing." So in his comedies. . . . The machinery is the usual Elizabethan machinery; Middleton is solicitous to please his audience with what they expect; but there is underneath the same steady impersonal passionless observation of human nature. . . . In Middleton's tragedy there is a strain of realism underneath, which is one with the poetry; and in his comedy we find the same thing. . . . Middleton was a great observer of human nature, without fear, without sentiment, without prejudice. . . . He has no message; he is merely a great recorder.

These excerpts tell their own story: Middleton is "merely a name," yet Mr Eliot after all knows, in essentials, just what manner of man he must have been. Middleton's tragedies and comedies have no connexion with each other, yet after all prove to be intimately connected both from their author's unique understanding of woman and from his success in uniting realism with poetry. Further, Middleton is "a great recorder," yet in another place Mr Eliot announces plainly that "a great recorder" is an impossibility, because the terms contradict each other. "The great vice of English drama from Kyd to Galsworthy has been that its aim of realism was unlimited." Moreover, "the art of the Elizabethans is an impure art," because "realistic drama, . . . the photographic and gramophonic record of its time, can never exist"; and "the aim of the Elizabethans was to attain complete realism without surrendering any of the advantages which as artists they observed in unrealistic conventions. . . . The Elizabethans are in fact a part of the movement of progress or deterioration which has culminated in Sir Arthur Pinero and in the present regiment of Europe."[10]

Thus Middleton and Elizabethan drama as well seem to be disposed of. Yet Mr Eliot has persistently exerted himself to demonstrate the unique greatness of Elizabethan drama, in despite not only of these remarks but of a general assertion elsewhere that "the progress of an artist is a continual self-sacrifice, a continual extinction of personality."

It is not a little instructive to see how this conclusion is reached, through observations on the quality of Massinger's

[10] Written in 1924.

verse. From a collection of instances provided by Cruickshank, Mr Eliot examines Massinger's borrowings from
Shakespeare, and thence concludes "that Massinger's feeling for language had outstripped his feeling for things; that
his eye and his vocabulary were not in coöperation." But
the greater Elizabethans were men in whom "the intellect
was immediately at the tips of the senses. Sensation became
word and word was sensation. The next period is the period
of Milton (though still with a Marvell in it) ; and this period
is initiated by Massinger." Mr Eliot continues:

It is not that the word becomes less exact. Massinger is, in a
wholly eulogistic sense, choice and correct. And the decay of the
senses is not inconsistent with a greater sophistication of language. But every vital development in language is a development of feeling as well. The verse of Shakespeare and the major
Shakespearian dramatists is an innovation of this kind, a true
mutation of species. The verse practised by Massinger is a different verse from that of his predecessors; but it is not a development based on, or resulting from, a new way of feeling. On
the contrary, it seems to lead us away from feeling altogether.
. . . Mr Cruickshank has given us an excellent example of Massinger's syntax—

> What though my father
> Writ man before he was so, and confirm'd it,
> By numbering that day no part of his life
> In which he did not service to his country;
> Was he to be free therefore from the laws
> And ceremonious form in your decrees?
> Or else because he did as much as man
> In those three memorable overthrows,
> At Granson, Morat, Nancy, where his master,
> The warlike Charalois, with whose misfortunes
> I bear his name, lost treasure, men, and life,
> To be excused from payment of those sums
> Which (his own patrimony spent) his zeal
> To serve his country forced him to take up?

It is impossible to deny the masterly construction of this passage; perhaps there is not one living poet who could do the like. It is impossible to deny the originality. The language is pure and correct, free from muddiness or turbidity. Massinger does not confuse metaphors, or heap them one upon another. He is lucid, though not easy. But if Massinger's age, "without being exactly corrupt, lacks moral fibre,"[11] Massinger's verse, without being exactly corrupt, suffers from cerebral anaemia. To say that an involved style is necessarily a bad style would be preposterous. But such a style should follow the involutions of a mode of perceiving, registering, and digesting impressions which is also involved. It is to be feared that the feeling of Massinger is simple and overlaid with received ideas. Had Massinger had a nervous system as refined as that of Middleton, Tourneur, Webster, or Ford, his style would be a triumph. But such a nature was not at hand, and Massinger precedes, not another Shakespeare, but Milton.

This is substantially the reason for which Massinger is cast to the dogs. But Mr Eliot is aware of a difficulty, and gives the appearance of facing it. The trouble is, that in comedy "Massinger was one of the few masters in the language." How came this about, despite his unrefined nervous system and consequent lack of personality? It must have been, says Mr Eliot, an accident;—and forthwith, on very slender and disputable evidence, he satisfies himself hastily that it was an accident. Upon which follows his conclusion: "Had Massinger been a greater man, a man of more intellectual courage, the current of English literature immediately after him might have taken a different course."

Now such a conclusion I believe Mr Eliot could not have reached had he not confined his inquiry to Massinger's command of technique. I say nothing about the conditional form in which the conclusion is cast, though I think that, in general, a very questionable device, because it lends itself easily to enormities of gratuitous insinuation. I refer, however, only to the accusation that Massinger lacked intellectual courage. Mr Eliot in this essay says much that is not only

---

[11] A quotation from *Philip Massinger,* by A. H. Cruickshank (1920), on which Mr Eliot's essay is based.

interesting but valuable. He sheds real light on one aspect
of his author. And it is not for me to enter into a dispute
concerning Massinger's nervous system. But that this second-
rate dramatist was a greater man than Mr Eliot has perceived, and possessed intellectual courage of a high order, is
not open to doubt, and will not be doubted by anybody who
studies all the evidence—or by anybody who studies, for
example, only the relation of a single play, *The Bondman*,
to contemporary events.[12] The plain fact of the matter is
that Mr Eliot's conclusions go far beyond anything war-
ranted by the scope of his investigation, so to call it, and
constitute a snap judgement. And I have presented this example of his critical procedure at some length because it is
characteristic.

Snap judgements, of course, are not always incorrect. Mr
Eliot's are sometimes faultless. The habit of making them,
nevertheless, is a habit of regarding truth lightly; and it
opens the way to indulgence in mere wilfulness disguised as
something better than itself. Mr Eliot is very earnest, but he
has fallen into this trap and made himself at home there. No
one would suppose that he formulated his conception of "the
perfect critic" with his tongue in his cheek, intending merely
to promote confusion, and not intending to pay the slightest
heed to his own precepts. Yet in all of his essays he does
the expressly forbidden thing: he makes judgements—and
"judgements of worse and better." And this, as I have indicated, through a few examples, is by no means his only self-
contradiction. He is full of contradictions and of wilfulness.
Yet to this his eyes are closed, because he does believe himself true to the goddess of "elucidation." And there is a sense
in which he is true—a sense illuminated by the following
confession, in his essay on Dryden:

When we try to isolate the essentially poetic, we bring our
pursuit in the end to something insignificant; our standards

12 The relationship has finally been worked out in detail by Dr B. T.
Spencer in his edition of *The Bondman* (1932). Its general character, however, was suggested long ago, by S. R. Gardiner, so that it cannot be regarded as a discovery made since the first publication of Mr Eliot's essay.

vary with every poet whom we consider. All we can hope to do, in the attempt to introduce some order into our preferences, is to clarify our reasons for finding pleasure in the poetry that we like.

The "elucidation," in other words, which Mr Eliot endeavours after is the elucidation of himself. This it is which gives a certain unity and consistency to his essays, because it is the real underlying motive of every one of them. It also explains many of the contradictions in which his work abounds. I do not think even this can explain all of them; but Mr Eliot has, along with some abiding preoccupations, an atomistic mind. Such a mind is not identical with the kind in which nothing is ever settled, but all is to be begun anew over and over, or got up quickly for each essay written. Nor is it the same as the kind of mind with which Mr Facing Both Ways is endowed. At times the atomistic mind resembles both of these types, but it is really quite different—it is the mind, or part of the mind, of the man of science. The scientist is concerned—within, of course, the limits imposed by the tests he can apply!—with absolutes. He can only find by a process of abstraction, or "purification," the things with which he is able to deal. If, for example, he wants to know what platinum is, he can only learn by separating it off from everything else, until nothing save "pure" platinum is left, which can then be described in terms which serve to distinguish it from everything else. Thus alone can you come to know platinum for what it really is—something hard, impenetrable, perfectly mysterious, which only begins to acquire meaning as you proceed, having separated it off, to relate it again to everything else. This, it would seem, is but dimly understood; but the process of abstraction is easy to grasp and has yielded such useful results that it has threatened to become the one good thing which shall corrupt the world.

The central preoccupation of Mr Eliot has been poetry. But he has had other preoccupations—the poet, criticism, philosophy, ethics, religion, and possibly still others. His notion has been that by a process of abstraction one could discover "pure" poetry, the "pure" poet, "pure" criticism, and the like. The further this attempt was pushed, the more completely criticism, for example, had to be isolated from everything else; and once Mr Eliot had determined to his satisfaction the nature of criticism, he felt bound, apparently, to conform to his own standard only in so far as it might be convenient—though the standard itself remained as a test, or club, to be applied to others. The point is that Mr Eliot has been interested in reaching Truth by methods of isolation, so that he has dissociated things—following, of course, that "great critic," Remy de Gourmont—and has delighted, as a theorist, in emphasizing their separateness. "Poetry is not a substitute for philosophy or theology or religion; . . . it has its own function." There is truth in this. Poetry has, at any rate, uses of its own, a "place," and should not be confused with "philosophy or theology or religion";—and protests against confusion are doubtless always in order. Stated absolutely, moreover, as Mr Eliot has been fond of stating it, this affirmation is intelligible, and implies that he has been converted to philosophical pluralism, or anarchism. The atomistic mind is, in fact, the mind that has been divided off into water-tight compartments.

But Mr Eliot, though he is very positive and assured in *using* his essences or entities, when it suits him, refuses to be bound by them. He will turn upon himself whenever that also suits him, and exclaim, "What is man to decide what poetry is?" Hence the impression he sometimes creates of being a slippery person; and this impression can only be corrected by remembering that his real and abiding task in his essays is the elucidation of himself. Thus a number of his pieces fall together as a series of suggestions for a new history of English poetry, the peculiarity of which, should it be written, would be the consistency with which poets, from Shakespeare to our day, would be praised or blamed accordingly as they can or can not be regarded as preparing the way for the kind of poetry which Mr Eliot himself has found it possible to write. But Mr Eliot's poetry is chiefly a particular technique, while Mr Eliot is much more than a technician, so that he has not hesitated to throw overboard "pure" poetry when it has already served one of his purposes and will not serve another. "It would appear," he recently wrote, "that 'literary appreciation' is an abstraction, and pure poetry a phantom; and that both in creation and enjoyment much always enters which is, from the point of view of 'Art,' irrelevant."

This is candour! And the man who tucked this admission away at the end of a long footnote[13] has both engaging and solid virtues of a high order. He has, too, put all thinking people heavily in his debt; and it is an ungrateful task to give reasons for anything other than an attitude of sympathetic admiration towards him and towards all that he has accomplished in the face of every difficulty. It must, however, be realized that the real interest and value of Mr Eliot's essays is more private, so to say, and personal than would at first sight be supposed from their ostensible form. Their interest and value is, in fact, very great, because their author's intellectual history is typical, if not of a generation, at least of many in our troubled time who have been irresistibly impelled to break through the iron bands of "modern thought." But the essays are only incidentally critical; and are only critical at all because Mr Eliot has generally disregarded his own requirements for criticism, and because his standards of judgement, while narrow, sectarian, and often tenuously related to his conclusions, have not always led him astray.

V

IN *Axel's Castle* Mr Edmund Wilson writes: "The criticism of our own day examines literature, art, ideas and specimens of human society in the past with a detached scientific interest or a detached aesthetic appreciation which seems in either case to lead nowhere." But, he adds, Mr Eliot, though his work is much of a piece with this contemporary criticism,

---

13 *Selected Essays*, p. 257. The same thing, in effect, is said in the Preface added to a new edition of *The Sacred Wood* in 1928; and in this Preface Mr Eliot speaks apologetically of his "assumption of pontifical solemnity" in his earlier prose pieces. The difficulty one feels in reading these pieces, however, does not arise from their "solemnity," but from their pert assurance of tone, not fortunate in itself, and the less fortunate in the light of Mr Eliot's subsequent changes.

has "largely succeeded in escaping the vices which it seems
to encourage." And he has done so, Mr Wilson thinks, because he is "passionately interested in literature," because
he has "real intensity of enthusiasm," and because he is able
"to see beyond his own ideas" and is willing "to admit the
relative character of his conclusions." Mr Eliot has also become a leader, we are told, "in spite of the meagreness of his
production," "because his career has been a progress, because he has evidently been on his way somewhere, when
many of his contemporaries, more prolific and equally gifted,
have been fixed in their hedonism or despair."

Mr Wilson's book is well written. Few volumes of essays,
indeed, have given me so much pleasure in the reading, simply from their workmanlike form. Mr Wilson has caught and
maintained what seems to me the right tone—serious, mod-
erate, and quiet. The strained liveliness, the vulgarity, the
wheezy enthusiasm so characteristic of much of our recent
critical writing he has entirely avoided. Yet he is not solemn,
or precise, or tiresomely detached. His style is easy, natural,
and lucid. And this is the more remarkable because he has
immersed himself in imaginative literature notoriously difficult and obscure, so that his book seems, in its clarity, a triumph of expository skill.

But the mastery of a technique, unfortunately, is not
everything, as Mr Wilson himself is ready enough to point
out when it suits him, and as his book demonstrates anew.
The verdict on Mr Eliot's criticism which I have reproduced
is significant because, as far as it goes, it is characteristic;
and it signifies compendiously and clearly that *Axel's Castle*
is, despite all its excellence of manner and form, a shoddy
piece of work. Mr Wilson knows as well as anybody that
"intensity of enthusiasm" is nothing apart from its object.
Men are capable of becoming intensely enthusiastic over
practically everything imaginable, from astrolithology to
paronomasia. There was an English nobleman who became
so intensely enthusiastic over water-closets when they were
first introduced that he not only had one placed in every
room in his palace, but even contrived to get one in his coach.
No surer way is known, in fact, of making one's self in-

tensely ridiculous than that of falling a victim to misplaced enthusiasm;—yet how many cranks, dangerous or merely harmless, does not every generation bring forth?

In the present instance the object of "passionate interest" is "literature"—just "literature." But what can this mean? By itself it would not serve to distinguish Mr Eliot from hundreds of people, estimable perhaps, but simple, who have no aptitude or desire for positive accomplishment of any kind, and whose minds are, seemingly, rag-bags. Evidently Mr Wilson means something more than he has said, and we are to infer his meaning from the context. Mr Eliot, we observe, has been saved from a kind of criticism which "leads nowhere." Yet his criticism is largely of this kind, but is distinguished from it by his "passionate interest" in "literature." The kind complained of "examines literature . . . with a detached scientific interest or a detached aesthetic appreciation." Does Mr Wilson mean, then, that Mr Eliot examines literature with passionate scientific interest or passionate aesthetic appreciation, or both? Or does he mean that Mr Eliot examines literature with passionate detachment? I do not see how he could mean either, since both possibilities are about equally self-contradictory, and I cannot help suspecting that Mr Wilson never really asked himself what he meant. The detached critics, Mr Wilson thinks, "lead nowhere" because, though brilliant, they are tiresome; and also because they expect one to do no end of reading. This, Mr Wilson says, is pedantry; and he considers Mr Eliot to be guilty of it. Nevertheless, somehow or other Mr Eliot is not tiresome, but lively.

Liveliness, however, is not Mr Eliot's sole distinction. He is also able "to see beyond his own ideas." One would suppose that the person blessed with this capacity must see something, and that what he would see would be another idea, or the tail of another idea. Seeing it, moreover, he would straightway proceed to make it his own. This, at any rate, is what Mr Eliot has done; and it is radically different from admitting the relative character of one's conclusions, as should be clear from what has been said above concerning Mr Eliot's critical work. Nobody, in truth, ever sees beyond his own ideas in the fashion Mr Wilson suggests. To admit the relative character of one's conclusions is to do one of two things—to try immediately to find better ones, or to acquiesce in an all-dissolving scepticism. The latter I do not think any human being has ever done consistently; so that in practice the sceptic also tries, though by his own route, to reach better conclusions. It is, of course, an entirely different thing to admit the relative character of all human knowledge, and this may be what Mr Wilson thought he was saying;—but, if it is, it is manifestly not true of Mr Eliot.

Mr Wilson's vagueness and carelessness of thought, resulting in a practically complete failure to explain why Mr Eliot should have at all succeeded in escaping the vices of aesthetic criticism, is, as I have said, characteristic of him. He would have done better had he seriously attempted to understand what the vices of aesthetic criticism are, instead of contenting himself with the assertion that such criticism is apt to become "tiresome" and encourages "pedantry." In that case, however, his book could scarcely have been written, save as an instance of what he deplores. The example of "pedantry" which he gives—parodying Mr Eliot instead of quoting him, and thus having things all his own way—is very surprising. It is one which tends to show that every work of literature has an historical background, extending as far as the historian's knowledge can reach, so that no piece can be fully "appreciated" in isolation. But this is just what Mr Wilson himself professes to believe, and just what he elsewhere complains that Mr Eliot does not sufficiently recognize.[14] He himself states, as we have already noticed, that his "idea" of literary criticism is that it should be "a history of man's ideas and imaginings in the setting of the conditions which have shaped them"; and he announces that his purpose in *Axel's Castle* is "to try to trace the origins" of symbolistic literature and to show its "development in the work of six contemporary writers." He takes pains, moreover, to suggest at intervals that he writes objectively in a detached spirit. His detachment, however, is a greatly vary-

14 *Axel's Castle*, pp. 124 and 121.

ing quality, which opens the way to an understanding of this self-contradiction.

For Mr Wilson avoids what he calls pedantry only by avoiding what any historian would recognize as history. His real object in *Axel's Castle* is to glorify symbolism, and his detachment puts in an appearance only when he thinks it desirable and possible to dissociate symbolism from the thought of certain symbolistic writers. Similarly his "history" puts in an appearance only when he wants to *use* it, either to discredit what he does not like or to buttress what he does.[15] He is not at all content, in other words, to "elucidate" in accordance with his professions, but is determined

15 Several passages in *Axel's Castle* simultaneously illustrate Mr Wilson's "detachment" and his use of "history," or "the conditions which have shaped" his writers. He does not like Mr Eliot's "incurable moral solicitude," nor his conversion to Christianity. Hence he reminds us that Mr Eliot, "though born in St Louis, comes from a New England family and was educated at Harvard." And, he continues, "he is in some ways a typical product of our New England civilization. He is distinguished by that combination of practical prudence with moral idealism which shows itself in its later developments as an excessive fastidiousness and scrupulousness." From this Mr Wilson concludes that Mr Eliot's "religious tradition has reached him by way of Boston," and that his relation to "the Anglo-Catholic Church appears largely artificial." His conversion, in fact, seems to "us" really "a reawakening of the New Englander's conscience, of the never quite exorcised conviction of the ineradicable sinfulness of man." This is a gratuitous attempt to fasten on Mr Eliot a label fabricated by the industry of Mr Mencken, Dr Lewisohn, and others. Again, Mr Wilson says that Proust's *"A la Recherche du Temps Perdu,* in spite of all its humour and beauty, is one of the gloomiest books ever written." Because of this, Proust ends "by goading us to the same sort of rebellion that we make against those dialogues of Leopardi in which, in a similar insistent way, Leopardi rings the changes on a similar theme: that man is never happy, that there is no such thing as satisfaction in the present. We have finally to accept with dismay the fact that Leopardi is a sick man and that, in spite of the strength of his intellect, in spite of his exact, close, sober classical style, all his thinking is sick. And so with Proust we are forced to recognize that his ideas and imagination are more seriously affected by his physical and psychological ailments than we had at first been willing to suppose." But only *some* of Proust's "ideas and imaginings" are thus disposed of—those which Mr Wilson disapproves. And we hear no suggestion that Corbière's poetry is sick, or de Nerval's thought, or Rimbaud's life. We are, however, invited to "consider the disproportionate size of the shadow-structure of speculation which such a writer as Eddington tries to base on some new modification of physical theory, itself suggested on most uncertain evidence"; while Professor Whitehead's speculations are accepted by Mr Wilson as the very heart of the newest and best science.

to judge symbolism and, what is more, to judge it favourably. I do not mean thus to imply that the whole framework of *Axel's Castle* is a conscious sham. I think this inconceivable in Mr Wilson, and it is as evident as such things can be that his book is written in good faith. But unconscious deception, alas, is self-deception, and the lie in the soul is most properly thought to be the worst lie of all.

Had Mr Wilson, indeed, not been unconscious of what he was doing, it is scarcely imaginable that he would have made mere novelty his principal standard of judgement. His standards in their entirety are, to be sure, aesthetic standards; and in this his work is exactly parallel to Mr Eliot's, and is open to the same objection; because the judgements he forms are by no means exclusively aesthetic, but go far beyond that field. Nevertheless, although strangeness is a real factor in artistic success, it is not open to question that when artists become chiefly engaged in a straining attempt to turn up something new, art has entered on a phase of exhaustion and decay. For with novelty it is the same as with enthusiasm, or "intensity." Everything depends, in both cases, on significance. It is, of course, precisely Mr Wilson's contention that his symbolists are significantly novel in their technique; but he tends constantly to assume or imply that because their methods are novel, therefore they are significant. This could hardly be said more plainly than in his introductory essay: "Mallarmé was a true saint of literature: he had proposed to himself an almost impossible object, and he pursued it without compromise or distraction. His whole life was dedicated to the effort to do something with the language of poetry which had never been done before." And the same note recurs again and again throughout the book, until one is forced to recognize it as a dominant factor, perhaps the dominant factor, influencing Mr Wilson's judgements.[16] Hence when he reaches the nadir of symbolism he has no protection against Miss Gertrude Stein and the Dadaists, but has to make the best of them, which he

16 See *Axel's Castle,* pp. 22, (23), 70, 75, (93), 96, 109, 112, 132, 147, 153, 154, 179, 189, 203, 204, 211, 220, 221, 222, 228, 237, 253, 255, 270, 272, 286–287, 292, 297, and 298. The references on the two pages within brackets

unhesitatingly does, with much arrant special pleading[17] and, in the case of the latter, with much emphasis on "the conditions" which brought them into being. And incidentally he shows, in his translation of the *Memoirs of Dadaism*, exactly where the cult of novelty finally leads its victims: "At the Salle Gaveau, at the Dada Festival, the scandal was also great. For the first time in the history of the world, people threw at us, not only eggs, salads, and pennies, but beefsteaks as well. It was a very great success. The audience were extremely Dadaist. We had already said that the true Dadaists were against Dada."

are in passages which Mr Wilson quotes from Mr Yeats and Mr Eliot. My list is not complete, and I have excluded references such as occur on pp. 95 ("Verlaine, . . . a less original and interesting personality") and 99 ("It must not be supposed . . . that Eliot is not original"). I add a few examples: "It is certain that this mysterious poem represents a genre which has never appeared in literature before"; "This is also its peculiar strength: it is one of the most original studies of love in fiction and . . . we recognize in it an inescapable truth"; "A literary personality of unmistakable originality and distinction"; Proust "has recreated the world of the novel from the point of view of relativity: he has supplied for the first time in literature an equivalent on the full scale for the new theory of modern physics." Mr Wilson makes a great deal of the remarkable discovery—whether or not it is all his own he does not say—that symbolism, especially in the hands of Proust and Mr Joyce, coincides with "the new physics"; and he has a vague dream of a good time coming when science and art may "arrive at a way of thinking, a technique of dealing with our perceptions, which will make art and science one." The dream, of course, is the dream of Zola over again, in a new setting; and the "discovery," which enables Mr Wilson to hint repeatedly that Proust and Mr Joyce are buttressed by "the new science," is another characteristic example of muddle-headedness. Does Mr Wilson really imagine that Professor Bergson and Professor Whitehead are philosophically on the same side of the fence?—and that "the new physics" is identical with an impossible conflation of the metaphysical speculations of these philosophers?

[17] I give an example: On p. 249 of *Axel's Castle* Mr Wilson quotes a paragraph from the *United States Courts-Martial Manual*. On p. 250 he quotes *A Patriotic Leading* by Miss Stein—one of the very few pieces of hers which is even partially intelligible. He then says (p. 251): "The difference between Gertrude Stein and the author of the *Courts-Martial Manual* is entirely a technical one: it is a difference simply of syntax and of the order in which each evokes his or her selected group of images." This is like saying that genius is a form of madness. Supposing Mr Wilson to be correct, he merely shows that technical differences can be, on occasion, crucially important. And this indeed he asserts, when it suits him, but in the present instance he plainly means to insinuate that they should make no difference in our reactions or judgements.

It is evident, surely, without going further, that neither Mr Wilson nor his readers have been well served by his "idea of criticism." That "idea" is one which cannot be carried out fully and consistently, aside from any question about the assumption it rests on, because the necessary facts can in no way be had. Mr Wilson's work does not exhibit clearly the difficulties to be encountered—as did, for example, that of Taine—simply because he makes no serious attempt to be faithful to his "idea," having, possibly, no real understanding of what would be requisite. This at least would seem to be the likeliest explanation of his casual methods. But it is to be observed that whether historical "elucidation" is seriously or light-heartedly undertaken it is bound to involve tacit judgements and evaluations. And the disadvantage under which it places even such an accomplished and able man as Mr Wilson is the grievous one of forming judgements while ostensibly doing, while doubtless honestly enough intending to do, something else. It would be astonishing indeed if, under these circumstances, this responsible and difficult task could be carried through intelligently. What actually happens, so far as one may see from the present instance, is that the critic is thrown back on his own limited, largely unexamined, largely emotional reaction to life, and is positively encouraged to regard this as a sufficient, self-evidently "true" basis for judgement.

Thus Mr Wilson obviously is disgusted with life as he has found it. He thinks it is tame. He has, like the great majority of his contemporaries in America and an increasing number in England, less than a little historical knowledge. He is bound by no ties even of sentiment to any institution or locality which might give him a real sense of the continuity of life. He is aware, of course, of vigorous "survivals," but, being outside of them, he is merely puzzled by them—or perhaps not even that, perhaps blindly contemptuous. For he is also aware of innumerable changes on all sides, startling, marvellous, and causing a great ferment of expectation. This was crystallized as long ago as the eighteenth century in the gospel of Progress, which Mr Wilson accepts. But he cannot understand why, when each wonder-

ful progressive change promises so much, it should perform
so little. It must be, as so many have said ever since the
eighteenth century, that "society" has put blinkers and
bridles on us all, and has so habituated us to them that we
insist on blinkers and bridles for everybody, even for artists.
If men would just "let themselves go," forgetting their ignoble prudence and fear, their "moral solicitude," their "excessive fastidiousness and scrupulousness," their "pedantry,"
things would be better. Life would become immediately more
colourful and exciting. And not only that; for the break
with all our artificial restraints and conventions, releasing
each man's full individuality and enabling it to expand
freely and spontaneously without limit, would reveal a deep
unity of feeling binding men together in a true herd-society,
no longer merely conventional, but in tune with absolute
reality. And *then* our progress, "through economic readjust-
ment, political reform, education or biological and psychological study," would bear the fruit it ought to. It is Adam
Smith's notion, which was developed in the doctrine of lais-
sez-faire, transferred from the economic sphere, where we
were so foolish as to suppose it could work well, to the intellectual, social, moral, and artistic spheres, where it is bound
to prove an ineffable blessing. The Russian communists are
already passing out of the desert, Mr Wilson hopefully believes; and amongst us the emancipated artists are heroically
showing the way;—and above all the symbolists, by their
new technique, and especially Mr James Joyce, by his conflation of symbolism and naturalism.

VI

THE confusion which results when a critic with such an
equipment, and with no liking for the scrutiny of himself,
thinks he is engaged in "elucidation," I have sought to illustrate. And I cannot close this survey without emphasizing
the fact that patent confusion of thought, always difficult
enough to avoid, is a rapidly growing vice of our time, precisely amongst so-called critics—and a vice which has been
directly and especially encouraged by the development of
modern science. To say this is not in any way to "attack"

science, because science is not in any way at fault in the matter. "Science," the President of the Carnegie Institution of Washington has recently written, "is only the truth about ourselves and the world around us";[18] and in this legitimate though archaic sense of the word—now being brought back into currency chiefly by controversialists—who can feel anything save unqualified devotion to it? We cannot have too much knowledge at our disposal, and anybody who increases our store is one of the true benefactors of the race. Nor need we inquire whether the distinguished spokesman whom I quote meant "absolute truth" or something less. He meant, we may suppose, well-established knowledge, or what he himself calls, as he goes on, "honest knowledge." But his phrase is an admission that there may be pretence to knowledge without the reality—the grand manner without the grand thing—and this danger is, in fact, exactly proportional to the prestige of the grand thing. Nor is this all. It is by no means easy to detect the empty pretender to knowledge; it sometimes is, but it becomes more and more difficult to do so as science grows more complex, or more highly developed. A far greater and more insidious danger, however, which has become acute as science has won its extraordinary triumphs in modern times, is the premature generalization; and akin to this, and equally dangerous, is the misunderstood generalization.

Both have become extremely dangerous because inevitably the most strenuous efforts have been made to enlarge the boundaries of science as much as possible. Very properly, science acknowledges no limits save those imposed by our means of acquiring exact information. And, impressed—as who can fail to be profoundly impressed?—by the extension of our knowledge of "the world around us" during the last several centuries, and by the changes thus brought about in our ways of living, men have eagerly attempted to increase similarly our store of "truth about ourselves," hoping that both the individual and society might thereby be improved

18 Extracts from the President's *Report* are reprinted in the *Bulletin of the American Association of University Professors* (March, 1932), from which I quote.

as greatly as have been, for example, our means of transportation. There has been, quite naturally, the utmost reluctance to admit that the two fields of possible knowledge—ourselves, the surrounding world—are not equally open to investigation; and in fact genuine additions to our knowledge of ourselves, and additions of the highest value, have been made. Nevertheless, it does have to be acknowledged that there are extraordinary difficulties in the way of carrying the "science of ourselves" much beyond the point where we can no longer be assimilated to "the world around us,"[19] because, aside from other considerations which I shall not here enter into, the factors involved are exceedingly complex, and the element of pure contingency correspondingly large. And parallel with this, it may be said by the way, is the fact that it is exceedingly difficult both to determine and to bring about a genuine social reform, and comparatively very easy to discover and secure the adoption of, for instance, an improved method of transportation.

Now the one point I wish to make is that in every field of scientific investigation knowledge of a certain kind is obtained, if it can be obtained at all, only by paying a certain price for it. Things are studied by men of science, not simply as they are found, but only in part, only in so far as they are amenable to exact observation, analysis, measurement, and the like. This does not mean that the parts of an object discarded by a man of science are less real than those he studies;—it merely means that they are not useful for his purposes, though they would have to be given a place in any *complete* account of the object in question. The consequence, until recently unseen, but very generally recognized to-day

[19] Thus we have sound, even though not complete, anatomical and physiological knowledge about ourselves. We know ourselves, in other words, very well, in so far as we can be regarded as physical organisms, like other animals. But psychological science, save as a branch of physiology or as the study of animal behaviour, has encountered difficulties which—whether ultimately insuperable or not—have hitherto retarded its progress. Through psycho-analysis remarkable advances have been made in quite recent years, but the significance of these advances is still, amongst psychologists themselves, a vexed question very far from solution;—and no one, save those (a large number) who are much more anxious to *use* psychology than to understand it, supposes that we are out of the forest, or near its edge.

by scientists themselves, is that "the truth" known through science, though immeasurably *useful*, is also fragmentary and special;—and altogether likely to be misunderstood by those who do not fully realize how it was obtained and within what strict limits alone it may contribute to our understanding of ourselves or of "the world around us." And this fact is more significant and important in proportion as the object studied is complex or many-sided. Thus the President of the Carnegie Institution, in the *Report* from which I have quoted, warns his readers that "truth in partial statement must be interpreted carefully and applied with every precaution"; and, he adds, "along with new information it is essential to have guidance regarding what to accept as fact and what to consider as merely tentative grouping of ideas for the purpose of testing theories."

There are some people—idolaters they should be called— who seek to cry down every attempt to understand science, or to regard critically the generalizations which from day to day are offered us in the name of science. They are, I am sure, the worst enemies science now has; and of all people they are furthest removed from the spirit of science, since their concern for truth has obviously been displaced by blind partisanship. This is the more unfortunate because we cannot get along without generalizations which, from the strict scientific point of view, might fairly be termed premature. We should like to have knowledge about ourselves as exact, as readily verifiable, as little open to dispute, and above all as nearly complete, as we have in the field of chemistry. There are reasons, to be mentioned in a later chapter, for thinking this desire vain; but in any event we do not have such scientific knowledge now, and we certainly are not going to have it soon. Hence there is an irresistible tendency, which was very evident amongst men of science in the nineteenth century, and is even more evident amongst those who look to science as to an universal oracle, to seize on scientifically derived "truth in partial statement," and to pretend that it gives us, at last, the real science of ourselves. It was, not so very long ago, phrenology. Preposterous as that seems now, it is not actually more preposterous than any one of sev-

eral competing successors to-day. But this is precisely what
our idolaters will not hear to; and nothing can exceed their
insolent self-assurance—just as nothing can exceed the
rapidity with which, from time to time, they change their
allegiance!

It remains, consequently, the task of criticism to weigh
premature generalizations, to guard as best it may against
their passing for what they are not, and to keep steadily in
view the practical knowledge of ourselves and of society
which can be derived from the accumulated experience of the
race. This experience is reflected in history, in literature, in
philosophy, and in religion; and it includes, of course, what
has also most recently been learned by scientific methods.
Such knowledge criticism should, indeed, welcome with a
very special gratitude;—but not indiscriminately, idola-
trously, or, in other words, uncritically. This, one would
think, should be self-evident. Yet the fact is that too many
of our critics are themselves amongst the idolaters, for whatever bad reasons. There can be no good reasons, though it is
true that a development so impressive as that of modern science exerts a contagious influence, or forms a current so
strong that, for a while, it sweeps all before it. Thus the
critical work of Mr Eliot has been strongly influenced, as we
have seen, by the example of science;—strongly, but not
happily, because, as he has begun to realize, the subjects he
has dealt with are not really amenable to the kind of simplification by processes of abstraction which he has sought to
impose on them.

Mr Wilson has vigorously protested against this simplification, in words which one wishes one might merely echo
with full assent; but, as we have seen, he does not appear to
know what to make of his own protest—and for the excellent
reason that he employs the simplification himself, and tries,
like Mr Eliot, to base extra-aesthetic conclusions on strictly
aesthetic judgements. We have also seen, moreover, that Mr
Wilson's entire book is involved in confusion because he professes to be doing one thing while he is really attempting
another, with the consequence that he has actually written
neither a historical work nor a genuinely critical one, but

rather a piece of propagandism. And Mr Wilson's initial trouble, clearly, arose from his apparent acceptance of a scientific generalization and apparent readiness to present it as the truth about men, while adhering to it, nevertheless, only in so far as he could make use of it for his own purposes.

This vicious trick—for it has come to seem nothing less and nothing more—of pretending to follow the Teachings of Science when one is really forcing the Teachings of Science to follow one's self, is practised, as I have said, not alone by Mr Wilson, but by a growing number of so-called critics, some of whom succeed in making Mr Wilson's confusion appear, by comparison, a trifling and almost innocent fault. I will cite, as an example, Dr Ludwig Lewisohn—not because his work offers the readiest and easiest means of illustrating a vicious tendency, but because Dr Lewisohn is, like Mr Wilson, a very able man who could have exerted a powerful influence in favour of straight thinking and significant criticism if he had ever fairly set about it. "To a philosophic eye," wrote Gibbon, "the vices of the clergy are far less dangerous than their virtues." And similarly it is because such men as Mr Wilson, Mr Max Eastman,[20] and Dr Lewisohn

---

[20] I mention Mr Eastman because I cannot help thinking better of his capabilities than he seems to want one to think. His recent book, *The Literary Mind,* suffers as a piece of literature from recurrent attempts to write down to a public which, I imagine, it has not after all reached. It is, besides, one of the most bigoted books I have ever read. Yet it contains sane, illuminating comment on some contemporary literature and criticism; and in a few pages reveals Mr Joyce, or an important part of him, much more clearly than Mr Edmund Wilson has been able to reveal him. Its central argument, moreover, is one which goes back to Plato, and which might very usefully have been restated in contemporary terms, instead of being childishly perverted. But Mr Eastman has axes to grind, and so merely ends by doing everything he can to discredit himself. He is a disciple of Karl Marx, and his book is transparently propagandistic. He is one of the idolaters of science of whom I have spoken, but really wants science to serve his political purposes—and does not hesitate, in different parts of his volume, depending on the immediate purpose to be served, to present contradictory descriptions of science. He disparages all philosophy, pretending that Marxian materialism is something else—science, of course—and thus silently *assuming* exactly what needed to be proved, as the essential basis of his whole book. But if he had made the slightest attempt to follow his own precepts he could not have written *The Literary Mind* at all. Instead of trying to meet those he opposes, he "explains" them by asserting that they are merely— without, perhaps, knowing it—fighting to preserve their jobs and their social

are setting an example of shoddy work and slapdash thinking that the tendency I speak of has become important.

In the Preface to *Expression in America* Dr Lewisohn
states that he has inevitably used "the organon or method of
knowledge associated with the venerated name of Sigmund
Freud"; because, he adds, "the portrayer of any aspect of
human life or civilization who does not do so to-day will soon
be like some mariner of old who, refusing to acknowledge the
invention of mathematical instruments because their precision was not yet perfect, still stubbornly sailed his vessel by
the stars." This is more emphatic than illuminating, but
illumination comes from the body of the book. At the beginning of its eighth section we read:

The nineteenth century was the century of easy solutions and
of eternal truths that lasted ten years. There is a deep human
pathos in this circumstance. For one kind of intelligible universe men desired at once to substitute another equally intelligible and stable in order to have a rest, however bleak, for their
souls. It is now clear, tragically clear, if one likes, that the
nineteenth century succeeded solely in asking the pertinent and
crucial questions. All its answers were absurdly premature; all
its solutions are strewn like withered leaves on an autumnal
road. The disillusion, be it remarked, is not with science as an

position. "We must lay aside all this motivated nonsense," he then cries. But
is his own work unmotivated? Indeed, however it may be with those against
whom he writes, how can he suppose that one with his views can be thought
of save as a person fighting for money and position? If what he says is true,
it must be true of him; if it is not true, it still remains his own self-con-
fessed belief that this is what all men really do, and so must at least be
true of him. And perhaps the desperateness of Mr Eastman's struggle for
money and position may be gauged from his attempt to impose on men a
definition of poetry which, as he actually admits, will not account for poetry
"throughout the historic period" (p. 91). "Pure" poetry is only to be found
in incantations of pre-historic savages and, by accident, in the works of a
few of our contemporaries. Or perhaps a still better indication of the real
nature of Mr Eastman's labours may be gained from his wonderful admission, after he has raised a veritable storm of dust, that the situation about
which he writes is one that may conceivably arise *"thousands of years
hence"* (p. 161). Mr Eastman pokes fun at professors who, as he has discovered, are merely advocating very elaborately and imposingly "the ordinary routine business of learning to behave yourself";—yet this is a lesson
which he, very evidently, has not been able to learn.

organon; it is with a type of mind that jumped to conclusions suiting its inner climate and then sought to impose its special interpretation, its sombre subjective poetry, upon the world as truth and fact.

This diatribe issues in the characterization of some of the work of Dr John B. Watson as "grotesque drivel," and of the behaviouristic psychology as degenerate "mechanistic dogmatism"—"a superstition as empty and as rigid as any previous superstition that ever plagued the mind." The Freudian psychology, on the other hand, though it is certainly as naturalistic as the variety thus denounced, Dr Lewisohn enthusiastically accepts, because it "approaches profoundly suggestive explanations" of human experience. In other words, Dr Lewisohn's attitude is somewhat similar to Coleridge's towards Christianity. The Freudian psychology "finds" him, or comes home to him, as behaviourism, for example, evidently fails to come home to him. I wish there were more evidence to offer on this particular question; but I can only record that Dr Lewisohn does not, as might be supposed from his words quoted above, merely accept psychoanalysis as a useful "method of investigation, an impartial instrument like, say, the infinitesimal calculus."[21] As such, it has, beyond question, proved valuable in the treatment of mental disease; though its employment is an extremely delicate matter, involving of necessity, I believe, the physician's inculcation of naturalistic philosophical assumptions. This may shed some light on it; but, in any case, Dr Lewisohn obviously assumes that the Freudian psychology, which has been elaborated from a basis of psycho-analytical investigation, is a body of valid scientific knowledge, doubtless incomplete, perhaps subject to modification in detail, but not conjectural, not a "merely tentative grouping of ideas for the purpose of testing theories," and not, like everything of the sort bequeathed us by the last century, "absurdly premature."

21 This is Dr Freud's own statement, in *The Future of an Illusion* (English translation by W. D. Robson-Scott), p. 64. I cannot help thinking the calculus a misleading analogy.

From the wealth of matter in *Expression in America* illustrating the consequences of this assumption, I choose two typical "explanations," both of which happen to be concerned with criticism:

Poe's critical theory is a defensive rationalization of his instinctive and inevitable practice, a justification, a glorification of his own lack of passion, humanity, ethical perception, continuity of power, imaginative sympathy, knowledge of man and of human life—of all the capacities and qualities, in brief, that give substance and import to a writer. Poe, like all persons whose inner self-esteem is abnormally low, needed to build a legend of greatness for himself. He made his own limitations the laws of art. Hence writers like Baudelaire, stricken by similar neuroses and driven to similar compensatory gestures, accepted his critical theories with profound satisfaction. Baudelaire [was] a psychical and physical masochist with the mentality of a monk of the dark ages. . . . It is needless to say that I feel no moral disapprobation toward such psychopathic types. . . . Hopelessly crippled in the most vital and pervasive of human functions by a trauma sustained in infancy, a pseudo-aristocrat of Virginia and an outcast, a prey to poverty and all its worst humiliations, greatly gifted, insanely sensitive, driven into the temporary release of intoxication by that first and most insupportable of human ills—Poe is worthy of tears and not of taunts. . . . The childish confusion at the heart of his critical theory is to be found in his use of the word truth. He uses that word as though it meant proposition, scientific statement, maxim or saw. With these forms of intellectual expression literature has in fact little to do. But Poe pretended to himself, for unconscious reasons of his own, that he was fighting a mean didacticism, when he was declaiming against the necessary and eternal content of literature, which he himself was incapable of achieving. . . . It was Poe's pathological flight from the realities of his own constitution and character and thus from all reality that blinded him to the confusion of his thinking and to the nature of the books which he evidently read. . . . It does not speak well for the intelligence of eccentric and aesthetic critics that they have taken Poe's theories to be more than the

rationalization of his own practice and have assigned to them
any validity in the world of thought. . . . As a critic he does
not exist. . . . His critical theories . . . are objectively considered absurd.

The second "explanation" may be given at once:

Howells yielded without so much as an inner protest to Boston and this pusillanimity of his is the worm that may hollow
out the otherwise extraordinarily fine structure of his best
work. There is in his treatment of the major human emotions
a shocking and contemptible moderation; there is in his attitude to marriage, above all, an unbearable stuffiness and creep-
ing prose. . . . What, alas, reconciled his contemporaries to
Howells and reduced the weightiness of his achievement was
that he assumed the limitations of his experience and his observation to be the limitations of truth itself. . . . Not content
with declaring all American humanity to conform to a certain
type of anaemic Bostonianism, he carried this standard into
the past with an amazing effrontery for so mild a man and declared three-fifths of the literature commonly called classic to
be "trash and often very filthy trash" and added his conviction
that "nobody really enjoys it." In other words, quite like Poe's,
Howells' critical theory is a rationalization of his practice
which, in turn, was the inevitable expression of his nature. So
that this critical theory has no critical, no objective value at
all. . . . Howells, like his age, was acutely and negatively sex-
conscious. We have no need to be always protesting against
that which does not trouble us. . . . Tradition and authentic
personal report have it that as he grew older he grew ever
sourer and more intolerant on this subject, . . . falling into a
kind of negative frenzy at the slightest suggestion of man's
mammalian nature and hence as obsessed by sex as a fighting
prohibitionist is by alcohol. . . . Howells' avoidance of human
passion in his works is clamorous in its significant and sultry
silence. Nor is tradition wholly ignorant of the aging novelist's
uneasy and unconsciously guilty methods of sublimation. But
these cannot yet be discussed with propriety. What one is not
surprised to find is that at the core of his long and in all outward circumstances happy and fortunate career, there is a note

of guilt and gloom, of preoccupation with death and with the disasters of the social order.

It is no part of my purpose in this place to comment generally on Dr Lewisohn's interpretations of Poe and Howells. They invite such comment, because they are open to serious question at a number of points. Their drift, however, if we pass by details, is towards something familiar enough and scarcely doubtful. We did not have to await the Freudian psychology for the discovery that man is a limited, conditioned creature, whose thought is dependent upon his capacities, including his capacity for experience. But Dr Lewisohn, of course, has more than this to say; and the remarkable thing which calls for special notice is his conclusion in each case that the critical theory under examination has no validity, because of the conditions back of it. The Freudian psychology, in other words, does not simply "explain" Poe and Howells—it explains them away—after which Dr Lewisohn rescues what he thinks serviceable in the work of each.

In the case of Poe we are definitely informed that the mental condition out of which his work issued was pathological. Not only his criticism, but his tales and poems also, are the products of a diseased mind; though Poe did have "rare and brief" "moments of insight, however troubled." Yet Howells is explained away in terms not different from those which serve for Poe, while it is not pretended that his was really a diseased mind. There are, to be sure, hints looking in this direction, dropped quite after the manner of gossipers who take pains to assure one that they could say more if they would; but on the other hand a great deal is said to show that Howells's mind was of a type common, or indeed practically universal, in his age and country. And, moreover, the process of compensatory or defensive "rationalization" of which Poe and Howells were the victims is detected by Dr Lewisohn repeatedly in Americans of every generation, and not only in literary people, but in whole sections of the population.

How, indeed, could it be otherwise? Zeal for law and order, we are told, is simply the expression of an unconscious desire to commit crimes which, nevertheless, one is "ethically inhibited from committing." The Puritans of early New England ferociously punished those who disobeyed their regulations because only such punishment could express the "smothered rebellion" of their "natural passions." "The conventional gloating of the 'pure' over the 'impure' " is the expression of envy, which, when it is otherwise impotent, vents itself in cruelty. The more "pure" one is, in other words, the more "violently sex-conscious" one really is. If one says that another person is "sex-obsessed," one really "bears witness to one's own obsession and to the agonized cry of one's soul: What I dare not do, you shall not do!"[22] In fact, Dr Lewisohn says, "this process of ambivalence, of simultaneous attraction and repulsion, of desire and fear, must be understood by any one who wishes to penetrate to the true character of men and their ways." And elsewhere he explains "the true character of men and their ways" when he remarks that our "ambivalence" "pollutes and sickens the soul from age to age."[23]

How, I may repeat, could it be otherwise? If things are thus with humanity, the wells of thought are indeed poisoned; and, of course, once the process of "ambivalence" has been discovered through the analysis of mentally diseased people, it can be seen wherever one may choose to look. Nothing would be easier than to exhibit the "fierce ambivalence" which animates Dr Lewisohn himself, because no one writes with more constant personal reference than he, so that the data in his case are not only abundant, but perfectly transparent. To follow his example, however, would chiefly gratify ribald spirits; and it is more to the present purpose to notice that, according to Dr Lewisohn and Dr Freud, there are some instances in which reason really is reason. Examples are to be found even in America, and include, amongst others, Mr Van Wyck Brooks, Dr Joseph Wood Krutch, and Dr Lewisohn. But here arises a difficulty. What is reason?

22 These statements occur on pp. 166, 14, 49, 238, and 482–483 respectively of *Expression in America*.

23 *Expression in America*, pp. 244 and 14 respectively.

Dr Lewisohn is perfectly frank and very insistent in asserting that he is wholly reasonable.[24] Hence I suppose, if he is correct concerning himself, we may discover the nature of reason from its operation in him. But how, on the basis of the Freudian psychology, can he know whether he is correct about himself or not? I am unable to see the slightest possibility of his knowing this, or of our knowing it.[25] If, however, we proceed to contemplate the operations of what we may provisionally call Dr Lewisohn's "reason," what do we find? I cannot, of course, give anything like a complete report in small space. I can only present a few instances showing the *way* in which Dr Lewisohn's "reason" works. It tells him, then, that there is an "enormous . . . cleavage between

[24] I do not exaggerate. A number of statements to this effect may be found in *Expression in America*—for instance, Dr Lewisohn's explanation of his own place amongst American critics (p. 425). There is also a sufficiently direct statement on p. 11 of *The Creative Life* (1924): "I am a radical in my notions about life and a classicist in my notions about literature. . . . A radical is one who insists that men shall live by the use of reason. (He means it. He does not stop using his reason when he is suddenly confronted by some particularly hoary and disreputable prejudice, taboo, superstition. It is at that point that he insists all the more on using his reason. Even at the risk of hurting some one's feelings. For by sparing this, for the moment, imaginary antagonist's feelings our radical gives that antagonist the continued privilege of spreading ruin and feeling righteous.)"

[25] I am aware that there is a place in the Freudian psychology for the reason which is alleged really to be reason, and that much is made of it. One may call it, not derogatorily, but descriptively, "animal cunning." To be perfectly rational is to have a mind wholly in tune with "reality." Lessons learned from the relief of mental disease are behind this, and mental health is conceived quite simply as freedom from tension or disharmony. The mind thus liberated does not foolishly ask what is "real." The question does not come up. One trusts one's instincts. I have been gravely informed by an intelligent student of psycho-analysis that the normal human being simply grows like a tree. Thus it appears that consciousness itself is the mental disease at which Dr Freud and his followers are really striking. And certainly the Freudian psychology riddles it, in a manner to suggest that the psychologist must be something other than human, if to be human is to grow like a tree. Dr Freud, I must add, realizes what complications are introduced when the human trees form themselves into a society, but he has a way of resolving these difficulties which seems to satisfy him. He is, however, too easily satisfied at more than one point, and clearly fails even to safeguard what he calls "reason" from the dissolving activity of his own psychology. Dr Lewisohn's "reason," for example, is constituted as Dr Freud's is, and bears a family likeness to it; but it cannot be the same "reason," because it reaches some quite different conclusions.

the past and the present," that real change is the rule, that discontinuity marks our world, and that man "has undergone changes which have transmuted the very groundwork of his character and outlook." Yet at the same time it tells him that there are "changeless elements" in man, in nature, and in human life; that "sound literature" has a "changeless character," and so "speaks permanently to men," because men have "eternally" the same "preoccupations"; and that "the effects demanded of literature have not changed in their *essence* from Isaiah and Euripides to, let us say, Dreiser and Shaw." Nevertheless, "there are no external or fixed standards by which either genius may be known from without or creative activity guided from within." Genius, in fact, "creates values as it goes along," working wholly from within; and what genius creates is inherently moral, beautiful, universal in significance, and imperishable. Criticism, however, "is the disengaging and weighing of these values into which men transmute their experience and from which alone experience derives both its *meaning* and its *form*." Criticism thus demands complete detachment, in order that the critic may "hold the balance utterly level." But that education is to be condemned "by which the gentleman withdraws himself from the mob." Still, it is true that "the minority that carries on a national culture is small," and that "the principles of the majority of men are mean and superstitious and barbarous." For this reason, doubtless, "all creative spirits are necessarily heretics." Yet "it is indeed quite open to question whether the greatest works of the human imagination have not been produced when the artist identified himself largely with the collective culture and tradition of his folk." And the real explanation of art is to be found in the truth that "the creative and the procreative instinct are one."[26]

This collocation of passages, which might be greatly extended, shows how easy it would be to make Dr Lewisohn's

[26] These statements are not drawn from works written at different times. I have purposely confined myself to *Expression in America*, where they will all be found, on pp. xi, 459–460, xvii, 296, 160, 185, 55, 403–404, 459, 458, 456, 416, 80, 43, 282, 405, 78, 274–275, and 536 respectively.

"reason" look ridiculous. He has impetuously said his say
as he has gone creatively and rapidly along,[27] trusting his
genius. When occasionally he thinks of his "reason," he is
apt to regard it as something supernal; but he is actually
guided by his passions, and does not even attempt consistently to "rationalize" them. In complete accord, like Mr Edmund Wilson, with a familiar modern belief, he takes it for a
certainty that if he can just be fully enough himself, without let or hindrance, he will strike a vein of fundamental
reality uniting him with what is similarly real in all other
men. This is the ground of his opposition to all standards, of
whatever kind—an opposition which, with other of his "cer-
tainties," allies him in his own despite with aesthetic critics
whom he has venomously attacked. This, too, explains how he
could write, in 1924, that "the function—perhaps the chief
function—of the American critic" "must be" the effort to
make a larger number of people understand why artists and
writers, or all "creators," of necessity lead irregular lives.[28]
And this, finally, accounts for his easy confidence that the
terrors of the Freudian psychology could be invoked against
others without recoil upon himself. He stood, like his venerated master, beyond the fateful circle. The Freudian psychology, in other words, was to be welcomed as a useful servant. Through it he could deliver knock-out blows, without
taking the trouble to argue any question on its merits. I do
not mean that this has been his conscious attitude. His truly
monumental self-righteousness is, I am sure, genuine. But he
is very easily satisfied when he wants to believe anything;
and I do not see how, if he had deliberately tried, he could
have made it more evident that in reality he has simply used
the Freudian psychology as a bludgeon, for his own purposes. And I do not see, in addition, how Dr Lewisohn could

[27] Frequently, too, he can only be read rapidly with any satisfaction. If
one hastens, one can feel fairly sure of his general drift; but if one stops to
look for the exact meaning one is likely, often, to be lost. I will quote a sentence from p. 420 of *Expression in America:* "So much the briefest self-
examination should have taught even an academic critic who himself cannot
imagine as the expression of his personality any opinions but those he has
come to hold embodied in any but the prose form which he actually masters."
[28] *The Creative Life,* p. 20.

have made it more evident that this fancied resource has in fact weakened and vitiated his work, encouraging him to write confusedly, thoughtlessly, and yet violently.

VII

THERE is a passage in one of Montaigne's essays which some of our critical writers seem positively bent on making one recall. "Nothing vexes me so much in stupidity," Montaigne wrote, "as that it is more pleased with itself than any intelligence can reasonably be with itself. It is ill-luck that discretion forbids you to be satisfied with yourself, and to trust in yourself, and always dismisses you ill content and faint-hearted, whereas opinionativeness and rashness fill their possessors with rejoicing and assurance. It is those who most lack ability who look at other men over the shoulder, always returning from the fray full of pride and gladness. And most frequently, too, this arrogance of speech and cheerful aspect give them the better of it in the opinion of bystanders, who are ordinarily of weak intelligence and incapable of judging well and discerning the real advantage. Obstinacy and heat of opinion are the surest signs of dulness: is there any thing so firm, resolute, disdainful, meditative, serious, and solemn as the ass?"[29]

Now I have tried to make it clear that I do not think of Dr Lewisohn as a stupid fellow; but it is something more than a piece of ill luck that Montaigne should have hit him off so exactly in this brief description. And it is at least a piece of ill luck, not only for them but for our generation, that other so-called critics who are by no means stupid fellows should nevertheless, for whatever reason, be writing exactly as if they were stupid fellows. For that is what it finally comes to. The late Professor Burnet of Scotland, a very learned, very simple, very honest man, delivered a lecture not many years before his death on the growth of ignorance in our time. And he has not been alone in perceiving that the very advance of knowledge has been attended by corresponding dangers—dangers of advancing ignorance

[29] *Essays,* Bk. III, Chap. VIII (G. B. Ives's translation).

and, equally, of thoughtlessness. In the earlier part of this chapter I have tried to show that there is nothing at all astonishing in this, but that, on the contrary, it is the inevitable result of increasing, successful specialization;—and it is a result which will plague us even more severely in the immediate future should our educational institutions continue blindly to promote it. Yet at present, as the latter portion of this chapter, I trust, makes sufficiently clear, the plague of ignorance and thoughtlessness has already attained proportions of great magnitude, and shows itself—not alone where we might have expected it, amongst cheap journalists and small specialists—but precisely amongst our most talented and most serious critics.

I am aware that no one cause is sufficient to explain this break-down at a crucial point in the structure of civilized society. I believe that specialization and the things going with it account for much.[30] But other causes enter in and are not unimportant.[31] And all of them together exert a formidable pressure. There can be no doubt about that, and it would be the height of foolishness to minimize the powerful influences which are to-day making for disintegration on all sides. But it matters not how formidable the pressure, disintegration is not thereby made a good and lovely thing. Let "the conditions" shape man for it howsoever strongly, shoddy work and slapdash thinking remain shoddy work and slapdash thinking. And as a matter of historic fact "the conditions" have always been unfavourable to excellence. The conditions may be as unfavourable now as any one may

[30] Not, I must add, that I am "opposed" to specialization. As I have earlier said, it is simply idle to talk of dispensing with it. But it is one thing to encourage it blindly, and another to see it for what it is and to attempt to keep its benefits while safeguarding society from its evils.

[31] For example, Dr Lewisohn insists, correctly, that "art is not a profession" (*The Creative Life,* p. 21; see also *Expression in America,* p. 456). Yet Dr Lewisohn is a professional man of letters, and was recently reported in a European newspaper as saying, at a public luncheon in Paris, that he was being forced to *double* his annual output, because of the decline in the sales of his writings brought about by the depression. Who can help thinking that this sheds light on the real nature of work which, nevertheless, we are invited to regard as "more significant than the struggle between armies with banners"?

care to claim—more unfavourable, possibly, than at any previous time we know of. Nevertheless, neither this extenuating plea nor any other can serve to excuse the thoughtlessness, the sheer unintelligence, displayed in such a passage as the following, written by Mr Wilson:

It is well to remember the mysteriousness of the states with which we respond to the stimulus of works of literature and the primarily suggestive character of the language in which these works are written, on any occasion when we may be tempted to characterize as "nonsense," "balderdash" or "gibberish" some new and outlandish-looking piece of writing to which we do not happen to respond. If other persons say they do respond, and derive from doing so pleasure or profit, we must take them at their word.[32]

It is very true that no human being is infallible, that even the best qualified persons will make mistakes, even in such definitely determinable matters as those with which, for instance, structural engineers have to do. It is true that sometimes a flash of sudden, inexplicable, sure recognition is worth more than the careful, deliberate verdict of the learned and thoughtful. It is true that discoveries, whether in the realm of literary art or in any other realm, have nearly always been greeted, at first, with opposition or scepticism, and that time has had to pass before they could be judged aright, and that this has often brought undeserved suffering upon benefactors of the race. All this and more is true, and is as deplorable as true, and shows plainly enough that in every generation more is demanded of intelligence than intelligence can well perform. But is this an adequate reason for supinely giving over all effort to be intelligent; for concluding that things must go as they will, hit or miss; for simply throwing up one's hands in acknowledgement that life in this world is too, too difficult?

Mr Wilson utters no word about his "other persons," or about the "pleasure" or the "profit" they may *say* they receive; he is concerned only to insist that "we must take them

32 *Axel's Castle*, p. 252.

at their word." It has always hitherto been recognized that,
when one said pleasure was the object aimed at by an art,
this was not an evasion of the problem of definition, but an
attempt rather to state the problem accurately. It is by no
means simple, and efforts to make it simple uniformly fail.
Hence it was proposed that the question should turn upon
the quality of the pleasure given. A work of art was to be
pronounced successful if it really did give its appropriate
pleasure to the *right* person, the person best qualified to feel
that kind of pleasure. But Mr Wilson will have none of this.
It shall not be ours to distinguish, to discriminate;—ours
not to reason why, ours but to accept or die. "Life is just so
mysterious, my dear children, that it's no use asking questions about anything. Really, my dears, the only safe course
is to try to live like a sponge. Nice sponges, you know, never
do anything—never even say anything—and so they never
do any harm, never make any mistakes, never hurt anybody's
feelings, never discourage their brothers. Because in addition
to the sponges, you remember, there *are* their brothers, the
creative fish. And the creative fish keep letting themselves go,
and throw off the most wonderful things, without even knowing what they are doing. And the nice sponges just receive
everything that comes, and if anything ever seems a bit queer
they never say anything—they just receive it anyhow—and
after a while they like it when they get used to it, the same
as everything else. And it would be a Terrible Wrong, children, both to the fish and to themselves if they did otherwise."

Of course it can be said that the context of Mr Wilson's
plea must be remembered—that he might never have gone
so far had he not been confronted by a very difficult situation. Having resolved to swallow the symbolistic technique
whole, he simply had to make out the best case he could for
Miss Gertrude Stein, and courageously risked everything to
do so. This, I imagine, is true enough—and has nothing
whatever to do with the question. It simply shows that Mr
Wilson was determined, not to deal with a problem, but to
make out a case. It shows equally that to concentrate one's
attention on relatively small questions, when one has not set-

tled with one's self the larger questions and does not hold general principles steadily in view, leads in the end to the most disastrous thoughtlessness.

But, it may also be said, Mr Wilson's plea has a background. It is merely the last term, or *reductio ad absurdum*, of an argument which goes back at least several generations, and for which there is something to be said. And this also is quite true. In 1869 Flaubert thought that genuine criticism was still to seek. "At the time of La Harpe," he told George Sand, critics "were still grammarians; at the time of Sainte-Beuve and of Taine, they are historians. When will they be artists, only artists, but really artists? Where do you know a criticism? Who is there who is anxious about the work in itself, in an intense way?"[33] From the time when these questions were asked until this day there has been a steady, widening current of what has looked to be the kind of criticism that Flaubert desired. And there is a need for such criticism, a very real need which gives it, when we get it, true importance. Flaubert wanted aesthetic criticism, directed at the reading public. If he was publishing a novel which, simply as a work of art, was distinctive, and perhaps superior in this respect to any other novels, he wanted critics to understand, discuss, and emphasize what to him, as an artist, was its real importance, and so to educate the public, leading it to appreciate in the right way what he had done.

For such criticism there is, as I say, a real need. The trouble is, as Flaubert himself realized, that it is most extremely difficult to produce. Hence aesthetic criticism is always likely, even with constant watchfulness such as we have scarcely had, to degenerate into something which may look like the real thing, which may satisfy artists, and which may be an unmitigated evil, because not criticism at all. From time immemorial there has been a living aesthetic criticism, most often not written, not published—the criticism by artists, from their own special angle, of their fellow-artists' work. It is what may be called the shop-talk of artists, and it is safe to say that no art can thrive without it, without a

[33] *The George Sand–Gustave Flaubert Letters,* translated by Aimee L. McKenzie, p. 121.

great deal of it. It concerns processes, the ways in which
different effects may be achieved. It is technical, minute, and
perhaps endless. Not all the king's horses nor all the king's
men can ever interest a large number of people in it. As soon
as it becomes public it is likely to become meaningless, because its life is in its actual contact with the concrete, genuine situation—with the work in progress, now lying on the
writer's desk, now fastened to the painter's easel.

But Flaubert felt—and rightly—that something could be
done, and should be done, to help the public to look at a work
of art as artists look at it. Yet we have not had, in England
and America, much criticism of this kind. We have had instead the development traced in this chapter, which has culminated in the pretence that literature is, so to say, the private concern of a coterie completely independent of all social
ties or responsibilities; that criticism is strictly confined to
the "elucidation" of what this coterie happens to write—and
should, as far as possible, be monopolized by the "artists"
themselves; and that the vulgar public "must" take one
artist's word for it that his fellow-artists' writings—*The
Wasteland, Ulysses, Tender Buttons*—are "works of literature which, for intensity, brilliance and boldness as well as
for an architectural genius, an intellectual mastery of their
materials, rare among their Romantic predecessors, are
probably comparable to the work of any time."[34]

It is writing like this—having its own boldness certainly,
if nothing else—which makes one wonder if some of our
critics may not have received part of their slender training
in a correspondence school of advertising. I do not think the
"creators" are any better served by it than the public. I
think the evidence is full and clear that much of our recent
"criticism" is not really criticism at all. I think the time has
come to recognize that, since criticism inevitably involves
judgements, the effort must be made, howsoever difficult, to
judge intelligently—which is to say consciously, deliberately, on the basis of the best standards, frankly acknowledged, that the critic can formulate. Such standards will not

[34] *Axel's Castle*, p. 297.

be absolute; they will be subject to amendment, to ever-renewed examination, as conditions change; they will not be held in common by all critics; they will not make criticism simple, easy, and instantly decisive. But at least critics will know what they are doing, and those for whom they write will know what they are doing.

I think it indisputable, then, that criticism, like charity, should begin at home. I think it indisputable, too, that when criticism ventures abroad it should do so, not for the sake of artists, but for the sake of men, for the sake of life. No small part of our trouble and confusion in recent years has arisen from claims which are indefensible only because they are exclusive and exaggerated. We actually have, as I have said earlier in this chapter, many kinds of criticism—and need them all, cannot do without them. It is the vainest of vain pretensions to assert that criticism can only be the concern of artists for the sake of art. There is a true aesthetic criticism without which art cannot thrive, and there is need for more of it than we have or are likely soon to have. But it is not the only criticism; it is far more limited in character than those imagine who want, not really to practise it, but to *use* it; and it is not primarily addressed to the public.

What happens, then, when the "creators" attempt to take criticism into their own hands and to refashion it to suit themselves, instead of submitting themselves and their work to it, is something disastrous to the "creators," to criticism, to sanity, and so to civilization. And what is disastrous to the "creators" is not their failure, but their degree of success. They have sought a freedom indistinguishable from the irresponsibility of childhood, and they have used it just as might have been expected—to create a hole-and-corner literature. And the trouble with the "criticism" that has sprung up along with this hole-and-corner literature is its wilfulness, its ignorance, its thoughtlessness, its lack of integrity. There is not, as I have tried to make clear, the slightest doubt or question concerning the real nature of the critical spirit, and its vital importance in human life. But in this one field where the name of criticism is still popularly known, and in which alone we can hope at present for that comprehensive criticism of life without which all specialized criticism, howsoever rigorous and successful, will ultimately prove vain—in this field of largest opportunity and responsibility we are asked gratefully to accept, for the convenience of the proponents, something which is simply the negation of the critical spirit. This, as I have shown, is not a matter of opinion, or open to argument. With a very great deal that Dr Lewisohn, and Mr Max Eastman, and Mr Eliot have to say I am myself in full agreement, but that is not the question under discussion. Nearly everybody can find himself in full agreement at some point or other with, for example, Dr Lewisohn, because, as we have seen, he contrives to be completely on both sides of a great many arguments. And this plainly arises from his success in attempting to be nothing whatever except Dr Lewisohn—Dr Lewisohn expounding Dr Lewisohn for the sake of Dr Lewisohn, and just trusting his genius, though calling in Dr Freud for expert assistance in destruction.[35]

Accordingly I do not wish to suggest that criticism should somehow be taken away from the "creators." You cannot take from men what they do not have. And I think, besides, that in the long run those who can be seriously harmed by the wilful, cocksure "modernists" are only themselves. But I do wish to suggest that since "criticism is as inevitable as breathing," and as important, we should look for it where it is really to be found. It has not in fact perished in our time. And not only does it flourish in many specialized fields, whence, as we have seen, we can learn both its nature and its vital place in life;—it also continues active in its field of largest opportunity and responsibility. And amongst those who are keeping alive the true critical spirit to-day I would

[35] On p. 422 of *Expression in America* we are told that Dr Spingarn, in formulating his theory of criticism, is really to be regarded as "a Jew . . . seeking to conquer America for his children." However this may be (I have received no pamphlet from Dr Spingarn on the subject) Dr Lewisohn could not have given his own game away more plainly;—though there has been, this long time, no excuse for doubt about it. In 1919 he was entrusted with the responsibility of editing *A Modern Book of Criticism*. He then judged himself worthy of much more space than he accorded any of the other twenty-four French, German, English, and American critics whose work is represented in the volume.

suggest that we can learn most from Mr Paul Elmer More.
I will say frankly that I am inclined to this belief because
I myself have learned most from him; but I make the suggestion with the more confidence because repeated and varied
testimony gathered through a good many years has convinced me that Mr More's work has only to be known and
understood in order to be respected, and recognized as having a very high importance, whether or not it wins full assent
from any reader or fellow-critic. This has, in fact, been fully
and generously acknowledged in England and in continental
Europe. It has now been fully and ungenerously acknowledged by Dr Lewisohn, in *Expression in America*. And it
has been no less fully though tacitly acknowledged by a large
number of other critical writers in America, who have felt
that Mr More could not be allowed to go unanswered, but
who have discovered no better method than consistent misrepresentation.[36] This campaign of misrepresentation will
make, some day, a not uninstructive study; and it has been
so far successful that, although Mr More himself is one of
the most widely known of American men of letters, and, as
Dr Lewisohn says, "one of the soundest of American prose
stylists," his work, notwithstanding, is less well known and is
generally misunderstood.[37] Hence I have come to feel that a
commentary on Mr More's writings should serve a useful
purpose, and such a commentary I have attempted to provide in the following pages, traversing in greatest detail the
early years and the preparatory work of that time.

[36] See Appendix B.

[37] As Mr More confessed several years ago, he used to solace himself with
the boast that he was at once the least read and most hated author in existence: "Other writers I admitted might be more hated, and I hoped that a
few were less read; but the combination I claimed for myself as a unique
distinction." (*The Demon of the Absolute,* 1928, p. 3.)

II. EARLY LIFE AND WORK

I

PAUL ELMER MORE was born in St Louis on 12 December, 1864. He is the seventh of eight children born to Katharine Hay Elmer and Enoch Anson More. Both the Elmers and the Mores are of English descent, but little is known concerning the history and connexions of the latter family. It appears that a certain Enoch More owned property in Cambridge, Massachusetts, in 1637. There is nothing, however, to show whether or not he was the direct ancestor of a later Enoch More—the great-grand-father of Paul More—who was a soldier in the Continental Army and who died of black fever in 1777, while in camp near Philadelphia. This Enoch More came from Greenwich, New Jersey, and his third son, Paul More's grandfather, was a mill-owner in Bridgeton, New Jersey.

Concerning the Elmers comparatively a great deal is known. The name is Saxon and appears, as Ælmar, in extant records dating from as early as 1009, whence it has been learned that one of that name was Bishop of Shearborn. The name was later written Aylmer, and in the first quarter of the fourteenth century an Aylmer was high sheriff of the county of Norfolk. From him was descended John Aylmer, Bishop of London from 1576 until his death in 1594. He in turn was the grandfather of Edward Elmer, who came to Massachusetts with other members of the church of Thomas Hooker in 1632. Four years later Edward Elmer removed from Cambridge to Connecticut, where he became one of the founders of Hartford. Early in the eighteenth century a grandson, Daniel Elmer, settled in New Jersey; and Lucius Q. C. Elmer, great-grandson of Daniel, was the father of Katharine Hay Elmer. Lucius Elmer lived in Bridgeton, was an officer in the American army during the War of 1812, was a member of the Twenty-eighth Congress (1843–1845), was later Attorney-General of New Jersey, and finally became a Justice of the Supreme Court of that state.

Katharine Elmer was an incessant and omnivorous reader throughout her long life;—born in 1825, she died in the spring of 1914, some fifteen years after the death of her husband. Like some other omnivorous readers, she was not really critical—was not, perhaps, in any important sense an intellectual woman at all. Yet her reading did much more for her than simply help to pass the time. Her life was by no means easy, and many women in similar circumstances—with the responsibilities of a large family, and with marked fluctuations in fortune to contend against—have become more and more creatures of routine, narrowly constricted in outlook, and content merely to get through the passing days without positive disaster. It was not so with Mrs More. Literature, in the most inclusive sense of the word, early opened the doors of her mind and kept them always open to the life of the world, while it deepened the springs of emotion, and refined her feelings, and nourished her imagination. She thus became a real force in the developing lives of her children, not by trying to mould them in accordance with strong convictions of her own, nor by trying, as she well might have, to send them out quickly into practical life, but by aiding them to see that existence was not wholly bounded or conditioned by material circumstance, by encouraging them to take large and long views, and by giving them in herself an example of the reality of spiritual life. By "spiritual life," it should scarcely be necessary to add, I mean nothing depending solely on religious belief, but rather, in a broad sense, the life of the mind experienced as something more real and more rewarding than the life of sensation, or of social distraction, or of struggle for power. Naturally, the home in which Mrs More's children were brought up was a home for books; and the young Mores, whatever else they at any time lacked, never failed of the opportunity to become reading creatures. It was, moreover, through their mother's determination and through her self-sacrifice that her younger children were enabled to complete their education.

No influence so direct was exerted, on his younger children

at any rate, by Enoch Anson More. He appears to have been of a type formerly not unusual in America. Whether or not he was deeply religious it is perhaps impossible to determine. He was certainly rigid in belief and in his way of life, while at the same time apparently a capable man of business—though, like many another, he found it easier to start a business than to keep it going. After his marriage he took his wife West, and established himself in Dayton, Ohio, where he built up a profitable trade as a bookseller. This he abandoned, to go to St Louis about 1860, largely so as not to be separated from a minister who had come to exert a considerable influence over both him and his wife. When the Civil War broke out he actively supported the cause of the Union, and attained the rank of Brigadier General in the Commissary Department. It is said he kept his records so well that they are still used as models by the Department of War. The remainder of his life was spent in St Louis, where he engaged with varying success in a number of business enterprises. Religion and trade, however, did not wholly absorb him; for he was, in addition, a lover both of shooting and of fishing. What he might have become in different circumstances it is useless to conjecture. It seems that he had wished, when young, to become an architect, and had turned to business only because his parents had made it practically necessary. That this youthful ambition, moreover, may not have been the expression of a merely idle or random desire is suggested by the ability he exhibited, throughout his life, both in arithmetical calculation and in drawing. He had, besides, a rather good instinctive taste, though he never attained any real knowledge of art.

It is tempting and perhaps not wholly fanciful to conclude that Paul More may have inherited from his father qualities and talents which needed for their fruitful development the influence exerted by his mother. That he was, at any rate, a born artist in words is evidenced by the power he had, when still a mere boy, to hold his comrades transfixed, sometimes for hours, by the vivid and thrilling tales he invented for them. They instinctively recognized in him qualities which they felt he alone possessed, and which made him their natural leader;—a leader, however, with no desire for domination and with little interest in merely childish pursuits, who swayed his subjects in spite of himself, by a power he did not understand, which had, in fact, something uncanny about it. What seemed most obvious was its intensity; but while it found expression in tales, to the delight of young auditors, which emphasized, often baldly enough no doubt, the residuum of mystery in human nature, it also took form in a burning confidence that life meant something, had a significance extending far beyond its apparent or earthly limits, and was in fact not a gift but a responsibility. The nearest analogues that suggest themselves, concerning which there is sufficient evidence really to aid understanding, are the cases of Coleridge and of Newman in their boyhood. These cases show, moreover, that it would be a radical mistake to think of the story-telling as something separable from the religious conviction which appeared alongside it. The latter, however, found immediately at hand a channel for its development and definite fixation, in the institutional religion of Paul More's parents. This, it must be said, was crude, narrow, over-positive, and plainly at variance with nineteenth-century science and its philosophic implications.

A child could not know that, of course; but even the merest youth, in the latter part of the nineteenth century, if he read seriously at all, could scarcely fail to hear of the conflict between science and religion precipitated by Darwin and Herbert Spencer, and carried on energetically by Huxley. And Paul More followed the example of his mother as early as it was possible to do so, becoming what he has remained, an incessant, unwearying, and extraordinarily retentive reader. As a consequence, the Calvinism of his childhood left him, never to return. He became a thorough-going sceptic, though without, at first, or for some time, realizing the full meaning of the change. He rejected, in other words, the authoritative claims of his parents' church, because he could no longer believe that the miracles described in the Bible had really occurred, and because in other respects also the Bible seemed clearly fabulous; yet this did not immediately cause him to question everything which had hitherto made up his world. No one who has been through a similar experience will suppose that it can ever have been taken lightly, and in this instance it assuredly was not. Such changes, indeed, especially when they occur in extreme youth, are likely to be violent as well as serious, and they almost invariably leave permanent marks.

That his abandonment of Christianity was not for Paul More a revolutionary or tragic event, though a most serious one, was due to the fact that his reading had already brought to bear on him other influences from the tangled skein of modern thought and literary achievement. At the same time that he was beginning to learn something of the meaning of modern science, he was also becoming acquainted with the poetry of the nineteenth century, with Carlyle, with Emerson, with Thoreau; and the progress of his education, too, was opening up to him German literature, which both Coleridge and Carlyle taught him to regard as the fountain-head of new life and light for the human spirit perplexed and deadened by "mechanical" philosophy and triumphant, vulgar industrialism. Romanticism thus appeared as a welcome refuge, and Paul More steeped himself in its imaginative and poetic embodiments, and particularly in its most characteristic and extreme German manifestations. It doubtless seemed at the time that he had discovered the real unknown goal and full expression of his own intense childish convictions, at once imaginative and spiritual; and he gave himself up to this congenial world of the imagination, much as Coleridge at the beginning of the century had yielded himself wholly, for a space, to the materialism of David Hartley.

The influences in these two cases were each the other's opposite, but the cases themselves are curiously parallel. For Coleridge thought himself wholly absorbed by Hartley when in reality only half of his mind, so to say, was converted— with the consequence that gradually he found he was assenting to fundamentally opposed propositions, and must make a decisive choice between his ill-assorted beliefs. In much the same way Paul More was, as far as he was aware, wholly converted to romanticism, while nevertheless deeply impressed by the philosophy of Herbert Spencer, and impelled thus towards a hard, scientific rationalism. He even formed the design of a rationalistic system which was to be more consistent than Spencer's, and was to fulfil what Spencer had not succeeded in finishing. A considerable part of this plan was actually carried out, though how competently or impressively cannot be known, as the completed portion was never published, and has since been destroyed. At almost the same time, moreover, he was composing romantic tragedies in verse, and a huge romantic epic—and these too were never published and were later destroyed.

Both the verse and the philosophical prose were, of course, the products of youthful excitement and discovery—not the products of experience and of mature reflection—and it may safely be assumed that they served their most important purpose simply in aiding their author to see his way beyond them. He meanwhile was growing to manhood in the city of his birth—a city which, as it then was, has been described best by Mr Theodore Dreiser in his *Book about Myself*. "I can testify," Mr More has written, "to his account of its streets and institutions, and to his characterization of some of its well-known citizens, as truthful and extraordinarily vivid."[1] Mr More attended the public schools of St Louis, and then proceeded to Washington University, in the same city, where he was graduated A.B. in 1887. Soon after his entrance into the University, his eyes failed him entirely, but this did not compel him to interrupt his studies. His devoted sister, Alice, read to him, and so enabled him to carry on, while he gradually recovered his sight. After graduation he immediately became a teacher in the Smith Academy, at St Louis, and held this position for five years, though one year out of the five he spent in Europe. At the same time he continued to study, fruitfully, though entirely without help and on his own responsibility. In 1892 he received a master's degree from Washington University, for a thesis written in Latin—and since destroyed.

During this period he also published his first book, *Helena and Occasional Poems*. It is a small volume of seventy-eight

[1] *The Demon of the Absolute*, p. 65.

pages, within which space Mr More included a tiny fraction
—all that he thought worth keeping—of the verse he had
written before 1890. The first thing to strike one who looks
into the book is that by the time the title-poem was composed
its author had fallen under the sway of a third influence; for
Helena is written in hendecasyllabics, and both its style and
certain of the incidents narrated show clearly that the piece
is modelled not only in metrical form, but in all respects, on
classical poetry. One can, in fact, be more specific, because
the poem's combination of idyllic elements with touches of
seemingly naïve, homely realism is definitely Theocritean.
And Theocritus, of course, and his followers, represent precisely that development of classical poetry nearest akin to
two important and distinctive aspects of romanticism—its
idealization of simple, unsophisticated people, and its proneness to turn away from the real world to some imagined
scheme of things nearer the heart's desire. To remember this
is to see more easily how two streams of influence which we
commonly, and not inaccurately, think of as antipathetic,
can nevertheless unite at one point or another, as they did
repeatedly in the work of various poets of the nineteenth
century. In the present instance one finds no idealization of
simple or primitive people, but one does find idyllic scenes
and situations represented, more than once with real if fragile beauty of conception and execution. Both of these aspects
of romanticism, moreover, are but particular developments
of sentimentalism, and a mild sentimentality is the pervasive
characteristic of the whole volume. It is, too, a volume of
echoes. Besides Theocritus, one hears, faintly and fragmen-
tarily, the voices of Coleridge, of Keats, of Landor, of Swin-
burne, of Arnold, of Longfellow. And this, I think, fairly
indicates the chief interest of the little book, though its
author dreamed, at this time, of becoming a second Heine on
the banks of the Mississippi. The volume does contain a few
moderately good pieces; but alas—candour compels one to
add—nothing in the least remarkable. There is some awk-
wardness, some flatness; there is nothing to make one value
these poems for themselves. They are worth recalling only

because they give us a glimpse of Paul More's intellectual history and earliest development.[2]

They give us, however, no more than a glimpse, for reasons which are not far to seek and are of some importance. They read too much like pieces written for practice. They served in this way, indeed, as we shall see, a useful purpose; but it may be taken for granted that, howsoever deliberate their composition, they were not written merely in experimental fashion and to gain facility. And the truth is that these poems fail because, as he grew to manhood, Paul More had become, in the manner I have sought to indicate, a deeply yet unconsciously divided person. By reason of his intensity and extreme sensibility he was more readily open to the appeal of romantic literature and thought than are the great majority of people at any time and under any conditions. He had yielded to this appeal without reserve—had learned, not by hearsay or by observation only, but in his own person, by experience, just what romanticism practically and essentially was. It had, however, brought him little peace, and no philosophical anchorage. By the time he wrote the poems in *Helena*, it only held him because of the lack of something better; and hence in these pieces we see him merely playing with a few pretty sentiments. From them alone no one could suspect the really characteristic qualities of their author which had sent him with such serious hope to the romantic fold, and which at the same time had made him a disciple of Herbert Spencer.

II

In Paul More's second book, *The Great Refusal*, which was published in 1894, a different note is struck. The volume is, like *Helena*, obviously immature; and its chief value, too, lies in the aid it gives towards an understanding of its author's intellectual history. Nevertheless, it has far more substance than its predecessor, and one feels immediately that

[2] Inasmuch as *Helena* has long been out of print and is practically inaccessible, I have selected several poems from the volume which are reproduced in the first section of Appendix A.

its author has undergone a real development in the interval
and now begins to speak from the centre of his being. For
this there is a reason. An event of capital importance had in
fact occurred, in 1891, which was to affect Mr More's whole
subsequent life and work. He has spoken of this event in his
essay on St Augustine, published eighteen years later.

No reader of Augustine's *Confessions* is likely to forget
the passage in which the Saint tells of the moment of his
conversion—how he heard a voice crying "Tolle, lege; tolle,
lege," how he took up a book of the New Testament and
read at random the first sentences that met his eyes, and how
the darkness of his doubt at once melted away, while Christian faith was born within him. In allusion to this, Mr More
opens his essay by saying: "It seems to be a pretty common
experience, among those who have passed through more than
one phase of belief, that at the critical moment of hesitation
some chance volume, falling in with the time and the mood,
should furnish a guiding impulse to the mind in its new
course; that in a lesser way we should all of us have our
Tolle, lege." And he goes on to say that the book which hap-
pened for him to mark the parting of ways was "no slender
oracle, but the ponderous and right German utterance of
Baur's *Manichäisches Religionssystem.*" "It would be impossible," he adds, "to convey to others, I cannot quite recall
to myself, the excitement amounting almost to a physical
perturbation caused by this first glimpse into the mysteries
of independent faith. It was not, I need scarcely say, that I
failed even then to see the extravagance and materialistic
tendencies of the Manichaean superstition; but its highly
elaborate form, not without elements of real sublimity, acted
as a powerful stimulus to the imagination. Here, symbolized
by the cosmic conflict of light and darkness, was found as in
a great epic poem the eternal problem of good and evil, of
the thirst for happiness and the reality of suffering, which I
knew to lie at the bottom of religious thought and emotion."[3]

What Mr More learned from the *Manichäisches Religionssystem*—which fell into his hands, apparently, by the

[3] *Shelburne Essays,* Sixth Series, Studies of Religious Dualism, 1909.

merest accident—can only be understood in the light of his situation at the time. Romanticism's sway over him was then beginning to wane, and he was undertaking in earnest by 1891 the study of classical literature, Greek as well as Latin. This, however, though it was to refashion his taste, and though it opened up to him an inexhaustible fund of sober good sense, did not yet answer to his innermost need;—and neither did the study of science, or of the philosophical interpretations of life suggested by scientific discovery. The increase of knowledge made possible by the methods of exact science impressed him, as it has inevitably impressed every child of the modern world, but he saw very early and very clearly what many of us only now begin to see, and what some of us still obstinately refuse to see—that science can answer no ultimate questions. It gives us a great deal which we must take into account, which conditions the form of our own answers, which invalidates some answers, but that is all. Its positive value is as high as any one may care to claim, because it is really inestimable; but it is a definitely specifiable, or limited, value; and only endless mischief arises from the failure to recognize these limitations. To accumulate facts by careful observation, and to derive thence, when possible, so-called laws of change, may be an inexhaustible pursuit; at least, after much activity of this kind, the end is not even in sight. It is, moreover, to many an absorbing occupation; and men of science are encouraged to follow it for its own sake because it is believed that every addition to knowledge, however insignificant it may seem, will sooner or later prove useful. Useful for what? Useful to whom? The questions scarcely need to be answered. Knowledge is only useful to men, and as a means enabling them to live better. Hence science is a good servant, but no more than a servant. It cannot tell us what it is to live well. It can only tell us how to achieve certain of our purposes, once we ourselves have determined them—and *certain of our purposes*, not all. For the field of science is not identical with the whole field of experienced reality, but only with those portions of it which can be directly observed and exactly measured. This is a serious limitation; and it means, too, that any attempt to interpret life exclusively in terms of exact science is doomed to failure; because science, by reason of its very nature, leaves out of account precisely those elements which give life its meaning and purpose, and render it distinctively human, and make man a being capable of attaining scientific knowledge.

Though this, and much more to the same effect, is rapidly becoming a commonplace to those "in the know," a critical or intelligent attitude towards science is still, as I have intimated, not usual amongst us. It is consequently the more remarkable that Paul More, as early as 1891, in almost complete isolation, perceived not only the spiritual emptiness of scientific naturalism, but the strictly limited and relative character of science itself, and the continuing validity of non-naturalistic interpretations of life which tried honestly to cover the whole field of experienced reality. How explicitly he did so, from the very moment when he became acquainted with Baur's treatise, may remain a doubtful question. It is not important. What was important for him, and what remains important for those who would understand this crucial turning-point in his development, is that the *Manichäisches Religionssystem* came to him at the right time, when he was profoundly dissatisfied, and when he had learned enough to feel confident that he was legitimately dissatisfied, both with nineteenth-century romanticism and with naturalism. And through Baur's massive learning his eyes were opened to the possibility of attaining, by the comparative study of religions, a philosophy less fatally exclusive than any then current, and one independent of dogma or revelation, depending solely on human experience and self-knowledge, and hence faithful to the spirit of modern science and harmonious with what was genuine in it—in conflict merely with its speculative fringe. And this possibility, obviously, stirred him like no other intellectual experience, before or since, because the dualism crudely but plainly embodied in Manichaeism answered absolutely to his own knowledge of himself and of others.

From his reading of Baur, accordingly, Mr More could date the discovery of himself, and his work and development henceforth were self-conscious and deliberate. In the following year, 1892, he went to Harvard, to equip himself linguistically for the study of religions which he now proposed to undertake. He remained there three years, receiving a second master's degree in 1893 and holding the post of Assistant in Sanskrit in 1894–1895. He did not seek the doctorate, because, as he has said, he was at Harvard to learn all he could within a limited period; and he could not afford to spend a large portion of his time in minute work on some small, isolated problem in linguistics;—a sacrifice which would have been necessary for the purpose of writing a dissertation. He had, in other words, a serious purpose in view, and no desire to pose as a budding "authority."

The strongest influence exerted on Mr More during these years came, not from any of his teachers, but from a fellow-student of oriental and classical languages, who was later to become one of the best known and most influential members of the faculty of Harvard, and, in addition, a courageous and incisive critic of modern literature and thought. This fellow-student was Irving Babbitt. The two young men were strangely complementary to each other, and their study of Indian religions gave rise to endless discussion, which often enough carried them far afield. Such intercourse, when fortunate accident brings it about, is usually the most effective stimulus conceivable to fruitful work. Paul More found it invaluable, and has more than once, both publicly and privately, acknowledged his indebtedness to this oldest and closest friend. In particular, he was powerfully impelled by Mr Babbitt in a direction which he had already taken, to be sure, before coming to Cambridge, but in which he was now fully confirmed;—he was led, that is to say, away from romanticism and towards classical literature.

The Great Refusal shows, as I have said, a considerable change undergone by its author since the publication of *Helena*. It shows equally, however, that Mr More, when writing it, was in a state of transition. The book is composed of letters and poems sent to a woman, named Esther, with whom the author believed himself to be in love.[4] These were written

4 Professor Frank Jewett Mather revealed the fact, several years ago, that these letters are genuine. Publication was an afterthought; and for this

at intervals during the year before Mr More went to Cambridge.[5] They were thus written after some progress had been made in the new studies suggested by Baur's treatise, but before the realistic and classical influence, represented by Mr Babbitt and by Paul More's study under the direction of Professor Goodwin, had yet made itself felt. They are consequently romantic, but romantic with a striking difference; and they have sources whose juxtaposition is unusual, though not inappropriate. The sources are explained by Mr More's having begun the comparative study of religions. He has said that Baur, whose treatment of Manichaeism is confined almost exclusively to its Western aspects, sent him at once to St Augustine. Thence he went on to study medieval Christian literature, while at the same time he began to acquaint himself with the sacred literature of India. Thus it came about that *The Great Refusal* reflects both medieval mysticism and the mysticism of the Upanishads. This is a heavy load for a book of love-letters contained in scarcely more than 150 small pages—and the heavier because the narrative, such as it is, is interrupted by several poems having no close relation to the theme. The narrative, indeed, would have required very different treatment to make it really plausible; and the fictitious writer of the letters described in the Preface is a mawkish fellow of whom his Esther, one thinks, was well rid when he finally renounced her in order to dissolve "in the vapours of mysticism."

The poems contained in the book, nevertheless, are on a higher level, with respect both to form and to content, than those in *Helena;*[6] and the letters themselves possess a genuine interest because of the extent to which they reveal, not merely Mr More's studies, but the man himself as he was at

purpose some alterations were made, and a fictitious character introduced as the writer, both to conceal the identity of the woman addressed, and to direct attention away from the merely personal aspect of the letters to their meaning. Thus Mr More appears in the book simply as its editor, but this is part of the fiction.

[5] The final portion of the book, which is entirely fictitious, and the Preface were written later. The Preface is dated November, 1893.

[6] Because this volume also is out of print, and copies can be found only with great difficulty, I reproduce six poems from it in the second section of Appendix A.

this time. We gather that the beautiful woman to whom he wrote had a warm, perhaps deep, regard for him, but distrusted his love because she thought it more fanciful than real; and that he gradually came to agree with her, though not for her reasons, as he became absorbed in his new world of Indian religion. He possibly dreamed, for a time, in his first excited apprehension of the profound human truth embedded in classical Hinduism, of actually and completely renouncing all human relations. From the beginning, moreover, his love for this woman was of the Petrarchian kind, and though he could later recognize that in effect he had become a Platonic lover,[7] this was only after he had experienced the failure of Petrarchian love and had passed beyond the possibility, as he thought, of all passionate desire. Now how far the woman was justifiably distrustful, and what mixed feelings excited her lover, may best be seen from the latter's own words:

It occurred to me in your presence last night as never before, that here after all, almost within reach of my breath, is that very strange something we call beauty, that elusive harmony of form which must have troubled the vision of Scopas when he carved the Roman statue; which was on the face of Beatrice, so that Dante was moved to say he would write of her such things as had never been dreamed, so that by the mere looking into her eyes he was upborne from planet to planet; . . . And on the long way home, the recollection of what things others had been led to accomplish by such a vision still haunted me. It seemed to me that this loveliness of form and spirit was too high for me alone, or for any other individual, to see and possess in his imagination; and a longing was born to speak of it in the ears of all men, that this feeling towards you might become a part of the universal admiration and love of mankind for beauty. But then the old doubts came back, of my weakness and distrust and ignorance, of my own unworthiness, and of man's nature

---

[7] Platonic in the true sense, not in the distorted and ridiculous sense which became current in the seventeenth century and which has persisted to our day. The distinction between Petrarchian love and Platonic is sharply and admirably drawn in *Shelburne Essays*, Second Series, pp. 10–12.

mated with all the base things of creation. For he who shall
bring new perception of beauty to men must have his own mortal vision purged of the doubts of this blinder age, which would
find nothing divine in man but only a more perfect animal. . . .
The doubts returned. And then I thought of you, and again my
heart sang within me for gladness. For I said, let doubt undermine the very pillars of the world, let there be no God, no eternal life, no moral purpose; let the realities about me become the
merest phantasmagoria of my own imagination, the thin shadows cast by the light of my own burning heart, fair or hideous
as my moods may shape them—doubt can go no farther than
that: yet will I bear within me the likeness of one fair woman,
whose beauty and loving-kindness shall rest upon these fleeting
images and whiten them to the whiteness of snow. Around this
one radiant thought of her, all thoughts and imaginations, and
joys and sorrows, shall circle in order. Then shall virtue become, as Augustine calls it, *ordo in amore*. . . . You will
say that I have idealized you. Be it so. Yet there is within me
only gloom: the glory must be all your own. My love is vision,
that is all. . . . You know better than any other what the
struggle of my life has been. Perhaps mine has been the most
unfortunate of human temperaments. A mind that always
doubts, united with an imagination that continually reaches
after the infinite and finds no abiding place among transient
things—such a union must form a most unhappy disposition.
What my searching has been, how I have striven to find peace
in the common faith of men, you know only too well. I have
boasted that through the intensity and breadth of my love for
you I would build up a faith in beauty able to bind the physical
with the moral world, and to content my heart. But you have
understood my words expressed more an ideal than a reality,
and have wisely held my love as a thing fair but insubstantial.
The completeness of your life will not be endangered if this is
withdrawn from it. . . . However sudden this decision may
seem to you, yet it is inevitable and has been well premeditated.
Of late I have pondered much, walking by night among the
crowded streets of the city, if perchance inspiration might come
to me from the atmosphere of humanity; and again walking in
solitude here by the sea, "that wilderness where sing the ser-

vants of God." And ever one word sounded through all my thoughts—one word which is the key-note of one of the great Indian philosophies, *Kaivalyartham, for the sake of abstraction, isolation,* sounded in my ears above all the uproar of the city; and again *Kaivalyartham* was the admonition borne to me from the turbulence of the sea. That philosophy teaches us of the duality running through all, and of the soul that abides in the body as a prisoner in his cell. The wise man, having knowledge of himself, strives after abstraction from the things of the earth. This is the final message for which all my life has been a preparation. Henceforth my way must lead through the solitudes of abstraction and meditation; no human care shall touch me more. What neither Christianity nor philosophy, neither art nor science, neither love nor friendship, has been able to afford, that I have found in the mystic *Brahma,* in the *Paramatman.* I have gone through the waking world of men as one walks in his sleep. I have not understood their words, nor the springs of their actions, nor their joys and sorrows. I have revelled in fantasies, insubstantial as clouds, gloomy at times, and again radiant with the splendour of the sun of love. Yet I have not found rest. It was but the pageantry of evening that precedes the night. Now I would enter into the silence of communion that is likened most unto deep sleep.[8]

The inward drama—it is nothing less—imperfectly summarized in these sentences is that of a young man, with sensibilities at once delicate and keen, struggling for a way of escape from the accepted implications of nineteenth-century science; and struggling against all odds because his spiritual nature was deep, intense, unconquerable. No regard for tradition or for established institutions entered at this time into his consideration. He was impelled to reject materialism and every other form of naturalistic thought because he found he could not help it. He was motivated singly by a wholehearted

[8] In quoting I have silently abridged several of these passages. It should be remembered that alterations were made in the letters when publication was determined upon. Hence it would be illegitimate to regard any isolated statements as literally representative of Paul More's thought. The letters do, however, accurately exhibit the drift of his feeling and thought, springing out of real experience.

devotion to truth, and would not be contented with any easy solution requiring him wilfully to deny facts established by modern science. He would take those facts honestly into account and abide by the consequences. Nevertheless, his own experience and self-examination showed with complete cogency that man's nature was not, and could not be, wholly explained by the external methods and necessary assumptions of exact science. There was something further. Man was an animal without doubt, but something else too. It was not that Paul More was determined to vindicate man's pride, or self-respect. It was just that he could not escape the evidence, as real as any other fact of observation, that human nature was dual—spiritual as well as physical—and could only thus be explained. The evidence from history, he was beginning to learn, was overwhelming, but the absolutely unescapable evidence came from within.

The problem, consequently, was how to be faithful to this evidence within the limitations imposed by science. Naturalism, whether idealistic or materialistic, simply evaded the problem, and so was fundamentally dogmatic and antiphilosophical. It was easy, illegitimate, and suicidal to accept exclusively either horn of the dilemma of human existence. But what *was* at once legitimate and saving? The sentences I have quoted from *The Great Refusal* exhibit Paul More's first groping answers. Obviously, however genuine his feeling, he was so deeply engaged with his problem at this time that he perforce subordinated everything to it, and so made the woman to whom he wrote chiefly a point of departure for the development of a cult of beauty spiritualized— a cult suggested by medieval attempts to convert woman into a bridge between earth and heaven. Mr More's desires, in addition, though they were so closely bound up with his problem, were not wholly thus absorbed; he had literary ambitions; and he was undoubtedly encouraged to offer a sentimental answer to his questionings, because such an answer promised a ready outlet to those ambitions. He was thus on the verge of the aesthetic heresy which engulfed many of his contemporaries in the later nineteenth century, and which, though since purged of sentimentalism, still receives its many

victims. From this he was saved;—though his early discovery
of the hollowness of such a solution seems to have owed quite
as much to the steady common sense of the woman to whom
he wrote as to his own insight, doubts, and further studies.
These, however, led him through the Upanishads to his second answer; and before we leave *The Great Refusal* several
further passages must be quoted to show aspects of his journey alluded to but not described in the sentences already
given, and also to show more definitely the nature of the second answer:

We who walk in the shadow of doubt know not which is the
sadder and which is the wiser, the fortitude and disdain of the
stoic who contemns pleasure and pain alike, or the anguish and
humiliation of the monk who deliberately loses his life to gain
life. Between the two lies the world of the indifferent, and, I
begin to surmise, the world of the artist who in his own way
would likewise escape from the trammels of earthly things. Reject me not as indifferent or shallow if I tell you that peace, if
it come at all, must find me also in this last manner. . . . You
say I am a sceptic and have no part in [Catholic Christian]
faith. It is just because I am a sceptic that it means so much
to me. I am a visionary also, a dreamer, an idealist, if you
please; and it is because I am both of these that a beautiful
conception like this of the Virgin Mary is a vital part of my
life. I live, not in a world of faith, but in a world of imaginations; and the sublime enunciations of Saint Augustine or the
vast dreams of Erigena may have more reality to me than to
many a good member of the orthodox fold. I measure such ideas
by their intrinsic beauty, and not by any meagre standard of
revelation or dogma. . . . Jacob wrestled until dawn with the
Lord as with a man, and in the end he received the blessing. It
was a priceless victory. But how many of us have wrestled more
than one night, crying many times, "Tell me thy name!" and
have grasped only shadows, heard echoes alone, and for our vain
efforts have gone halting through life, unfamiliar to its pursuits—for the great struggle, though futile indeed, has made
the lesser prizes of the world quite despicable to us. . . . At
one time in my life I was ready to give up liberty and ambition

of thought in order to become a disciple of the faith that promised peace in this world and resurrection in the next; but, thank
God, the pride of my intellect revolted from such a betrayal of
its nobler, if yet austerer, aspirations. Let me bear my bitterest
doubts with me to the end rather than succumb through lassi-
tude to an easy belief promising repose. It is possible to submit
with the heart when the intellect rebels: it is the abnegation of
all that is divine within us, a moral cowardice not to be counte-
nanced. . . . Strange, is it not, that these Hindus, of all
peoples in the world, should display the greatest shrewdness in
their epigrammatic verses. From the windows of their silent abstraction they were yet able to cast piercing glances into the
world of action about them. The verses that follow,[9] however,
do not, so much as others I might have selected, exhibit this
phase of their understanding, but hint rather at the deeper
spiritual insight which forms the true wisdom of the east. In
this, I begin to suspect, must lie the consolation of those who
find our western religions superficial and our philosophies mechanical; for here is taught in its purest form the method by
which the individual soul, shaking off the trammels that bind it,
may mount upwards unto true communion with its infinite
source. . . . The wisdom of the east may be summed up in three
mystical words: Brahma, Atman, Om. Brahma signified originally the swelling of the heart in the fervour of prayer, the
feeling of exaltation which ever comes to a man in seasons of
earnest worship, when the walls of his personality are broken
down and the infinite powers of the universe sweep over him.
At such times the soul knew of the God that encompasses the
barriers of the senses, and the word describing the condition of
the worshipper was naturally extended to this nameless power
with which he communed. So this God was called Brahma, the
infinite, eternal, unchangeable, all-embracing, all-pervading.
And he who in times of ecstasy felt his spirit rapt into communion with this God was said to know Brahma. And as knowledge with the Hindus, and forsooth with all men of insight, is a
manner of identification, and what we know, with that we are

[9] A group of eight epigrams, seven of which are reprinted, with some
minor alterations, in Mr More's *Century of Indian Epigrams* (Nos. 17, 41,
56, 67 [first stanza only], 79, 98, and 99).

made one; so he who knew Brahma was said to be united with Brahma, to be Brahma. Our Jesus meant no more than this when he said, *The Kingdom of heaven is within you;* and when he avowed that *I and my father are one.* . . . Atman is the breath, the breath of life, and thence easily enough life itself. It is the anima, the soul, the spirit. It is what remains when everything else is stripped away; it is the inmost being, the *Self.* It was the aim of those forest-dwelling philosophers, who gave up the world that they might surrender themselves to uninterrupted meditation, to penetrate through the outer trappings of man's nature into the secret places of the heart. And there they found this Atman, sitting in solitary state, a king hidden from the gaze of the idle, passionless, unmoved, while the faculties of the mind and the organs of the body, like ministers of state, served his bidding. And then looking out upon the world they perceived a similar power dwelling in the innermost shrine of nature, a higher Self to whom this natural world was what their bodies were to them. And while the ignorant were busy trafficking with the phenomena that were the mere underlings of his court, they put aside these things that their Self might hold converse with him, the greater Self, Paramatman or simply Atman, as they called him. And again, as he who knew Brahma became Brahma, so he who knew the Paramatman was raised into union with it; and Brahma and Atman were but different names of the one Spirit. This conception of the inner and the outer Self, and their essential unity, is undoubtedly the ultimate achievement of thought. And this is clearly to be distinguished from a philosophy that would exalt the individual *Ego* of a man. For the *Ego* says within us, *this is I! this is mine!* and is but a fiction of the brain, rising and perishing with the body: but the Self is precisely that within us which is least individual, which suffers not nor enjoys, which knows neither birth nor death, which is not a portion or emanation of the Eternal, but is that eternal Self.[10]

10 What is said of the meaning of Om is not quoted, because it adds nothing which contributes materially to an understanding of Mr More's thought at this time. I have again silently abridged several of the passages reproduced.

III

In 1895 Mr More became an associate, or instructor, in Sanskrit and classical literature at Bryn Mawr College. In the
following year he contributed a short paper, entitled *The
Influences of Hindu Thought on Manichaeism*, to the sixteenth volume of the *Journal of the American Oriental Society*.[11] Any one who turns from *The Great Refusal* to this
will at once feel that the author had in the interval made
significant progress in the art of writing. The paper on
Manichaeism is straightforward, lucid, workmanlike. Above
all, it is not consciously "literary." However this lesson was
learned, it was a necessary one, no matter what Mr More was
to write.

The article, in addition, deserves our notice for another
reason. It was the earliest fruit, in the field of exact scholarship, of Mr More's comparative study of religions—and it
was also the last. He set out to establish, "First, that Mānī
was influenced not by Buddhism alone, but by that whole
movement of Hindu thought of which Buddhism is a single
part; and, secondly, that this influence is seen not so much
in the addition of new rites and dogmas borrowed from
Buddhism as in the subtle spirit of India permeating those
already adopted from Persian and Christian sources." He
found it easy to make out a good case. He found it, in fact,
entirely too easy; and this frightened him. At such a rate,
what was it not possible to "prove"?—and what lay at the
end of an indefinite accumulation of "proofs" except, perhaps, scholarly reputation? He concluded that in this field,
as perhaps in some others, the methods of exact scholarship
really lent themselves to very deceptive activity—to the
"establishment" of results which *looked* like science, but
which actually were speculative. And such speculation seemed
entirely unprofitable, the moment it was recognized for what
it actually was. Hence he further concluded that for any one
whose interests were serious and went to the centre of this or

---

[11] What he considered substantial in this paper was much later incorporated in his essay on St Augustine (*Shelburne Essays,* Sixth Series).

similar subjects, methods at once more tentative and more general were requisite.

From this experience and from the exacting study that led up to it, Paul More thus learned enough to be critical— to see that scholarship was false both to itself and to science when it aped the methods and certainty of science in fields where those methods were inappropriate and where scientific precision was unattainable. What was needed, if men were not to blind themselves to truth instead of finding it, was balance, a sense of proportion, a candid recognition that exhaustive treatment was an empty pose in fields where exhaustive data were not to be had, or, equally, in fields where the data were so complex and elusive as to defy rigidly objective and systematic investigation. It was necessary, in other words, to beware of absolutes. More than this, it was necessary, one might almost say, to *multiply* distinctions— not, of course, for their own sake. And the extension and refinement of the processes of sceptical criticism became more important, not less, with the increasing prestige of science, because the temptation was now created to hide a new and subversive dogmatism under the cloak of pretended absolute knowledge.

Thus actual experience once more, and honest self-examination, were crucial factors in determining Paul More's career. Meanwhile, he was teaching the elements of Sanskrit to young ladies. If, in 1893, his heart had "found the mystic haven of rest," as he supposed, he himself had not—for an easily discoverable reason. When he had created a fictitious writer for his letters before publishing them, he had endowed this young man with independent means, and had also granted him an early death. But he himself had no money, and good health. Hence complete retirement for the sake of abstracted mystical contemplation was not a real possibility; and death, very fortunately, was far distant. He had, then, to submit himself to life on such terms as were offered by the society into which he had been born. When his means of studying at Harvard were exhausted, he had to take what came. He duly went to Bryn Mawr, and tried to look forward hopefully to a professor's chair. His article on Manichaeism was a first step towards it, of the orthodox kind. But what effect that had upon its compiler has just been mentioned—and teaching itself he found no more congenial than when he had served as instructor in Latin at the Smith Academy.

He had felt in 1892, as he has recorded in *The Great Refusal*, "that such a life was worse than death, was beyond his powers of endurance." He was now older, but found the American teacher's slavery to trivial duties, to incessant lectures, and to endless committee-meetings no more endurable than before—and again he was constrained to rebel against it decisively, after giving it a second fair trial. Now by no means everybody is called to be a teacher, even where conditions are more favourable than in many American colleges and universities, and notoriously the profession harbours some discontented men and women, who are there only because they know not where else to earn their bread. In Paul More's case, however, discontent did not gradually eat itself out in grumbling and indolence. It was fundamental and uncompromising, and it reveals matters of importance concerning the man. Superficially its two manifestations were very similar;—not the least significant fact revealed by scrutiny is the underlying difference of temper which distinguishes the second act of rebellion from the first.

On the occasion of his earlier abandonment of teaching, Mr More was in revolt not alone against that occupation. He had come to feel "that any active life among men was for him impossible." He felt outraged by any claims upon him that society might make, interfering in any way with his own free activity—and so outraged that any external pressure induced in him a state approaching sheer desperation. The words are not too strong; and Mr More's revulsion was in fact an expression of that exaggerated and hypersensitive individualism which, in men more aggressive and wilful, during the last generation or two, has found an outlet in anarchism or, as Dean Inge and Mr More himself have acutely observed, in Marxian materialistic socialism. It has also, during the same period, in literature found an outlet in symbolism.

That Paul More was thus on the road which had been

travelled by Gérard de Nerval, by Tristan Corbière, and by Jules Laforgue, to mention no others, and which has since been travelled so far by Miss Gertrude Stein, is clearly enough proved by his confession in *The Great Refusal:*

I knew not where to turn. The enigma of existence, of my existence, pressed upon me. The men of the street upon whom I looked out seemed in some way the cause of my mental torment. It was to satisfy their ideals that the dream-life of my soul must be roused into painful activity. Their factitious world of daily routine and sordid cares bound my spirit as in an iron chain. I began to hate them. As always happens with me, my vision was affected by my emotions, and the stream of faces that flowed past became like so many diabolical apparitions, distorted, grimacing, threatening. The rumour of their voices and footsteps became like the noise of a tumultuous victorious army charging over me.[12]

This is the description of an experience; it is at the same time a succinct yet singularly complete expression of one of the characteristic developments of the romantic movement. Concentration upon the self, encouragement of spontaneity as the road to truth, consequent high regard for the dream-life of aimless reverie, hatred of restraint and of conventions, the corresponding tendency to uncontrolled expansiveness and thus to the dissolution of the self in a chaos of disordered impulses and impressions—all the familiar elements are here, explicitly or by plain implication, and this single brief passage even shows how easily romanticism passed, through such men as Gérard de Nerval, into the symbolism of the later nineteenth century and of our own day. "I ended," wrote Rimbaud, "by finding sacred the disorder of my intelligence," and this is precisely what Paul More was encouraging himself to do. The same fanatical absolutism, having the same root in uncontrolled egoism, expresses itself in politics by the demand for unrestricted personal freedom, by the dogmatic denial of inequalities and distinctions, by the sym-

---

[12] In quoting, I have omitted from this passage two inessential statements which would have required a larger context to be understood.

pathetic projection of the wronged self as the symbol of the real society, and by murderous hatred of all who stand in the way—ending, if it is given scope, in such absolute tyranny as the Russian communists have established on the graves of several millions of their brothers shot down in the name of humanitarianism. And this aspect, too, of romantic individualism is not uncertainly reflected in the confessional sentences which I have quoted.

Paul More, however, stopped short. Although he was in evident danger, he never quite lost the capacity for sane reflection; and he had learned enough to be aware that "of all untruths the worst and most deadly is, not the falsehood we utter, but the falseness with which we deceive ourselves . . . when the truth is hard and unwelcome."[13] His mind thus remained open to the saving suspicion that his trouble might be of his own making. The personality formed on romantic literature might be a personality malformed;—and this suspicion had in fact sent him to the study of classical literature, as we have already seen, before 1890. The new influence, however, could not instantly bear fruit, even though it was soon strongly reinforced, when Paul More became acquainted with Irving Babbitt, who in the early eighteen-nineties was as much the enemy of romanticism as he remains, essentially unchanged, to-day. But, as has been shown above, when Mr More went to Cambridge he was at first powerfully drawn to the Hindu gospel of renunciation, which was in its fashion as sheer a piece of absolutism as the world has ever seen, and romantic too in its affiliations. And this was the earliest expression of his reaction away from the other romantic gospel which had brought him to the verge of ruin.

Professor Babbitt is fond of a remark to the effect that nothing resembles a hollow so much as a swelling, and Mr More's complete change of front would seem at first sight to illustrate it. Both extremes to which he went were equally far from realistic common sense, and both made equally little of conditions which constantly reassert themselves in the

[13] *The Great Refusal,* p. 96.

actual world, as much to the discomfiture of self-flattering
doctrinaire revolutionists as to that of ascetic pantheists.
But there was also in this instance a most important difference between the swelling and the hollow. The mysticism of
the Upanishads, whatever its ultimate theoretical bearings,
did practically make for the integration of the self in holding up steadily a principle of broad distinction, or valuation,
as the touchstone of reality. Even in its own despite it was,
in practice, dualistic in its distinction between the realm of
illusion and the realm of Brahma; and its demand for renunciation gave it a sharp edge and was, within limits, wholly
tonic in its effect. And this was the point where it differed
from Mr More's earlier romanticism—the point where extremes did not meet. For the romanticism of the modern
Western world with which we are all familiar is bent passionately upon dissolving the self instead of integrating it.

Hence it was that Mr More's change was helpful in the
task of regaining self-possession, and proved to be a useful
means of transition to his further studies at Cambridge, both
in Indian religious thought and in Greek philosophy and
literature. Hence it was, too, that though in 1897, when he
abandoned teaching for the second time, he felt as deeply
as in 1892 that "any active life among men was for him impossible," still, he was not now in a state of sheer desperation. On the contrary, his mind was now equable, his intention deliberate and well defined, and his proposed course of
action sensible in the circumstances. He has briefly described
his manner of life after departing from Bryn Mawr, and the
reasons therefor, in the opening pages of the first series of
Shelburne Essays; and no one can fail to perceive the great
difference in temper, or tone, between this confession and the
earlier one which I have quoted above:

Near the secluded village of Shelburne that lies along the
peaceful valley of the Androscoggin, I took upon myself to live
two years as a hermit after a mild Epicurean fashion of my
own. Three maiden aunts wagged their heads ominously; my
nearest friend inquired cautiously whether there was any taint
of insanity in the family; an old grey-haired lady, a veritable

saint who had not been soured by her many deeds of charity, admonished me on the utter selfishness and godlessness of such a proceeding. But I clung heroically to my resolution. Summer tourists in that pleasant valley may still see the little red house among the pines—empty now, I believe; and I dare say gaudy coaches still draw up at the door, as they used to do, when the gaudier bonnets and hats exchanged wondering remarks on the cabalistic inscription over the lintel, or spoke condescendingly to the great dog lying on the steps. As for the hermit within, having found it impossible to educe any meaning from the tangled habits of mankind while he himself was whirled about in the imbroglio, he had determined to try the efficacy of undisturbed meditation at a distance. So deficient had been his education that he was actually better acquainted with the aspirations and emotions of the old dwellers on the Ganges than with those of the modern toilers by the Hudson or the Potomac. He had been deafened by the "indistinguishable roar" of the streets, and could make no sense of the noisy jargon of the market place. But—shall it be confessed?—although he discovered many things during his contemplative sojourn in the wilderness, and learned that the attempt to criticize and not to create literature was to be his labour in this world, nevertheless he returned to civilization as ignorant, alas, of its meaning as when he left it.

This could be a little better written—one thinks of that because so much of Mr More's later prose is really perfect in its kind—but I do not believe any one could describe more simply, naturally, and reassuringly an episode which, after all, was extraordinary in the United States in 1897;—if it was not, indeed, the exploit of a mere crank. And this it was not. Despite the "cabalistic inscription," there was no taint of affected singularity in Mr More's decision. He was profoundly troubled. He felt that men were being carried through life without knowing what it was; that practically none cared to ask until too late; that, instead, men intently followed their noses, or intently chased phantoms; and that thus they were the blind victims of circumstance while supposing they were carving out their own destinies. What they really lived and toiled for who could know? They themselves were perpetually discovering that their aims, when achieved, did not yield them the satisfaction they wanted. Had not Hawthorne's daguerreotypist, in *The House of the Seven Gables*, spoken, not literally but truly, for whole generations of up-and-coming Americans?—"I find nothing so singular in life," he had said, "as that everything appears to lose its substance the instant one actually grapples with it." But, then, Paul More asked himself, who was he to judge? He did not think his education really deficient. He had not learned what he knew of "the old dwellers on the Ganges" until convinced that their thought was still living and pertinent. Yet when he saw how he stood, apparently alone in his own generation and country, how could he be sure? Had men actually changed? Had they actually discovered that life had some genuine meaning and worth, expressed in their work and in modern civilization, of which he alone was ignorant?

Such questions, questions about himself as much as about modern civilization, would not let him alone. He remained, in spite of everything, acutely aware of needs which seemed to be left out of account in the solidifying structure of American life; and he was also aware of capacities within him, or at least of creative desires, for which too there seemed to be no outlet in the more usual or recognized occupations open to American men. Hence while there was yet time, before he found himself too deeply entangled in the stream of events, should he not deliberately stand aside, to see if undistracted thought might bring any certain answer to his questionings? At least he might thus, and only thus, determine what he himself was good for, whether or not he accomplished any larger purpose. And so, led by the spirit of honest inquiry, troubled but not defeated by life's complexities, he went to Shelburne.

I think the one point needful to make about this proceeding is that Paul More acted simply as any man should act, and on occasion must act, who takes seriously the great central questions concerning life which no one who is human can entirely escape before he dies. This is the whole meaning of his withdrawal from the busy common life about him, as it is also the meaning of those years of study and questioning thought and experimental activity which led up to it. Withdrawal, moreover, was itself an experiment, entered into with no thought that it could, or should, become permanent. It could, as far as he was able to see ahead, last only so long as the hermit's savings from his period of teaching might last. And that on this basis it continued for two years and three months is explained by the small cost of retirement into New Hampshire at the end of the last century. The little red house was rented for $3.00 the month, and other expenses were correspondingly slight. The hermit might, indeed, when the time came, have remained amongst the pines for a longer period, because by then he was earning, not much, but something, from literary work. He felt, however, that the purpose which had brought him thither had been accomplished, in so far as was possible, and that it was time for him to return from the wilderness.

IV

WHAT, really, had been accomplished? Mr More's allusions to the period are few, and in the passage quoted above he confesses that he returned to civilization "as ignorant of its meaning as when he left it." He admits, however, that this is not the whole story; and he has in fact provided means—not of telling it with any fulness—but sufficient to make possible an answer to our question. Of his life from day to day two glimpses are to be had, one in the "Notes on Thoreau" with which the *Shelburne Essays* open. In this essay Mr More tells of his own walks in the pine woods, and lets us see him, by the side of a mountain brook, reading *Walden*—and discovering that Thoreau, heard as one hermit to another, and in the midst of a New England forest, was a better and greater Thoreau than he had known before. This is a summer glimpse, and altogether pleasing. The second, one surmises, is of another season and a later time. Practically the only novels at his command at Shelburne, he says, "were a complete set of Dickens in the village library. One day, being hungry for emotion, I started on these volumes, and read them through—read as only a starved man can read, without pause and without reflection, with the smallest intermissions for sleep. It was an orgy of tears and laughter, almost immoral in its excess, a joy never to be forgotten."[14]

There is a picture in these sentences, for understanding eyes, which itself cannot soon be forgotten; but, for the rest, one can only record work accomplished during this period, and certain decisions reached. The first task to which Mr More turned was the completion of a small book on which he had been engaged, intermittently, for several years. It is entitled *A Century of Indian Epigrams*, and was published early in 1898, with a long dedicatory letter addressed to Irving Babbitt.[15] Though the facts are stated clearly enough in this letter, I do not believe the book has ever been recognized for what it is;—and its importance in relation to Mr More's later work has certainly not been realized. It is, on its face, a collection of short poems translated from the Sanskrit—and translated to perfection. Mr More's early attempts at verse-composition have probably served him well, in more than one way, in his later writing; but most conspicuously they bear fruit in the *Century of Indian Epigrams*. He warns readers that they cannot expect, in his translation, "any reproduction of the delicate art, the subtle intricacies of rhythm, the interwoven assonances, the curiously wrought style, of the original." "Our language," he says, "is not capable of these, and must compensate them by artifices of its own." Some difficulties of the kind are inevitable in translations, and must be specially great when the language of the original is as different from English as Sanskrit. The translator's achievement, consequently, is the more remarkable in giving these poems an English form which seems perfectly appropriate to their character and makes them, in a most real sense, a part of our literature. Only a practised writer of verse and genuine poet, who had made himself thoroughly at home, not merely in the language of ancient India, but in the very spirit of Brahminical thought and feeling, could have done

[14] *Shelburne Essays,* Fifth Series, p. 43.

[15] It was designed by Mr Bruce Rogers and printed at the Riverside Press. Copies of the first edition, when they can be found, are expensive, but a new impression was issued in 1926.

this;—which is to say that no one else amongst American writers or scholars, not even Emerson, could have hoped for the success attained by Paul More in this difficult and exacting task.

The *Century of Indian Epigrams*, however, is something more than a singularly excellent translation. On its title-page it is said to contain poems taken chiefly from the collection traditionally ascribed to Bhartrihari, a reigning prince of Oujein near the beginning of our era, who was awakened to thoughtfulness by an intrigue within his palace, and who thereupon resigned his throne to a younger brother and withdrew to the forest, to pass the remainder of his life in undisturbed meditation. In the letter which serves the book as preface, however, readers are told that Professor Babbitt and Mr More, when they were students together in Cambridge, found "the life of the ancient Brahmins an unfailing subject of argument, and were fond of comparing their doctrine with the discipline of Buddha." "And now," Mr More continues, "as an aftermath of those days, I have attempted in these translations to bring together the verses I used to quote in illustration of my views, or should have quoted if memory had been faithful to her call. And, first of all, do not demur on reading the name of Bhartrihari at the head of these epigrams. Count them up, and you will find the greater part taken from his work, while precedent from India itself justified me in substituting other stanzas where his own were not to my purpose."

This book, in other words, is altogether more personal than a translation of the usual kind. It fairly represents the conclusions which Paul More had reached by the time it was completed. It presents these modestly, in the words of others. It presents them, moreover, not systematically or argumentatively or dogmatically, but in simple, untechnical language, in the form of detached observations which are the fruit of actual experience. This is not the result of accident, but is a significant indication of one part of the compiler's thought. The poems hang together, and are in effect a commentary on man's progress from youth to old age, and from the sway of illusion through worldly prudence to wisdom, but they present no complete or rigidly defined philosophy. On the contrary, it is of their essence to suggest that the scheme of things is larger than our measuring instruments; and that man must accept much in life as purely given and somehow make the best of it. They suggest, consequently, that experience is not to be avoided, but *is* to be understood and so made the pathway to wisdom; and that wisdom is the knowledge which gives a man peace. Such knowledge is not complete knowledge, not absolute knowledge, but knowledge genuine as far as it goes. And it is suggested that knowledge, imperfect but sufficient, is attainable by reflection, and bears its own certification in its fruitfulness; that reflection is only possible when one breaks the chains of instinct or impulse, when one stands aside from the stream of perpetual change or action, when one stops in one's headlong course really to see what one has done and was about to do; that through reflection comes the discovery that one sought a happiness never to be attained by bending things or people to one's will, or by immersing one's self slavishly in the stream of distracting change, which leads on endlessly from one delusory promise to another, but only to be attained by renunciation. And this, it is particularly to be remembered, is not a doctrinaire conclusion. There is not the slightest pretence that renunciation is in some mysterious way a good thing for its own sake. Mystery, to be sure, presses us in closely from every side; but renunciation derives its warrant simply enough from the discovery that, when other pathways to felicity have been tried and found to fail, it has in practice succeeded.

When a man is young, however, and the world young with him, he will be swept irresistibly by the strong current of desire;—and he will find in everything—even in the freezing blasts of winter—a symbol and a confirmation of that which he feels:

> This Winter gale will play the gallant lover,
> And meeting careless girls,
> Will pluck their gowns, and with rude fingers hover
> Among their tangled curls.

He'll kiss their eyelids too, their cheeks caress
Till they are all a-tremble;
He'll tease their lips till murmurs soft confess
The love they would dissemble.

Experience shows that even at the best love is not the simple
and pure delight youth supposes; and so arise questionings:

But to remember her my heart is sad,
To see her is to know
Bewildered thoughts, and touching driveth mad,—
How is she dear that worketh only woe?

And disillusionment follows inevitably, perhaps beginning
with a question which men have had to ask in every generation, in all places:

With one they laugh and chatter, yet beguile
With luring eyes a second;
A third they cherish in their heart the while,—
Their true love who hath reckoned?

Thus we begin to know the deceptions with which life itself
leads us a chase, planting them, we find, within us as well as
about us; and so our conception of what we need is deepened
and our demands upon the relationships we form are rendered at once more discriminating and more exacting:

Communion with the good is friendship's root,
    That dieth not until our death;
And on the boughs hang ever golden fruit:—
    And this is friendship, the world saith.

Ourselves we doubt, our hearts we hardly know,
    We lean for guidance on a friend;
Ay, on a righteous man we'd fain bestow
    Our faith, and follow to the end.

Hence, thoughtfulness once really awakened, we begin to
perceive the true values embodied in men; and so high a

value do we set on righteousness, when we have begun to understand what it actually is, that we may even fancy:

> By truth the righteous guide upon his course
> The rolling sun, and stay the earth by force
>   Of penitence austere.
> They are the refuge of the worlds outworn,
> And worlds that lurk in darkness still are born
>   Because they tarry here.

Many, too, are the shrewd observations upon men and things which the awakened mind and alert eye now conspire to make. We may not here pause over these, but must at once go on to notice the central characteristic of "the righteous," which life teaches the discerning man to regard as above all price:

> Better from the sheer mountain-top
> Headlong the ruined body drop;
> Better appease the serpent's ire
> With thy right hand; or in the fire
> Behold thy riven members tost,
> Than once thy mind's integrity were lost.

Thus, also, one comes at length to see a truth too simple for unpurged eyes, and so begins to know wisdom:

> Like an uneasy fool thou wanderest far
> Into the nether deeps,
> Or upward climbest where the dim-lit star
> Of utmost heaven sleeps.

> Through all the world thou rangest, O my soul,
> Seeking and wilt not rest;
> Behold, the peace of Brahma, and thy goal,
> Hideth in thine own breast.

And with wisdom comes peace:

> Who is the Brahmin?—Not the mother's womb
> Declares him, nor the robes that all assume;
> But the true heart that never greed beguiles,
>   Nor turbid lust defiles.

Who is the Brahmin?—He who trembleth not
When snaps the cord that bound to human lot,
Who losing all is glad, whose peace is known
    Unto himself alone.

With peace, finally, comes that perfect liberation which the spirit of man unceasingly—but how blindly!—searches for:

Through many births, a ceaseless round,
I ran in vain, nor ever found
The Builder, though the house I saw,—
For death is born again, and hard the law.

O Builder, thou art seen! not so
Again thy building shall arise;
Broken are all its rafters, low
The turret of the mansion lies:
The mind in all-dissolving peace
Hath sunk, and out of craving found release.

It was said above that the *Century of Indian Epigrams* fairly represents Paul More's thought at the time when the book was completed, and a very considerable change can be seen since the publication of *The Great Refusal*. The sentimental attitude which had found expression suggested by medieval mysticism has been definitely and finally abandoned. And mysticism itself, though there is still a place for it in Mr More's scheme of things, has been decisively subordinated to dualism, which, also, has become more realistic. It is presented, of course, in its Brahminical form, and it may be asked whether or not the hermit of Shelburne at this time was really converted to Hinduism, and whether or not he really supposed that Indian dualism could be transplanted to America at the end of the last century.

Mr More has left the answers to these questions in no doubt. Even in 1897, when the influence exerted upon him by Indian religious thought was at its height, he wrote: "To call ourselves disciples of Buddha or believers in Brahma—as some unstable minds are prone to do—would be superstition and not spirituality." He had no notion, at this or at any other time, that it was either possible or desirable for men to turn the hands of the clock backward. But he did believe that the Hindus, during one period in their development, had shown a profundity and grasp, a depth of true insight into the enduring realities of human nature, which gave their religious writings unique value. The truth they had learned they had expressed in their own characteristic way, appropriate to their time and place. Their manner of expression had a local and temporary value; but that which was expressed, in substance, he believed, had a permanent and universal value. To forget this, to turn aside from Hindu dualism because it was ancient, and foreign, and entangled with a mythology we could not, even imaginatively, make our own —this was to throw away, prodigally, an unequalled achievement of the race, and to condemn ourselves to retrogression and blindness in the conduct of our own lives.

By this time Mr More had come to believe that the Greeks in the age of Pericles had achieved a similar classical finality in the fields of literature and art; and his position may be better understood if it be remembered that of them too he wrote: "Their forms have passed away with their civilization, and cannot be revived or imitated; but whoever would seek inspiration in art and poetry at their fountain head must now and always turn back to Athens and laboriously learn her ancient speech." Nobody has realized more vividly than Paul More that we live in a world of ceaseless change, and that it is the height of futility to suggest that we should stand still, or revive or repeat an ancient, and in fact unique, achievement of the human spirit. But he realized equally, by 1897, that change itself takes place in constant ways; that there have hitherto been, throughout the whole duration of the human race in so far as we know its history, constant elements and constant needs; but that these elements have by no means always or everywhere found equally complete expression, and that needs likewise have been most unequally satisfied. Hence he realized what the history of the Western world during the last three thousand years proves as conclusively as anything can be proved—that the cause of civilization is inseparably bound up with the effort to preserve, and make available anew for each new age, the genuine or definitive

achievements of the past, in order that we may build upon
the experience of the race. Those achievements were not easy,
not common, not ordinarily possible at all. Their loss to us
would be much more calamitous, much more truly a wanton
impoverishment of life, than would be the sudden loss of all
our sources of electrical energy and the lapse of all knowledge of the means and methods of replacing them.

In this spirit, consequently, Paul More published the *Century of Indian Epigrams*—regarding the book as a slight
but real contribution to the forces opposing themselves
against barbarism in our time. And in the same spirit he went
on while at Shelburne to make two other contributions of
somewhat similar character;—both of these, however, issuing
out of the Greek studies which were increasingly to occupy
him in the years to come. The first was a volume entitled *The
Judgement of Socrates*, which was published in 1898. It contains an introductory essay and translations of the *Apology*,
the *Crito*, and the closing scene of the *Phaedo*.[16] Ten years
later Mr More was to write: "Those who, intent upon the
abstruser problems of Plato, neglect the biographical message of the *Apology* and the *Crito* and the closing scene of
the *Phaedo*, have missed the heart of his doctrine." And from
this it can be seen that *The Judgement of Socrates* is, exactly
like the book of epigrams, a more personal document than
appears on the surface, in the sense that it puts forward tentatively and unobtrusively an evaluation of Plato which was
already taking definite shape in Mr More's mind, though it
was only much later to be worked out and explained.

Mr More published in the following year a translation,
into prose and verse, of the *Prometheus Bound* of Aeschylus,
with brief notes and with an introduction. The latter fills
some forty pages, and competently gives the information
needed by the English student for an understanding of the
tragedy and of its historical background. Both this volume
and its predecessor of 1898 constituted in different ways
severe tests of the translator's Greek scholarship, as the epi-

[16] The introductory essay, on Socrates, and the translation of the *Apology*
were later reprinted in *Shelburne Essays*, Sixth Series (1909). The opening
paragraphs of the essay, as it now stands, were added at this time.

grams had severely tested his proficiency in Sanskrit. He met
these tests with ease—he has, I think, produced the best
translation of the *Apology* in English—and could now consider himself adequately equipped to make his public appearance as a man of letters. He was in fact much more
adequately and broadly equipped than any American predecessor or contemporary, and this not unimportant source of
distinction has made itself strongly felt in all his work.

That work, Mr More determined at Shelburne, was to be
critical and not creative. Both Professor Babbitt and Dr
Spingarn have protested against the popular delusion that
these terms are mutually exclusive and that critics are of no
importance in comparison with creators, who are "divine";
—and fortunately, as this conjunction of names indicates,
such protest does not depend for its cogency upon any one
special, or perhaps questionable, interpretation of the critic's
function. Professor Babbitt, however, admits that the usual
distinction between creation and criticism is, for practical
purposes, "convenient and indeed inevitable."[17] Moreover, it
is safe to say that practically no one—in fact, I should think,
no one without exception—if given the choice, would hesitate: everyone, if he could, would become a great creative
writer. Certainly it is clear in Paul More's case that he really
wanted to become a poet, and that he turned to criticism
only after going through nearly half the normal span of
life, and expending much energy in a series of efforts to find
himself, as the phrase goes.

His difficulties were those of the thoughtful and serious
men of our confused age. Only shallow and contentedly ignorant people have entirely failed to experience them. There
were not a few capable writers in America during the eighteen-nineties, yet on the whole the verse they produced was
merely pretty, and their fiction merely diverting. Some actually believed that all of life's deeper problems were completely settled; others, not so deceived, thought it would be
beneficial and possible to pretend that there were no un-
settled problems; and still others, a smaller number, with

17 *On Being Creative*, p. 23.

some true sense of life's realities and a real desire to face them, found that they were addressing sealed ears and soon grew discouraged. Questions concerning the energies of men are extremely complex, and are not made easier to discuss by our inveterate propensity to mistaken valuations both of contemporaries and of those who have lived any time within a hundred years of us. Nevertheless, it is scarcely open to doubt that an unusual number of men in the United States, ever since the days of our Civil War, have shown genuine intellectual or artistic promise which has not borne real fruit. The abilities of these men have withered after a brief flowering, or else have been drained off into some easy, well-marked channel—into commerce, or merely factual investigation, or sport, or simple antiquarianism. This has, indeed, been remarked upon by many observers, and is a sign of the times by no means confined to America, though it has for several reasons been specially noticeable in the United States.

The case of Mr John Jay Chapman is a capital illustration. When comparatively young he wrote one brilliant essay, a vigorously and even beautifully phrased interpretation of Emerson, unmatched for discriminating, firm emphasis upon what is best in that oracular sage. This in itself was no small achievement, but Mr Chapman has never since equalled it or even approached it. He has not been driven into silence or fanaticism; he has continued to read, to think, and to write with penetration; he deserves fuller recognition than he has had from his contemporaries. But he has failed to *force* recognition—and has failed, not because of slight powers, but because of some inner confusion or disharmony which has distracted him and prevented him from developing in accordance with his promise. Hence his subsequent writings have tended to be spotty, fragmentary, sometimes aimless, sometimes unexpectedly weak, exhibiting only gleams of insight. He has not been able to find a genuine centre, about which he could organize himself, and so—it may as well be said—has failed to become a *person* in the true and full sense of the word.

And Mr Chapman's virtual self-defeat is significant because, as I say, it illustrates a common tendency. *The Edu-*

cation of Henry Adams attained, some years ago, instant
fame, because it was implicitly recognized—even by those
who took it, quite wrongly, for simple autobiography—as a
classical expression of the life we all tend to live now. And
that life is a constantly baffled life, never reaching a solid
basis or true centre; never attaining coherency, continuity,
wholeness; never, consequently, exerting itself with full
strength; tending to make its victims merely passive, cynical
spectators of other lives which seem meaningless or deluded,
certainly anarchic, and finding no real satisfaction in that
enforced role.

Mr More, at the end of his essay on Adams,[18] quotes some
words written by John Fiske when he was a youth. "When
we come to a true philosophy," Fiske asserted, "and make
that our standpoint, all things become clear. We know what
things to learn, and what, in the infinite mass of things, to
leave unlearned; and then the Universe becomes clear and
harmonious." This discloses but too frankly what Fiske actually did, and what many another has done—what even Emerson, despite all his scrupulousness and real wisdom, notoriously did. And we rightly feel that the "harmony" attained
by a man who simply closes his eyes to all that is disharmonious is worthless. Better anything than this, we cry, with all
the fortitude of the author of *A Free Man's Worship;*—and
then, too often, we straightway temper our fortitude with
the same Free Man, roaming with him in all his own disarm-
ing simplicity through a veritable Wonderland of what-
might-be-may-be-will-be-must-be. It is perilous in the land
of romance to stop even for a moment to think, and those
who do so cannot fail to see that Bertrand Russell's day-
dreams have their origin in a philosophical method identical
in effect with Emerson's, or Fiske's, though the opposite of
theirs in appearance. For Bertrand Russell has simply gathered up what is disharmonious into his philosophy in order to
dispose of it, to acknowledge it once for all and forget it, and
thus to free himself for irresponsible holidays in Utopia.

That which the boy Fiske was really driving at, neverthe-

18 *Shelburne Essays,* Eleventh Series.

less, in the words quoted by Mr More, is a significant truth.
Even a partially sound philosophy, if it take account fairly
both of man and of his surroundings, enables one to begin
making sense, as we say, of life. And Mr More, at Shelburne,
for his most important achievement there, was engaged in
seeing if he could now make sense of life, after his long
search, his changes, his years of study, his doubts and growing disillusionment. The record shows clearly, as I have tried
to indicate, that he could not rest satisfied with any facile
solution of the enigma of existence. It was not only that war-
ring solutions were too much in the air, and forced their
claims on the attention of serious men; there was also a something, an intensity of need coupled with a compelling honesty, driving Paul More from within, which forced him really
to take to himself the solutions that were offered and try to
live by them. He had at first no conscious demands. He accepted in good faith what came to him. He turned from the
full-blown romanticism of his youth only because he found
it actually undermining the roots of his being. And similarly
through the remainder of his years of search he was driven
in spite of himself from one point to another, until he
reached, as he thought, bedrock, in his early thirties. But he
was conscious then that his journeying had brought him to a
lonely place, and he was on that account assailed by fresh
doubts. Hence his retirement to the wilderness, where he
might without distraction come finally to know himself, and
so to know also in what relation he must stand to his busy
contemporaries.

And evidently Paul More's decision to become a critic
took shape as the inevitable consequence both of that deep-
seated confusion which has characterized our age of rapid
change, and of his own efforts to fight his way through it.
The comprehensive study and hard discipline of the years
from 1887 to 1897 were the penalties paid by a conscientious, reflective man of very unusual sensitiveness for being
born in an outpost society at a time when the traditional
foundations of life were being uprooted in the centres of
Western civilization. That study and discipline equipped
him for criticism as few have been equipped in any age, and

coincidently made him in effect a critic, really whether he
would or no. And the outpost society of his boyhood and
young manhood contributed to this end by reflecting the
crucial issues of the day sharply, just because it lacked
any rich and living tradition into which a man might uncritically and comfortingly sink himself. This society offered, too, little scope for any save politicians, traders, and
those who ministered to the convenience, pleasure, or self-
respect of traders and politicians. But if it thus made devotion to poetry of any serious kind seem otiose, it exhibited
the more clearly the need in which the age stood of genuine
criticism.

In the circumstances, Paul More's decision was so plainly
written on the wall that, as was just said, it seems inevitable.
The Western world was already in possession of a great store
of unsurpassable poetry. It had at hand a veritable family
of literatures, ancient and modern. At the moment it was in
much greater danger of losing its heritage—as indeed it is
still—than in need of doubtful additions. Its obvious and im-
perative need was criticism, as thoughtful men on both sides
of the Atlantic—Arnold and Lowell, for example—had
clearly perceived. Poets, novelists, and dramatists, moreover,
seemed to be even more plentiful than ever before, while critics remained as rare as they had always been.[19] In addition,
Paul More's long effort to make sense of life was ending as
such efforts nearly always must end when they have been
honest and thorough. It was forcing him away from the in-
coming tide of popular thought. It was forcing him to turn
and challenge the age, at more points than one;—to challenge its philosophical leaders as well as certain of its typical
creative writers and certain of its general tendencies. And
such a position most naturally found expression in criticism,
especially because Mr More had no ready-made philosophical system, in terms of which everything he encountered
could be neatly placed; but merely a philosophical principle,
which time had cut loose from its historic embodiments, and

[19] Professor Babbitt has recently reminded his readers of Tennyson's remark that great critics are more rare than great poets (*On Being Creative*,
p. 23).

which was to gather meaning for our age only as it might be found applicable and illuminating in concrete instances independently examined and discussed.

Hence it was, finally, that Mr More "returned to civilization as ignorant of its meaning as when he left it." He had a definite intention in admitting this. It has been seen how he was impelled, when he first became acquainted with Indian thought, to turn away entirely from secular and temporal things, on the ground that they were simply meaningless. The author of one of the *Century of Epigrams* wrote:

O World! I faint in this thy multitude
Of little things and their relentless feud;
No meaning have I found through all my days
    In their fantastic maze.

It is one thing to conclude with absolute logic and austerity that the whole phenomenal world and all that it contains is sheer illusion; it is a very different thing indeed to conclude, with humility, that the system of things is beyond one's grasp. The great illusion, Mr More had since learned from Plato's Socrates, is to suppose that we know more than human beings can know; and henceforth Platonic thought was increasingly to influence him, undermining the sway of oriental philosophy. The fruitful consequence was this confession of ignorance, of readiness to learn from whatever sources, of determination to elaborate gradually and concretely a picture of man and of the meaning of his earthly life based solidly on the widest possible examination of the records of human experience and reflection. There was thus implicit in this confession a program of criticism, which involved at the outset only one general exclusion. The critic was steadily to repudiate all easy philosophies which pretended, whether after the fashion of a John Fiske or of a Bertrand Russell, to reach universal or absolute conclusions by impatient, cavalier denial of troublesome facts.

V

In the autumn of 1899 Mr More left Shelburne and spent the winter in Cambridge, where he could use the Harvard

Library. He had already written a few critical essays, and he was to be steadily engaged in the work of criticism from this time forward. But, though the question of his life's work was now definitely settled, the important practical question of a dependable income was not. For the time being, indeed, it was not pressing. One could live cheaply in Cambridge, and some money was coming in, from a minor post he now held at the University,[20] from the sale of essays to periodicals, and from other literary work. During this winter, in fact, Mr More was writing for Messrs Houghton, Mifflin, and Company—and for a consideration of some $300.00—a short life of Franklin, which was to be included in "The Riverside Biographical Series."[21] He also undertook at this time to edit Byron for the series of "Cambridge Poets" published by the same house, and completed the work promptly, though the volume was held back for half a dozen years in order to get the benefit of any new matter to be contained in the definitive edition of Byron's *Works*, presently announced as forthcoming in England under the editorship of E. H. Coleridge and R. E. Prothero.

Such a way of living was well enough while it might last, but obviously precarious; and the question of income became urgent after Mr More's marriage in June, 1900. Within several months, however, it was settled, in a not unsatisfactory way, through the instrumentality of William Roscoe Thayer. Thayer had formed a highly favourable opinion of Mr More's promise as a critic from an essay published in the *Atlantic Monthly*, and he introduced the new essayist to William Hayes Ward, then editor of the *Independent*. Ward was much pleased with a review of Barrett Wendell's *Literary History of America* which he commissioned Mr More to write, and, after giving him several other books to review, made him Literary Editor of the *Independent*, early in 1901.

20 He had been appointed an assistant to Professor Lanman, for the year 1899–1900, in order to enable him to engage in translation from the Sanskrit.

21 It was published as Volume 3 of this Series in 1900. It is a well and sympathetically written brief study, implying no extended research—which would have been inappropriate to the character of the Series—but exhibiting a competent acquaintance with the subject.

Mr More was now fairly established in his proper work, but before an end is made of this chapter some account must be given of a book undertaken while he was on the staff of the *Independent*. The volume was published anonymously in the spring of 1904, and was entitled *The Jessica Letters*. It was written by Mr More in collaboration with a Southern woman, Mrs Corra May Harris, who later became well known as the author of *A Circuit Rider's Wife* and of other books. Mrs Harris had contributed an article to the *Independent* in 1899, and, after Mr More joined the staff, wrote concerning the possibility of doing other work for the magazine. The suggestion was made that the opportunity should be given her to write a review, and Mr More sent her a novel, which was soon followed by others. Out of correspondence connected with the reviewing sprang the design of a romance, in the form of a series of letters exchanged between an editor in New York and a girl, imagined as the daughter of a country preacher, living in "Morningtown," Georgia. The part of the book directly suggested by genuine correspondence is small, and its limits are easy to determine. The action which serves as a framework for the letters is entirely imaginary, and both the hero and the heroine are much disguised, though certain facts from the lives of the writers are made use of. Mrs Harris, for example, was really the wife of a Methodist preacher, a circuit rider, whom she had married, at the age of eighteen, in 1887. But, while all the circumstances and even the characters are thus really imaginary, the romance served both authors as a means of expressing their own opinions, feelings, and convictions.

It is because of this fact that the letters contributed by Mr More still have a considerable interest. He had not the natural aptitude for the undertaking that Mrs Harris so evidently had. Her creation of Jessica and of Jessica's surroundings is charming; and her language is vivid, often beautiful, nearly always highly individual—indeed inimitable. By comparison, Jessica's editor-lover, Philip Towers, is almost tame. Something here, to be sure, must be allowed for the necessities of the plot. Nevertheless, Philip is certainly not so successful a creation as is Jessica, and his creator's gift for expression had to find outlet in a quite different kind of writing before it could show itself fully. This granted, however, Philip's letters possess real value for what they disclose concerning Mr More.

Some part of that which is disclosed relates to his early struggles, doubts, and long search for some valid objective confirmation of his own inner spiritual promptings. This portion of the book, consequently, merely tells over the story which I have tried to tell in the present chapter from fuller and earlier sources. But it may have been remarked by some readers that Mr More apparently was not at any time tempted, in his efforts to make sense of life, by what was, in the nineteenth century, and is still, in the twentieth, the characteristic modern substitute for traditional religious faith— the gospel of humanitarianism. He did not, of course, fail to encounter it, but he felt compelled to reject it decisively; and in *The Jessica Letters* one finds his earliest attempts to explain his attitude. These attempts are the more illuminating, in addition, because the creator of Jessica vigorously champions humanitarianism, in the earlier portion of the book, and accuses her correspondent of heinous selfishness, callousness, and blindness.

Mr More replies, in the person of Philip, that, as a matter of simple fact, his "hatred of humanitarianism does not spring from selfishness or contempt, but from sympathy for mankind." Humanitarians, of course, always take the position that what they feel is precisely such sympathy, and that therefore if one does not join them one must be coldly selfish. This, as was just said, is the conclusion to which Jessica jumps. This is also, I should suppose, self-righteousness incarnate, which normally expresses itself in blindness to distinctions and in bigotry. Those, however, whose minds are not closed should find it easy enough to understand Mr More's position. He recognizes, in these *Letters*, as clearly as any one could wish, the necessity of fellow-feeling if men are to live together in communities—its necessity and also its beauty. He points out that such "social sympathy" has continuously been recognized, as something indispensable, by thinking people in the Western world from Aristotle to the present day—that there is nothing novel here, and that, if it needs renewed attention and encouragement in every generation, there is really no reason whatever to fear that it will fail to receive it. But there are better ways and worse ways of inculcating the need for fellow-feeling, and this too should be recognized. The novelty inherent in humanitarianism is something which makes of it "a cloak for what is most lax and materialistic in the age." For humanitarianism sets up material well-being or comfort as the ideal aim of mankind, to which all are called to devote themselves, and is based on the assumption that everybody will be happy and "good" when everybody is well fed, well clothed, and well housed. "Good" and "evil," according to this view, are wrongly used terms. "Evil" is merely the incidental consequence of social inequality. People are greedy, at present, only because there is a universal feeling of insecurity. Remove this, by equalizing incomes, and "evil" will become a meaningless word;— "good" also, because you cannot get rid of the one without the other. Thus, as Mr More perceived when it was much less obvious than it is to-day, humanitarianism melts into, and is finally indistinguishable from, Marxian socialism or, as it is now called, communism.

And that which Mr More uncompromisingly opposed was not the need always to encourage our fellow-feeling, our compassionate love for those in distress; nor did he oppose enthusiasm for "universal justice," or for improving the condition of the masses. It is no less than amazing, indeed, that this should have to be said; but Jessica, unfortunately, is not the only humanitarian who has eagerly hastened to level false accusations against Paul More, and it is needful to be as explicit as possible. What he did oppose was simply the naturalistic philosophy underlying humanitarianism, which found expression in its materialism and its sentimentalism. It was not compassionate feeling that he hated, but the fanatical exclusiveness with which it was exalted as the one thing needful for the salvation of mankind. And it was not material well-being that he hated, but the equal exclusiveness with which this was set up as the salvation mankind strives for. He felt that the humanitarians, by cloaking their materialism under

the fine sentiment of brotherly love, were unconsciously playing straight into the hands of a "sordid plutocracy." And
the sordid plutocrat he liked no better than the gullible senti-
mentalist. Both "sought to buy the gift of God with a price."

What he wanted was a less superficial and doctrinaire
reading of human nature, reached with due regard for the
experience of the race. Humanitarianism, he learned, from
examples beginning with Rousseau and John Howard and
extending to his own personal experience, promoted neglect
of "the simplest rules of honesty and decent living"—their
place being taken by beautiful feelings about "humanity"
and corresponding hatred for existing society. He continues:

Let me illustrate this tendency to forget the common laws of
personal integrity by allusion to a novel which comes from a
college-settlement source. It is a story called, I think, *The Burden of Christopher*, published three or four years ago,—a clever
book withal and rather well written. The plot is simple. A young
man, just from his university, inherits a shoe factory which,
being imbued with college-settlement sentimentalism, he attempts to operate in accordance with the new religion. Business
is dull and he is hard-pressed by competitive houses. An old lady
has placed her little fortune in his hands to be held in trust for
her. To prevent the closing down of his factory and the consequent distress of his people, he appropriates this trust money
for his business. In the end he fails, the crash comes, and, as I
recollect it, he commits suicide. All well and good; but in a
paragraph toward the end of the book, indeed by the whole
trend of the story, we discover that the humanitarian sympathy
which led the hero to sacrifice his individual integrity for the
weal of his work-people is a higher law in the author's estimation than the old moral sense which would have made his personal integrity of the first importance to himself and to the
world.[22]

This tale was evidently a trivial enough affair, and it has

[22] Mr More returned to this illustration some ten years later in his essay
entitled "The New Morality" (*Aristocracy and Justice, Shelburne Essays,*
Ninth Series, pp. 193–194).

long since been forgotten; but it aptly illustrates the point
Mr More wished to make. To aim at the material well-being
of the greatest possible number of people is not in itself evil.
Nevertheless, it becomes evil when it is considered more important than anything else. Both for the individual and for
society, he believed, personal integrity is something vital.
Moreover, he saw no warrant whatever in either history or
science for supposing that misery, and the evils which produce it, are not inevitable in human life, bound under any
circumstances to persist while our race endures. Consequently he felt that the humanitarians encouraged an entirely fallacious hope at the expense of those personal virtues
which alone preserve not only the individual, but society,
from dissolution. And he concluded that man's only way of
deliverance from misery and evil lies, in our time as in the
past, in devotion to ideal ends more important than the
earthly life of any individual and, by that much, more important than any man's, or all men's, material comfort. Life, in
other words, points unmistakably beyond itself; and for its
real fulfilment poverty and renunciation—though not good
in themselves—may be indispensable means, because of our
proneness to become absorbed in earthly things, forgetting,
until awakened too late, that they are at hand for us, not we
for them.

It was, in the end, their attempt to substitute sentiment
for intelligence, and their sheer wilfulness, against which Mr
More complained in his arraignment of the humanitarians.
And towards the close of *The Jessica Letters* he drew a picture of them which, though somewhat rhetorical, is so acute
as to seem prophetic in the light of developments since 1904.
With it, then, I will end this account of his attitude:

Humanitarians are divided into two classes—those who have
no imagination, and those who have a perverted imagination.
The first are the sentimentalists; their brains are flaccid, lump-
ish like dough, and without grip on reality. They are haunted
by the vague pathos of humanity, and, being unable to visualize
human life as it is actually or ideally, they surrender themselves to indiscriminate pity, doing a little good thereby and a

vast deal of harm. The second class includes the theoretical socialists and other regenerators of society whose imagination has
been perverted by crude vapours and false visions. They are
ignorant of the real springs of human action; they have wilfully
turned their faces away from the truth as it exists, and their
punishment is to dwell in a fantastic dream of their own creating which works a madness in the brain. They are to-day what
the religious fanatics were in the Middle Ages, having merely
substituted a paradise on this earth for the old paradise in the
heavens. They are as cruel and intolerant as the inquisitors,
though they mask themselves in formulae of universal brotherhood.

III. THE SHELBURNE ESSAYS

I

IN 1903, when Mr More left the *Independent*, he immediately became the literary editor of the *New York Evening Post*. This position he held until, in 1909, he was appointed editor of the *Nation*. During the period while he was connected with these journals they were both controlled by Mr Oswald Garrison Villard, and were closely related to each other. Though the *Nation* never lost its separate identity, its editorial comment on public affairs was at this time drawn each week, with occasional alterations and amendments, from the columns of the *Post;* so that the responsibilities, and opportunities, of its editor were largely confined to the field of criticism. Henry James, in his *Notes of a Son and Brother*, has told how the *Nation* under the care of E. L. Godkin, almost immediately after its inception in 1865, had "enjoyed a fortune and achieved an authority and a dignity of which neither newspaper nor critical review among us had hitherto so much as hinted the possibility." And James goes on to say that the journal "had from the first, to the enlivening of several persons consciously and ruefully astray in our desert, made no secret of a literary leaning." It was predominantly as a critical review that it continued, under the editorship successively of Garrison, of Hammond Lamont, and of Mr More, to hold the unique position which Godkin had won for it.

Mr More gave up his post in 1914, though continuing for some time thereafter to act as advisory editor of the *Nation*. It is impossible here to discuss in any detail his work as an editor; but mention must be made of his success in holding together and notably strengthening a very distinguished group of regular contributors. No body of reviewers at all comparable for finished scholarship, integrity, and unfailing common sense has ever been attached to any other journal in the United States; and as the *Nation* was gradually transmogrified, during the years immediately following Mr More's retirement, there passed from our scene the last effective, organized centre of resistance against the forces tending to make journalistic criticism a mere article of commerce.

Amongst the writers whom Mr More attached to the *Nation* the most brilliant was Stuart Sherman;[1] and sufficient matter has been collected by Professors Zeitlin and Woodbridge, in their overgrown though valuable biography of Sherman, to form a chapter in itself—and a very instructive one—concerning Mr More's positive influence on his reviewers. The character of this influence and the manner in which it was exerted are clearly set forth by Professor Zeitlin:

Sherman admired in Mr More a critic of wide learning, definite philosophical vision, secure judgement, and imperturbable temper, and an editor who inspired his contributors to say the best that was in them. He expressed the feeling that in having him for an audience, one had enough, and that if one had his approval one needed no other. The desire to please was all the greater because of the freedom from editorial pressure. Mr More exacted no conformity of opinion from his writers. Once they had gained his confidence sufficiently to be enlisted among his regular contributors, they were at liberty to utter their individual views. An editor of this type exerts his influence by virtue of his intellectual force alone, and there is no doubt that Sherman's thinking on literary and social questions was for a number of years deeply coloured by his sincere respect for the character and point of view of Mr More. But as he could not deliberately accommodate his views and temperament to another's in all important respects, there appears in his utterances of these years a tendency to wavering and inconsistency for which his editor was quick to chide him.

[1] Sherman, it is true, began writing for the *Nation* during the editorship of Mr More's predecessor, and was on the staff of the *Evening Post* in the summer of 1908. He received every encouragement, including the offer of a permanent position, from Lamont and Mr Rollo Ogden. Nevertheless, it was Mr More who succeeded in attaching him as a regular contributor to the *Nation*.

On one occasion Mr More took him to task because he sent in an unmeasured indictment of democracy, flatly contradicting earlier expressions of faith in "the People." Evidently, Mr More said, he had not yet quite found himself. And this, it should be remarked, is one of many instances in which Professor Zeitlin fairly presents evidence going counter to his own interpretation of Sherman's career; for on this occasion Sherman's self-contradiction arose wholly from within. And in general it is strikingly clear that the nearer Sherman came to finding himself the less he found, so that his earlier writing, accomplished while he felt most strongly the influence of his editor, is decidedly his most vigorous, acute, and important.

Mr More's work as an editor, though characteristic and significant, was not, however, his principal achievement during the period while he was actively engaged in journalism;—for the *Shelburne Essays* were mostly written during the years from 1901 to 1914. The first series of these was published in the same year as *The Jessica Letters*, 1904, and at present there are eleven volumes—the last of which appeared in 1921—and one volume of *New Shelburne Essays*, published in 1928. The twelve volumes contain, besides several long prefaces, one hundred and seventeen essays and two translations—the *Apology* of Socrates, mentioned in the preceding chapter, and *Sâvitrî*, a tale forming an episode of the *Mahâbhârata*.

The essays fall naturally into several groups, though their titles, in a number of cases, very imperfectly indicate their scope. Only one essay, for example, is wholly devoted to a German writer—that on Nietzsche—but German romantic writers, both imaginative and philosophical, of the early period of the movement, receive extended treatment in the essay on Thoreau's *Journal* and elsewhere. Paying heed, however, simply to titles, for a rough classification, we find two essays concerned with ancient India, five on classical Greek literature, one on St Augustine, one on Tolstoy, and three on French writers—Pascal, Rousseau, and Sainte-Beuve. But the great majority of the essays are devoted to the literature of England and America from the latter part of the six-

teenth century to the present time. Of those concerned with
England, there are eleven essays on writers of the Elizabethan period and of the seventeenth century, fifteen on
writers of the eighteenth century, and forty on writers of the
nineteenth and twentieth centuries. Twenty-three essays are
devoted to American writers. And there are, in addition, fifteen essays on such subjects as Dualism, Humanitarianism,
"Property and Law," and "natural Aristocracy."

Taking them as a whole, these essays constitute a critical
literature without a parallel in England or America. They
are unique not only in their range and variety, but equally in
their sustained quality, in their faithfulness to the spirit of
sceptical, disinterested inquiry, and in the light they shed on
ancient and modern letters, on thought, and on the deep-
lying perennial problems with which all men are confronted.
Matthew Arnold's work is similar enough to Mr More's to
invite comparison. Arnold possessed certain gifts quite lacking in his great successor, but these were gifts not of primary
importance for criticism, and I think it incontestable that
the *Shelburne Essays* are more significantly and consistently
critical than the Englishman's pieces in any or all of the
fields into which he made excursions. The *Shelburne Essays*,
in addition, cover far more ground than Arnold did, and are
written in a style which, while fully as lucid and easy as
Arnold's, is more appropriate to the tasks of criticism. It
would not occur to anybody, I believe, to call Arnold the
Doctor Universalis of the nineteenth century, though he
more nearly deserves such an appellation than any other
English or American critic of his time. But this title has been
conferred, not alone by the French, on Sainte-Beuve; and
the only critic of the twentieth century who has won a place
for himself alongside of Sainte-Beuve is Mr Paul More.

There are real enough differences between the two—differences which register time's alterations and the influences of a
man's intellectual climate, besides ultimate and personal differences. The resemblances, however, are striking and important. Mr More himself has pointed out[2] that Sainte-

2 In his essay on Sainte-Beuve, *Shelburne Essays,* Third Series. In subsequent references to or quotations from the *Shelburne Essays* in this chap-

Beuve as a young man was exposed to varied currents of thought and doctrine, mutually exclusive, more or less contradictory, yet flourishing side by side—to social and intellectual conditions, in brief, essentially the same as ours and the counterpart of our modern specialization of every conceivable kind. And Sainte-Beuve, precisely like Mr More, after listening to a number of gospels preached with the utmost confidence, became sceptical of all, and so was impelled to a fresh study of man, in an effort to discover some central, fixed point which might serve for guidance through life. He hoped, in other words, at least to strike through surface-appearances, and by processes of careful discrimination to lay bare the roots of human nature—the abiding elements which so variously manifest themselves from age to age—and thus to discover a connecting thread and a meaning in the natural history of humanity which he believed himself to be composing. And he was forced into this attempt, which took him far beyond what had been regarded as the sphere of literary criticism, and indeed over all boundaries comparting men's activities, because literature is itself the reflection of life, and cannot be judged apart from it, and carries the thoughtful critic who is in earnest with his task inevitably back to its source in any time of confusion when traditional standards are challenged or disregarded. Hence it may be said that Sainte-Beuve had to become a critic of life and of society whether he would or no, since his age offered him only a choice between this and some blind partisanship—between the most fundamental criticism and slavery to some passionately maintained yet evidently ill-based piece of dogmatism. And this again at the close of the last century was the choice offered Paul More.

When I say that as a consequence Mr More devoted himself in the *Shelburne Essays* to sceptical, disinterested inquiry, it may appear that I am characterizing his work in terms used by Mr T. S. Eliot and quoted in my first chapter. Mr Eliot's "perfect critic," it will be recalled, was to be a

ter I have not thought it necessary to give volume and page. A brief index to the *Essays* is printed at the end of the eleventh volume (*A New England Group and Others*).

"free intelligence" "wholly devoted to inquiry." But the trouble with this monster of "pure" curiosity is that he has never existed outside of Mr Eliot's imagination, and cannot, in fact, even have been imagined save in the vaguest fashion. For Mr Eliot, and others like him, positively wish us to believe that a man develops a genuinely inquiring turn of mind only in proportion as he has no reason for inquiring into anything. Whether or not this would be a desirable human characteristic may be a debatable question, and may be debated by those with a taste for the inane, but assuredly it is not thus that men are now, or ever have been, constituted. Childlike confidence characterizes us, invariably, in the absence of experience. By no means everybody is capable of experience—that is, of learning anything from it. But the great majority of men learn, if nothing else, that things are not always exactly what they appear to be. It is, however, impossible to see why this should make the slightest difference save because men have interests which turn on the question whether or not appearances are deceptive. And certainly a considerable number of human beings—if not all who attain real maturity—value for their own sake, or have a connatural affinity for, truth and goodness and beauty, at least in some of their forms;—though it is not unusual to find men who value one member of this famous Platonic trinity above the other two. Hence, although disinterested inquiry may very well be undertaken, and not infrequently is, inquiry for inquiry's sake is an absurd, meaningless locution.

We are, in other words, moved to inquiry only by disillusionment, which, however, of necessity has its positive aspect. And whether inquiry is disinterested or not depends upon the nature of this positive aspect. If one is devoted to truth, regardless of personal fortune, one is disinterested, even though one may have an unqualified faith that to forward the cause of truth is best for one's self "in the long run," or eternally. If, on the other hand, one is devoted to one's self, to the advancement of one's earthly fortunes, to self-expression, inquiry takes on a very different colour—so different that it is often said not to be genuine inquiry at all. Mr Mencken has frankly proclaimed himself an example of devotion to Henry L. Mencken. Truth, he thinks, "is the adoration of second-rate men"—the first-rate men adoring themselves. And his motive, he says, when he takes up the work of some writer to criticize it, is "simply and solely to sort out and give coherence to the ideas of Mr Mencken, and to put them into suave and ingratiating terms, and to discharge them with a flourish, and maybe with a phrase of pretty song, into the dense fog" that covers the United States. He calls his collected essays *Prejudices*, so that it is not his fault if his readers have been deceived into thinking him a critic.[3]

Mr Isaac Goldberg has pointed out that Mr Mencken, in his first critical treatise, published in 1905, "reads himself into Shaw." "Through this book on Shaw," Mr Goldberg continues, "Mencken speaks largely and unconsciously for H. L. M.; . . . at the height of his expository enthusiasm for the Irishman, he discovers and reveals himself." And both Mr Goldberg and Mr Ernest Boyd have said the same thing about Mr Mencken's second treatise, *The Philosophy of Friedrich Nietzsche*. "It is," writes Mr Boyd, "*his* Nietzsche rather than Nietzsche whom he expounds"—a Nietzsche "created" by Mr Mencken "in his own image."[4] Both of

---

[3] He was described, in the thirteenth edition of the *Encyclopaedia Britannica,* as "the greatest critical force in America," though the word has since been passed around that he is a great satirist rather than a critic, and this correction has been duly incorporated in the last edition of the *Britannica.* Dr Lewisohn (*Expression in America,* p. 444) informs us that "Henry Mencken's best satiric pieces are among the best in the world," ranking him "with Juvenal and Dryden"; and he quotes the following little masterpiece of characterization to clinch the matter: "Wilson: the self-bamboozled Presbyterian, the right-thinker, the great moral statesman, the perfect model of the Christian cad." One can understand the appeal this makes to Dr Lewisohn, but is there anybody else who would stultify himself by placing such rant alongside of, for example, Dryden's portrait of the second Duke of Buckingham? Dr Lewisohn, on the other hand, condemns Mr Mencken as a critic unqualifiedly, and with characteristic violence (he "simply does not know what either religion or literature is," p. 448). Mr Mencken is judged much more temperately, as well as discriminatingly, by Professor Babbitt, in his essay entitled "The Critic and American Life" (reprinted in *On Being Creative*). The passages quoted in the text above come from Mr Mencken's "Footnote on Criticism," in *Prejudices,* Third Series.

[4] *H. L. Mencken* ("Modern American Writers" series), pp. 27, 29. Passages quoted from Mr Goldberg are taken from his *The Man Mencken, A Biographical and Critical Survey.*

these students declare, moreover, that in his first two critical
books Mr Mencken traced a pattern which he has since followed without real change. He has always used his subjects
as pegs on which to hang pictures of himself, or as spring-
boards from which to dive into the sea of his aversions.[5] And
in his book on Shaw there are passages, owing much it is true
to Mark Twain, yet written in his own peculiar style, which
was later to achieve a kind of celebrity. Speaking of *Man and
Superman*, for example, he declares:

No one but a circus press agent could rise to an adequate
description of its innumerable marvels. It is a three-ring circus,
with Ibsen doing running high jumps; Schopenhauer playing
the calliope and Nietzsche selling peanuts in the reserved seats.
. . . It is a tract cast in an encyclopaedic and epic mould—a
stupendous, magnificent colossal effort to make a dent in the
cosmos with a slapstick.

With the passage of time Mr Mencken's style has so far developed that he has created a special vocabulary—"clearly
the vocabulary of an artist and a scholar," as Stuart Sherman once wrote in the *Nation*, quoting the following list to
prove it: "multipara," "chandala," "lamasaries," "coryza,"
"lagniappe," "umbilicarii," "Treuga Dei," "swamis," "ge-
maras," "munyonic," "glycosuria." To these should be added
certain other words and phrases, to make a representative
selection: "scare-monger," "word-monger," "osseocaput,"
"malignant morality," "natural kneebender," "kept patriot," "snoutery," "snoutism," "Boy Snout," "snouteuse,"
"baltimoralist," "uplifter," "chemical purity," "bozart,"
"boozehound," "smuthound," "booboisie," "wowser."
   Whether or not these are "suave and ingratiating terms,"
they have certainly been discharged with many a flourish, to
the delight of young readers, in the course of Mr Mencken's
campaigns. For he has been a soldier, a crusader, throughout his career, stung by "a sort of insatiable desire to help

---

[5] On p. 246 of *The Man Mencken* Mr Goldberg says: "Writing of men,
women and things, he writes, all the time, of himself. This he knows; this he
wants you to know."

along the evolutionary process." Some part of his "philosophy" has been derived from Huxley and from Herbert Spencer, and he concluded long ago that the best kind of man, anxious to aid the cosmic forces, must feel, like himself, "a sort of restless impatience with things as they are."[6] It was in fact the iconoclast in Nietzsche who attracted him and whom he expounded, and he has seriously conceived himself —despite what Mr Goldberg calls his "innate cynical levity" —as another "great emancipator."[7] His ways of thinking, however, are as peculiarly his own as is his literary manner. With an admiring eye, perhaps, on his own exploits, he has written:

The liberation of the human mind has never been furthered by . . . learned dunderheads; it has been furthered by gay fellows who heaved dead cats into sanctuaries and then went roistering down the high-ways of the world, proving to all men that doubt, after all, was safe—that the god in the sanctuary was finite in his power, and hence a fraud. One horse-laugh is worth ten thousand syllogisms. It is not only more effective; it is also vastly more intelligent.[8]

In substance this is nothing new; it is Rabelaisian doctrine; but it betokens an assured conviction that The Truth is resident within one—and this conviction Mr Mencken has enjoyed as fully as the Reverend Billy Sunday, or the late W. J. Bryan, or John Calvin. Yet at the same time he has

[6] I quote from Mr Mencken's portion of *Men versus the Man* (1910).

[7] M. G. L. Van Roosbroeck, in his interesting *Reincarnation of H. L. Mencken* (1925), has explained the seeming paradox created by the fact that the iconoclast's abuse of them is welcomed by readers with enthusiastic approval. Mr Mencken informs us "that the American people, taking one with another, constitute the most timorous, snivelling, poltroonish, ignominious mob of serfs and goose-steppers ever gathered under one flag in Christendom since the end of the Middle Ages, and that they grow more timorous, more snivelling, more poltroonish, more ignominious every day." (*Prejudices,* Third Series, p. 10.) Such pronouncements, M. Van Roosbroeck points out, are always sure of a ready welcome, because "we simply apply the abuse to our neighbours and enemies, who seem to us always more or less humbugs, and grasp the eulogy [always accompanying these abusive utterances or implied in them] for ourselves"; and this, he adds, "gives us a delicate pleasure."

[8] *Prejudices,* Fourth Series, pp. 139–140.

been no less firmly convinced that truth is wholly inaccessible to the human mind, that life is meaningless, and that the battles of criticism are all illusory; so that he can find nothing quite insulting enough to say about any one who "knows congenitally what is right and what is wrong."

Where, then, behind such contradictions, is one to find the real man? Possibly Mr Mencken has died under the burden. This has in effect been suggested by several friendly observers, including Mr Burton Rascoe and Dr Lewisohn, both of whom, in closely similar language, have asserted that Mr Mencken has so completely identified himself with ephemeral modes of thought and ephemeral causes as to have become inseparable from them, with the consequence that his *Prejudices* already have only an historical value. This, of course, is the penalty usually paid by those who concern themselves exclusively with issues or conditions produced by special and rapidly changing circumstances; and it is likely enough that Mr Mencken's volumes will find a permanent place only in the social historian's museum, alongside other monuments of vanished American eras—such monuments, I mean, as the *Police Gazette* and the dime novel.

Nevertheless, Mr Mencken has vulgarized, if not really popularized, more than one good cause; and it seems evident that once upon a time, at least, he was a man of simple, direct, and honest perceptions, diffident but nerved by strong feeling, with a positive hatred of cant and hypocrisy, and with a vein of tender sentimentalism of which he was defiantly ashamed. Doubtless his transformation, for purposes of public exhibition, into an undiscriminating hard-boiled ranter proves that there was from the start an element of weakness and shallowness in him, which might have rendered him incapable under any circumstances of significant achievement; but certainly whatever solid possibilities he may have had were vitiated by his wilful determination to trust himself, worship himself, and exploit himself.[9] He would honestly accept himself just as he was, would blurt out whatever came into his head, and so would at least, as Polonius had

[9] Mr Goldberg speaks repeatedly of Mr Mencken's "canny sense of showmanship and self-advertising." (See pp. 210, 212, and 259 of his book.) Self-

advised, be true to himself. The consequences, as in some other modern examples of self-adoration, have been illuminating. Mr Mencken has never thought anything through, has never really examined anything, has only by accident seen anything fairly or truly, and so has never even learned to know himself. I do not mean that self-knowledge is easy to come by; it is in fact rarely attained; but without it a man engaged solely in self-expression would seem to be badly off. And Mr Mencken is in truth one of the most inconsequential of writers, without much to express save often very disparate temperamental reactions.

The contrast between a man of this type and Mr Paul More is obvious; and I do not know that Mr More's temper could be better expressed than in these words from the *Meno* of Plato: "Some things I have said of which I am not altogether confident. But that we shall be better and braver and less helpless if we think that we ought to inquire, than we should have been if we indulged in the idle fancy that there was no knowing and no use in searching after what we do not know—that is a theme upon which I am ready to fight, in word and in deed, to the utmost of my power." The man of science, the scholar, and the philosophic critic are united by one common conviction and pledged to one common cause, and Plato's words stand as well now as when he wrote them for the spirit animating these, at once the true leaders and the faithful servants of mankind. Amongst them, in our time, Mr More's distinction arises not so much from his unwavering persistence in attacking the most difficult and most important of all our problems—that of man's nature and destiny—as from his steady grasp of the conditions to be met by any answer, and his success in framing one which does satisfy those conditions. We shall accordingly consider this problem and Mr More's solution, and in so doing shall find the key to a right understanding of the *Shelburne Essays*.

worship and self-trust are written indelibly into most of Mr Mencken's books, but, concerning his vanity, reference may be made to p. 127 of *The Man Mencken*. And the following sentences quoted by Mr Goldberg (p. 240) from a letter written by Mr Mencken to Mr Rascoe have a bearing on the matter of self-trust: "I do not believe in education, and am glad I never went to a university. . . . I never learned anything in school."

II

BECAUSE literature is a reflection of life, the problem we are to take up is, in the field of literary criticism, the problem of standards, and we may best approach it from this direction. We have learned enough, I think, to be bound to agree with Mr More when he says, in his own discussion of the question in *The Demon of the Absolute:*

The simple truth is that every man, unless he be a dumb idiot, has a standard, more or less consciously chosen, by which he judges, and when the "irresponsibles" exhibit such fury at the sound of the word, they are merely throwing dust in our eyes to confuse the issue. The real question is not whether there are standards, but whether they shall be based on tradition or shall be struck out brand new by each successive generation or by each individual critic.

It is a fact, of course, that if each human being, or even each successive generation, devised a new and different system of weights and measures, we should say that there were no standards of weighing and measuring; but we should say this because there were too many, not because there was none. There is thus a real possibility that society may be without standards;—though the individual cannot under any circumstances be without them, and the only question which arises in his case concerns his method of obtaining them. No one, however, can conceive of a society entirely without standards. All men are agreed, I should suppose, that the standard pound and the standard yard are necessities of social life. Not even the petty scoundrels who use false weights or yardsticks are of a different opinion. Hence these standards are given an authority which may fairly be called absolute, and which is rendered effective, as are laws in general, by the force at the disposal of the state. Again, our railway companies, after an initial period of free experiment, have adopted a standard width of track, upon which circumstances themselves have conferred an overwhelming authority; so that there is not now, in this matter, the slightest opposition to order, in favour of anarchy.

A multitude of additional examples will occur to every reader; and it is obvious that without order, without at least a minimum of uniformity, in human conduct and thought as well as in things men use, no society could be formed or could persist. If some ancient writers, and some also in modern times—Hobbes, for example—have felt more keenly than ourselves the necessity of order, and have been willing to sacrifice everything to it, this is merely because they had experienced, to an extent that none of us has, the intolerable evils of social disorder. It was, moreover, the perception of order reigning in the universe, and of this inherent correspondency between nature and society and the mind of man, that gave ground for the hope that men might attain demonstrable knowledge, or science. And knowledge is valued above everything else only, in the last resort, because, if it is knowledge, its authority is unqualified.

Now it is true that whenever, as far back as history carries us, men have for any reason become critical, or sceptical, of received beliefs, they have sought for knowledge, endeavouring so to obtain an impregnable foundation for social and individual life. It is also true that while there can be no sense of certitude save on a basis of evidence, believed to be unassailable, still, there are differing kinds of evidence and, equally, differing kinds of certitude. Rationally or experimentally established knowledge has been sought, from the time when it was first distinctly conceived as a possibility, because it alone is open to no question, being readily and fully communicable and verifiable. Hence it is not at all surprising that strenuous and repeated efforts should have been made to attain a science of ethics and a science of imaginative literature—or, in other words, rational standards, universally valid and absolute in their authority—nor is it surprising that the relationship of literature to ethics should have been assumed to be close.

Their relationship is in fact close, though open to the most serious misunderstanding. And such misunderstanding has been persistent throughout the Christian era, until finally it has provoked a reaction as extreme and unintelligent as itself. At the same time, all attempts to create a science of ethics and a science of imaginative literature having decisively failed, for reasons which will later become clear, a similar reaction against standards has taken place. We hear it said again and again, in effect, "that there is no knowing and no use in searching after what we do not know." And the view is spread abroad by our forceful anti-critics and their satellites, whom Stuart Sherman used to call the street Arabs of the press, that any one concerning himself about standards is a would-be autocrat who fancies that we live in a static universe, who would gladly stifle all creative genius, who hates change and desires only to fasten us in a Chinese stagnation. Standards, in other words, are imposing shams and those who use them whited sepulchres, or, as Mr Mencken says, what amounts to the same thing, professors. These inferior persons, with an ignoble passion for setting themselves up as judges over their betters, use pretended standards only to destroy what is good and living in favour of what is old and dead, and, by an easy extension, also to strengthen "special privilege" in its horrible warfare against righteousness.

Mr More, as we have seen, gives these anti-critics the benefit of the doubt they raise concerning their intelligence and says "they are merely throwing dust in our eyes to confuse the issue." And it is certain that they not only, as he points out, utter "the most savage and exemplary judgements against those who disagree with" them, but also utter the most confident and sweeping verdicts on literature, reached by the use of their own individual, largely unformulated and unexamined standards. They arc, then, in fact, however unconsciously, attempting to promote confusion and to profit by it; and in this they are evidently playing an ignoble— indeed, to speak frankly, a contemptible—part in our common life, no matter what their intentions may be.

The anti-critics, nevertheless, are dealing, according to their lights, with a real problem, and perhaps the most important problem which men have to face. It may be true that order is a necessity for social life, and that what we know as modern science is really a search for rational order in the phenomenal universe; but it is also true that to cry "Peace,

peace," when there is no peace is a vain expense of energy, and that on every side we have evidence which no man of our age can fail to be aware of, proving that perpetual change and novelty characterize our world, that nothing is fixed or stable, that everything we know and do and are is relative to circumstances which are never two minutes exactly the same, that yesterday's "knowledge" is ridiculous nonsense to-day, that what is one man's meat is another man's poison, and that of course there is and can be under these conditions no accounting for taste. Such semblance of order as we have is wholly artificial, consequently, not "natural," not "real"; and this is capitally illustrated by the example here used— the standard pound—which is purely arbitrary, and depends on nothing except mutual agreement and convenience. It is, besides, neither very ancient nor really convenient, and, as it once supplanted some other standard, it should now be superseded by the kilogramme. Hence it is that life is fundamentally changeable, a process of spontaneous variation, exhibiting real discontinuity and real novelty in its successive moments, and thus in a sense anarchical, certainly "wide-open," adventurous, full of surprise, incalculable. Hence, furthermore, we can learn nothing from the past. "Everything said in the world up to date is 'bunk,' " Professor James Harvey Robinson has been heard to declare;[10] and indeed he is so confident of it that he thinks any differing conclusion indicative of a pathological condition. For conservatism, says Professor Harry Elmer Barnes, summarizing the profound thought of this odd teacher of history, who boastfully confesses that he has been unable to learn anything from it— conservatism "is partially a savage and primitive trait and partially a sort of collective neurosis through which mechanism the guardians of the existing order seek to avoid facing the dynamic social realities of the present day."[11]

Though I must admit an inability to understand just what "a sort of collective neurosis" may be, there is doubtless truth in these words, as there is indisputably truth in the general contention—familiar enough since the time of

[10] *Life and Letters of Stuart Sherman,* p. 311.
[11] *The New History and the Social Studies,* p. 211.

Heracleitus—that we are changing particles in a world of
perpetual change. And if it is also true, as I have said, that
all efforts to erect absolute standards of judgement have
proved futile, the case for our modern apostles of the flux
may seem to be complete. But, aside from the morass of contradictions into which these apostles invariably sink, because
in their own despite they cannot avoid forming judgements
and using standards of a kind, it is a fact that, running
along with the incessant variableness of life, there are also
elements of continuity. In *The Demon of the Absolute* Mr
More cites, as an example of capital importance, the traditional supremacy of Homer amongst poets. His place above
all others he very early attained in the estimation of the
Greeks, and he has held it to this day, not without some real
variation of opinion in the long interval, but, still, without
successful challenge. And this continuous tradition can be
matched with additional evidence which gives impressive
weight to Mr More's conclusion "that in the matter of taste
there is still that which is not confined by the boundaries of
space or nullified by the process of time, and which makes
the whole world kin." In truth, the traditional supremacy of
Homer is itself enough to prove "that the law of taste is the
least changeable fact of human nature, less changeable than
religious creeds, far less changeable than scientific theories."

There is, then, at least one constant element in life, making against the absolute sway of change; and at least a
strong presumption is created that the *Iliad*, the *Odyssey*,
and other literary pieces similarly sanctioned by tradition
"embody qualities which it is very much our concern to appreciate, and which we have every reason to use as a criterion." Nevertheless, it is impossible to speak of a "law" of
taste quite as one speaks of a "law" of gravity. The latter,
though in our time shorn of its grandeur, is still applicable
to all bodies within our universe moving with something less
than the velocity of light. Hence, whether rightly or not, it
will certainly seem like a mere quibble to point out that both
"laws" are only operative in the case of "objects" possessing
respectively "gravity" and "taste." For by no means all human beings have taste, and those who do may have more or

less of it, while to possess it at all a favouring union of in-born capacity and of education is required. This is aptly illustrated by a confession which Mark Twain made in 1902, in the course of an address to some art students in St Louis. He told how, once upon a time, he had inquired of a man "who was away up in art" what he found to admire in Titian's Venus in the Pitti Palace, and admitted that he had received this answer: "It is not worth while for me to tell you. Because certain qualities are required in order that you shall see the marvels in that picture, and you are not quali-fied to see them. You are born with a lack that cannot be supplied by education. You cannot learn, and you may as well give it up."[12]

Mr More is fully justified in speaking as he does of a "law" of taste; but this undeniable fact that taste varies, and that, besides, some men do not have it and cannot get it, raises a difficulty. For how, then, are we to judge whether a man has it or not? We may agree that the tradition of Homer's supremacy amongst poets is such as to give it a strong presumptive authority; we may even say there is much reason to suppose that qualified persons will continue always to judge Homer the first of poets; nevertheless, to become qualified one must be capable of profiting by instruc-tion and must be instructed, and one must be capable of learning the right things from experience and must be expe-rienced;—and how are we to tell about these matters? If we say that one mark of a successful education is a "just" appreciation of Homer, we seem clearly to be involved in a vicious circle;—and, though the traditional valuation of Homer may be entirely correct, there would appear to be no way of bringing it to a genuine test. For all we can really *know*, it may be that the great, impressive tradition cited by Mr More is just "a sort of collective neurosis," or something else equally mysterious.

We are thus brought face to face with the thorny question of knowledge, which bedevils the thinking portion of man-kind, and has been productive in our time of the most com-

---

[12] I quote from a review (*Times Literary Supplement,* 19 January, 1933) of *Mark Twain, the Letter Writer,* by Cyril Clemens, Boston, 1932.

plicated attempts imaginable at self-elevation by tugging at
one's boot-straps. It is perhaps for this reason that, as Professor Lovejoy has observed, epistemology is a subject which
"many men of science and certain philosophers seem to consider not merely unprofitable but repulsive"; yet, he goes on
to say, no less justly than pointedly, "since those who profess
this antipathy manifestly have epistemologies, tacit or explicit, of their own, it must be assumed that what they are
really expressing is a dislike for inquiries into the subject
which do not begin by accepting their conclusions."[13] There
is, in other words, no defensible way of evading the problem;
though we, happily, do not need to enter into the empty
warfare of the schools with which Professor Lovejoy has self-
sacrificingly concerned himself in the famous book from
whose Preface I quote. For our present purpose it will suffice
to recall certain familiar facts which I do not believe any
one would wittingly attempt to dispute, but which, apparently, are always forgotten by some of our contemporaries.

There are, for example, few things more foolish than the
assumption, made conspicuously but not only by Professor
James Harvey Robinson and Professor Harry Elmer
Barnes, that anything can be disposed of by contemptu-
ously calling it "savage and primitive." Breathing is "savage and primitive"; eating is "savage and primitive"; self-
adornment is "savage and primitive"; singing, dancing,
boat-building, cloth-weaving, carving, painting, the domes-
tication of animals, medical treatment, education, and the
love of novelty are all "savage and primitive." And if conservatism has persisted as a constant trait of human beings
from remotest times to the present day, as it undoubtedly
has, this is an excellent reason for concluding that it is indispensable in life, and for seeking to understand it. To exhibit
instead a weak and vain anger, is merely to exhibit one's
enslavement to some dogma palpably at variance with fact.
To cry loudly that all is change in this our life and then to
turn with unqualified condemnation upon all life's constant
elements may be incorrigible stupidity, or impudence, or a

13 *The Revolt against Dualism*, pp. x–xi.

shady political dodge, but it is not wisdom and it is not science. Nor is it ever done consistently. Many, for instance, who talk as if the doctrine of progress invalidated everything that is done, thought, or said as soon as it has been done, thought, or said, appeal with the next breath to a real or supposed past that appeals to them. We hear the same persons confidently arguing from day to day that something is to be adoringly accepted because it is new, that something else is to be adoringly accepted because it is ancient and "elemental," that something else is to be rejected with horror because it is ancient and "savage," and that everything is to be rejected as soon as it is turned up because it is already out of date or because nothing can be known except that nothing can be known.

What is to be concluded by any one with a serious concern for truth? It seems clear that neither newness nor age can in itself serve as a criterion of validity. It seems equally clear that neither change nor constancy alone characterizes the scheme of things in which we are temporary participants, but that both together, inextricably commingled, are present wherever we may look. Both, moreover, qualify each other, so that nothing in the phenomenal universe, as far as we can ascertain, is either absolutely constant or absolutely inconstant. The "law of taste" may be, if not "the least changeable fact of human nature," at any rate one of many facts of human nature no more changeable than itself and at once more evident than it and more obviously constant; nevertheless, in the form in which Mr More expounds it, it relates to human beings and cannot endure longer than our race. But constancy co-extensive with the life of our race, and real continuity extending far beyond that limit, may be predicated of much entering into our humanity, with all the confidence which we accord to any well-established result of scientific investigation. For modern science has been as much concerned with constancy as with change, and in fact, as I have suggested, has been really concerned to discover constancy in change. And it has taught us that, despite all contrary appearances, there is no complete break between living

objects and lifeless; that animal life, again, shades off into
vegetable, with no sharp dividing line between; and that man
is an animal, linked with closest ties to other animals and by
identity of substance to the earth itself. Although, moreover,
no two men may be completely alike, still, all men are much
more like each other than like the family of animals closest
to man in physical and perhaps some mental characteristics.
By virtue, furthermore, of this real constancy and continuity we can, even from very meagre remains, recognize as men
essentially like ourselves, with whom we could have established social relations on the human level, beings who lived
probably ten thousand or even twenty thousand years ago.
Perhaps, indeed, contemporary anthropology's most significant contribution to our store of well-based information is
its discovery—emphasized by such competent investigators
as Professor Robert H. Lowie—that the differences between
so-called savages and ourselves are not nearly so great as
had formerly been assumed.

Such differences as there are, besides, are superficial in
comparison with even that minimum of constancy in human
nature which takes care of itself. The instinct of self-preservation is a part of that minimum, and we may reckon conservatism as another. The latter is more evidently variable
than the former, in that it is much more intense and active
in some men than in others, and also under some circumstances; but at the same time it persists through the generations, and remains a present reality no matter how shrilly
conceited dogmatists may rail at it. Taste, however, as we
have seen, is on a different footing. By no means all men
have it, and some there are who cannot acquire it, whatever
their opportunities. Perhaps every age has its many examples, but certainly our own time is rich in them. A great deal,
in fact, not only in the aesthetic, but also in the social and
political developments of the last hundred years and more,
is only explicable by the way in which certain groups or
classes have succeeded in reaping advantage of a kind from
their very disabilities, thanks to widespread sentimentalism
and prosperity. Mark Twain at times won success by play-

ing up some real or alleged lack in himself, thus winning
sympathy, which he turned to his advantage by insinuating
in the end that somehow there was sterling virtue in a dis-
ability which he shared with the common run of men. He
verged upon this trick in the confession I have quoted,
though really meaning, on this occasion, to show himself
aware of a genuine limitation which he genuinely regretted.
He has, however, been followed by a host of aggressive persons who have learned his trick without suspecting their own
deficiencies—who have discovered that they may be sure of
a sympathetic audience when they boast that Homer is Greek
to them, and when they ask loudly why they should admire a
poem or a play just because it has been admired through
many generations. And these fellows who make capital out of
their tastelessness teach us that, beyond the minimum of constancy in human nature which takes care of itself, there is a
possibility of a further continuity which depends upon our
own desires and effort.

Upon the maintenance of this further continuity, moreover, depends the difference between civilization and the
most abject, impoverished barbarism. For civilization is in
some ways analogous to an organic growth, and may instruc-
tively be compared to one of the giant redwood trees of California—for a very different reason, however, from that
which causes the muddle-headed psycho-analyst to attempt
to assimilate men to trees. The redwood attains its majestic
form and grand solidity only by a continuous life of several
thousand years, during which it is always adding to its mass,
conserving that which is sound and casting off that which,
though it is lovely to the eye and transiently great in mere
bulk, is destined quickly to rot. By its side the seedling of a
year and even the tree of three score years and ten look
almost equally abject and impoverished. And so with human
beings: It is only, as Charles Keary wisely wrote in a book
which should be better known, "It is only folk stupefied by
vanity who think they are equal to the task of creating a
new world out of chaos."[14] The civilized world into which

14 *The Pursuit of Reason,* p. 338.

all of us were born is a growth, slower than that of a red-wood tree, and a growth achieved by conserving, despite the never-ending challenge of stupidity, of ignorance, of vanity, and of changing circumstance, what is perdurable in the lives and deeds of the best men who have successively appeared amongst us. "The aim of culture," Mr More has said, "is not to merge the present in a sterile dream of the past, but to hold the past as a living force in the present."

To entertain such a design is to exhibit an understanding as true as it is rare of the social character of life; and the execution of this "aim of culture" is easily the most important social task of each generation. For thus to keep our heritage is to be able to use it, to build upon it if at all possible, but at least to save ourselves from the untold emptiness, futility, and misery of chaos, and from the perfect slavery to rigid, all-embracing convention which is, of necessity, the earliest stage of the escape from chaos. Hence to preserve human continuity as fully as may be above the level of the minimum which takes care of itself is not to condemn ourselves to the carrying of an always heavier burden;—it is, on the contrary, to secure to ourselves the only real freedom man can win. Who will pretend that it was in any sense an enlargement of Mark Twain's personality or powers that he was so nearly shut within the boundaries of his own time and place, and had so little help in enlarging those bounds at the period of his life when help might have been useful? It was, but too obviously, a pure loss that much which constitutes culture meant nothing to him—a narrowing circumstance lessening both his enjoyment and his understanding of life, and equally lessening the value of his work.

Mark Twain's trouble was ignorance, perhaps in the beginning not incorrigible. But in the world of absolute change and discontinuity which some metaphysicians and popular misleaders of opinion think they think we live in, neither could Mark Twain have become aware of his limitations nor could any one else become aware of his own or any man's. In that world no one could have any motive for self-correction or self-development, or even any understanding of the significance of such terms. In fact there could be no persons at all in that world, because not only would society be impossible and non-existent but every animate being would become a totally new creature from instant to instant. Under such conditions there could be, of course, no history, no science, no art, no intelligent activity of any kind. A world of absolute change is, in short, really unimaginable, since it is as far removed from our experience as a world of absolute constancy.[15] And it is constancy, as real in our experience as change, which alone makes experience itself, and hence knowledge, as we ordinarily use the word, a possibility.

When we say we *know* something we mean that we are entirely certain about it. When we believe something we regard it as *practically* certain or very probable, and belief shades off into opinion, which in turn shades off into mere conjecture. But how do we become certain? The feeling of certitude, unfortunately, carries with it no guarantee that it arises from knowledge. It doubtless always comes, as I have earlier said, as an inference, more or less conscious, from evidence which seems conclusive. There are, however, endless

15 It will doubtless be said that I push the theory of discontinuity to an absurd extreme. But to say this is, in the present connexion, to imply that those insisting on a theory should not be expected to accept its consequences; and the point I seek to make is precisely that the apostles of discontinuity either do not know or do not believe what they say. This theory is closely related to the anti-critical campaign discussed in my first chapter, and, like the theory there examined, it is in practice used as a club, and to bring in chaos, because its exponents are the kind of people "who think they are equal to the task of creating a new world." What they and their pronouncements really signify is well set forth by Keary in the following passage: "We have been richer in schemes for the future and in prophecies than in originality and the creative arts: so that there is truth in Ruskin's saying that our generation has conceit sufficient to question the designs of a universe, but not honest self-confidence enough to carve a cherry-stone with an original pattern. For my part I do not object to mental activity. Let Reason try all things, and if she have modesty therewith (and *Reason* always has) she will hold fast that which is good. But the universal 'speculation' which characterizes these times is no work of Reason's, but a part of the disintellectualizing of our age. It is the work of people too lazy to think their notions into a sequence; greedy to be titillated with 'suggestive' literature; incapable of enough application to reach a definite conclusion. 'Speculation' of this kind in the world of thought is the exact counterpart of speculation in the world of industry and un-industry. It is a throwing the dice into the air on the chance that they will come down a good number." (*The Pursuit of Reason,* pp. 372–373.)

possibilities of one's being deceived in the interpretation of evidence, whence arise the most painstaking and elaborate efforts to circumvent human fallibility by eliminating, as far as may be, the "personal equation." Thus specialized methods of criticism are built up, in the manner described in my first chapter. But, as was there pointed out, although we only come to know such a substance as platinum by a process of analysis through which it is effectively isolated, still, once we have it, it remains something wholly indescribable and incomprehensible save in so far as we can then relate it to other substances. That which characterizes platinum is that which differentiates it from other metals, and that which characterizes metals is that which differentiates them as a class with common properties from non-metallic substances; but in every case we learn what can be learned by comparison, and express it in relative terms. Were we confronted with an object or conception entirely unrelated to everything within our experience, we should be able to make nothing at all of it. Yet equally were there not partial discontinuities within the field of our experience we should be unable to distinguish anything from anything else. And it is in fact the commingling in our world of change and constancy, of continuity and discontinuity, which alone enables us to make any sense of it, and so to build up a body of knowledge;—and we call this mental structure knowledge because it meets the most rigorous tests we can devise, yielding under experiment the results predicted. The feeling of certitude thus induced is held to be legitimate for the simple reason, in the last analysis, that experimental verification is irresistible, we ourselves being so constituted as to find it irresistible.

It may be said, against such an assertion, that the conclusions enforced by experimental verification often are resisted, or are simply neglected, if they are in conflict with currently received beliefs;—and the fact is undeniable, and might be illustrated as easily from the behaviour of some dogmatic men of science to-day as from that of some guardians of religious dogma to-day and in the past. Pope wrote of certain medieval school-divines that "none had sense enough to be confuted," and, however open to question his verdict, it is unfortunately true that there are in every generation whole groups with more sense and much stubbornness. But it is also true that there are others in every generation cursed with a perverse love for what is not, full of hatred against what is, restless and eager for novelty at any cost, who are as wilfully blind to evidence, as little capable of sound judgement, as those who are the creatures of convention and inertia. Thus the people who would judge, not from evidence, but from temperamental inclination of this kind or that, hold each other in check in a rough fashion productive of constant re-crimination, and little commendable, though useful; while only those who are qualified by inborn capacity and educa-tion are able to see evidence for what it really is. Such per-sons are always a minority, and the conditions of our time, as I have said in my first chapter, press them harshly to con-fine their training and the exercise of their talent to small, sharply defined fields. But their authority in those fields is widely regarded as final—though even the most expert judges do not become infallible—and in the long run it is as irresistible as the evidence on which it is based.

This, however, brings us round once more to the qualified person, and at the same time enables us to see that we are no better able than any earlier generation of men to live without faith and without dependence at every turn upon authority. For, as regards faith, the "knowledge" under dis-cussion is relative knowledge, in more senses than one. Whether or not men will ever cease chasing the phantom of absolute knowledge is an unanswerable question; but as-suredly, as Mr More has said, "there are no absolutes in nature." And not only is our knowledge incomplete, approxi-mate, and never beyond the possibility of further improve-ment; it is also, unescapably, *our* knowledge—a construction built in accordance with the nature of human minds and human senses. Wherever it is possible so to do we control and reduce the human factor to the limit of our ability; but to get rid of it entirely is not possible, so that we cannot know what things would be like if there were no one to know them, nor how we would ourselves seem without senses or minds, or would seem to some imaginary being capable of unmediated and infallible apprehension.[16] Consequently we remain dependent upon faith, rendered as conscious and critical as may be, but, still, upon faith in our senses and our minds. Socrates, as we shall have occasion again to notice in the following chapter, declared before the court which condemned him that " a life unquestioned is no life at all for a man," and I have tried to make clear the indispensable place of scepticism in the development and activity of intelligence; nevertheless, even scepticism is here brought to a stop, because you cannot declare that nothing can be known without implicitly declaring in the same breath that at least this can be and is known—while if anything at all is really known a foundation is laid for further knowledge.

Faith, then, in this real sense, we cannot dispense with, nor can the individual move a step towards development, maturity, and real freedom without its extension. For while the stream of human life is continuous and carries on through the generations many constant elements, just as a river is always changing yet remains always essentially unchanged, still, with each individual, life makes a new beginning under conditions to some extent unprecedented and not to be repeated. Hence arise endless diversities and inequalities separating individuals, while their common humanity holds them together. But it is only as the individual accepts, by an act of implicit faith, the presumptive authority of the conserved experience of the race, and succeeds in appropriating this experience, that he can become fully human. This requires submission to prolonged discipline, whose end and possible reward cannot be known in the beginning, nor by any one who evades it. Some, who apparently have persuaded themselves that men spring full-grown into being, complain that submission to discipline must warp and stunt individuality. It would be as sensible to complain because knowledge destroys the notion that the moon is made of green cheese.

16 It is a fool's mission of this kind upon which some symbolistic writers have embarked, though the conscious tendency of the school as a whole is towards a complete individualism and subjectivism. The results in the latter case tend to become equivalent to simple insanity; in the former case they are, in so far as the mission is thoroughly carried out, exactly what could have been predicted—indistinguishable from pure nonsense.

Individuality is nothing in itself, or worse than nothing, like indiscriminate enthusiasm, and when deliberately cultivated is mere eccentricity and blind wilfulness. Significant individuality, which alone is valuable, comes solely as a development, through the subtle, pervasive relationship between the race and its members which does incalculably much to give life its distinctively human quality. If comparatively few men in any generation exhibit significant individuality, this is simply because, as far as can be known from all available evidence, comparatively few men are capable of developing it. Certainly some conditions are more favourable to this end than others, and discipline may be foolishly administered, as things are with us, more often than wisely, and the right ordering of education is an endless task, requiring the utmost delicacy, patience, sympathy, and intelligence;—nevertheless, it is certainly not by stubborn ignorance and attempted withdrawal from association with the human family, but by submitting to learn and by assimilating all that can be assimilated from the race's experience and achievements, that a man is formed and comes to have, properly speaking, a self, which at the same time and by the same means he is enabled to know. Self-knowledge, as I have said before, is not the simple and easy matter it is often supposed to be, and requires, besides, a real self to be known. For a child is a mere bundle of hidden possibilities, and these are brought to light and tried and developed, not by asking it to consult its inclinations when, in any true sense, it does not yet have any, but by compelling it early to bring order and purpose into its activities, to speak and write and read correctly and easily, to conform to accepted social conventions, and to enter, when a sufficient age has been attained, into the closest possible relations with humanity through history, literature, and science. And thus while that full continuity is assured which at once humanizes the youth and gives fresh life to civilization, the developing individual learns to know himself by learning his capacities, his limitations, his strangely close union with others, and his none the less insurmountable isolation and loneliness.

I sketch most summarily, it will be realized, the process of

personal development; and what has to be said runs counter
to the reigning popular theory of the day. But I cannot discover that the species of education, so-called, associated with
the name of Professor Dewey makes its appeal to facts. It is
rather a "speculation," designed, so far as facts are related
to it, to provide a plausible way of escape from education,
which cannot be imparted equally to all the children of our
overgrown democracy. Hence this theory, whose bearings
have become plain despite the cloud of words in which Professor Dewey is accustomed to veil his meaning, has not the
slightest interest to any save the dwindling number of
"speculators" who think they are pure equalitarians. And
wherever we may turn, to consult facts, we find that society
is dependent upon the authority of the qualified person, and
that the qualified person is one who has submitted himself, in
faith, to the discipline of learning and carrying on the accumulated experience of the race, and who has thus attained
the capacity for independent or reasoned judgement. If, to
take an example suggested by Dr Johnson in *Rasselas*, we
look at such a modern ship as the *Bremen* or the *Conte di
Savoia*, we may easily be lost in admiration, likely to be the
greater in proportion as we can understand the intricate
engineering problems so triumphantly solved by contemporary shipbuilders. And those are scarcely to be blamed who
take these great floating cities—to use the term not unjustly
applied to them—as convincing evidence of the gulf that
separates our age from all past time;—nor would anybody
desire to lessen the praise bestowed on the modern designer.
Yet neither this nor any similar achievement is at all miraculous. The thread of continuity is unbroken between the earliest rude boat, fashioned probably by hollowing out a tree
trunk, and the swift, enormous vessel of to-day with ribs and
sides of steel. And each step of the way between the two has
been relatively a small one, made possible by those preceding
it, so that the *Conte di Savoia* is, in fact, the product of
efforts made by innumerable men through thousands of
years. Development, it is quite true, has been extraordinarily
swift during the last century, dwarfing earlier progress;—
and this means that the rate of change in shipbuilding has

been similar to the rate of change in mass observable when one rolls a snow-ball. But it does not mean that historic continuity has been broken. Who, moreover, is the best judge of ships and of projected improvements? Who is the successful builder? Is it the man who turns his back on all that has been learned in the past, guarding his precious individuality, trusting his own unaided genius, writing "Whim" over the door of his draughting room, and spinning out his design with the aid of a perfectly "free" imagination?

The question does not need to be answered. And I believe one illustration is as conclusive for the present argument as a thousand could be;—since, as soon as we are forced to think about what we all know, we cannot help seeing for ourselves that in every walk of life the qualified person is formed, and can only be formed, through that submission to presumptive authority which at first looked to us as if it might condemn humanity to travel perpetually in a vicious circle. And it should now be clear that this it does not, because human beings are not mere floating particles of the stream of life, "instruments of the life-force," but individuals, with the possibility of becoming individually more or less significant, purposive, and constructive. Men are, unescapably, not complete in themselves, but members of a continuing family. They do carry on the stream of life, and in fact can realize or fulfil themselves individually only as, by their own participation, they help to insure the richest, most complete *human* or cultural continuity; but when they thus discover themselves as it were by losing themselves, they are capable of standing apart from the stream for detached observation, and even of moving against the strongest current if so they must. The continuous interaction of the stream and the individual is, in other words, the fruitful source of character, of integrity, of reason, of critical judgement, and of constructive leadership possessing high authority because it is ready and able at all times to give a full account of itself to those who have understanding.

Clearly, moreover, our exact sciences are attempts—and, within limitations, successful attempts—to confront the phenomena of our universe intelligently, removing both thought and activity as much as possible from the region where one man's guess is as good as another's. So far had this effort gone, by the close of the nineteenth century, that it seemed possible to construct a highly unified picture of the universe as a vast mechanical organization, following consistently, in all its parts, a single determinable course of development. It was recognized that portions of the picture were still blank, that other portions were only provisionally sketched, and even that there were some difficulties to be overcome; but it was very generally felt that the evidence accumulated during the seventeenth, eighteenth, and nineteenth centuries was overwhelming, and that the final solution of man's questionings concerning himself and his environment was definitely in sight. During the present century, however, the further progress of scientific discovery itself has effectually overturned this view, so that to-day it is realized by an increasing number of people, and especially by the most competent men of science, that the account of knowledge given in these pages is applicable without exception to all fields of inquiry. And this is of the utmost importance, because it means that human experience is the only absolute with which we are directly acquainted, and that no amount or kind of knowledge open to us can legitimately be used to destroy one part of our experience in favour of another. The effort to obtain knowledge, in other words, is an effort to convert the data of observation into an harmonious and intelligible form. When this is successfully done, the knowledge obtained can be used to fulfil human purposes, and therein lies the reason why it is so eagerly sought. But the test of success is and can be nothing other than verification through experience, our one court of last resort.

Thus modern physical science has been simply an attempt to describe the structure of the universe mathematically. This could only be accomplished by a process of abstraction—by silently discarding those aspects of phenomena which could not be exactly, though symbolically, expressed in quantitative terms. We have earlier in the present volume noticed that this selective process is a necessity in all scientific investigation. In this instance the data of observation which could be put into usable mathematical form proved to be sufficient for extraordinary triumphs of unifying constructive endeavour, successful in the sense just defined. And in this fashion the most diverse phenomena were, one after another, forced to take their places as parts of a coherent, intelligible system; —until in very recent years, as I have said above, further discoveries have conclusively shown that the familiar mechanistic pattern is not adequate to its purpose. Meanwhile, however, by the latter part of the nineteenth century its prestige had become so great that there was a general disposition to accept the mechanistic pattern as something absolute, final, and complete, and consequently to "explain" everything inconsistent with a mechanistic materialism as mere delusion. But to explain is one thing, while to "explain away" is another and very different undertaking, in a case like the present only to be justified by proof that man has attained a standpoint transcending the level of experience, from which the latter can be adjudged true or false. And this is precisely what men are always imagining they have somehow done, and are always discovering that, after all, they have not done and cannot do. In the case under discussion the "explanation" sufficiently showed its character by creating a far greater difficulty than it solved; for to assert that man was simply a piece of mechanism and consciousness a mere epiphenomenon was to render it wholly impossible to understand how this same man could have consciously discovered this or anything else. The feat was incomprehensible and unbelievable save on the absurd assumption that the man of science had contrived to get outside of himself—or, we might say, beside himself— and so to obtain a standpoint, or standard of judgement, from which he could evaluate himself as something other and less than himself—a creature adequately to be known from abnormal behaviour when attacked by disease, but incapable of knowledge or of responsible activity.

What really occurred has for some time been quite clear. The achievements of the exact sciences were such as to create a very strong prejudice in favour of defining reality as simply that which these sciences could make something of, or could use. There were reasons for this, positive and negative,

which cannot be set forth here, but whose impressiveness
one would not wish to deny. Nevertheless, the proposal led
straight to the absurdity just mentioned; and it did so because it was an attempt to make reality conform to science.
This, though perhaps inevitable, was arbitrary and wholly
illegitimate, as we have seen, since the science in question concerned only some aspects of the phenomenal world as given in
experience—aspects selected merely because they lend themselves to exact investigation. There was nothing in such a
procedure even to suggest that other aspects might be less
real; they were simply less tractable. The very possibility of
our having any science at all, moreover, depended on our
being in a genuine sense outside, though at the same time not
completely outside, of the field of such science, able to stand
apart from that which we could know, yet able to bring conjecture, or hypothesis, to the final test of verification through
experience. Hence there was not—and there is not now, and
there never can be—any remote chance that our science could
really undermine or destroy our distinctively human character as responsible, purposive, intelligent beings, or our
direct experience of this character in our own lives.

This elementary consideration has never been successfully
challenged; it has merely been ignored. But it cannot be
ignored without disaster which engulfs all science as well as
humanity. And in truth it was not science, in the last century
and in the early years of our own, which led up to the crucial
absurdity we have noticed, but false philosophy, pretending
that in physical science it had found a basis of absolute and
universal truth, and hence attempting to force everything
given in experience into a rigid mould obtained by consulting only one part of what was thus given. Not a single
achievement of science, furthermore, need be called into question or ignored by one who resolutely disavows this and all
other efforts to find a cheap and easy way of satisfying man's
vain wish for absolute and complete knowledge of the scheme
of things in which he finds himself enmeshed. It is not science,
for example, which has imposed on us the notion that we are
particles in a chaos of discontinuity, or the notion that we are
independent of the past and can learn nothing from it, or the

notion that man is a kind of mechanical toy, or the notion that humanity is not different save in its illusions from animals and vegetables and rocks. These and kindred notions are all "speculations," some frivolous, some disingenuous, some desperately serious, though none the less empty for that —because not one of them arises from anything other than an effort to *use* science, as if it were absolute knowledge, in order to obtain a starting-point for some variety of metaphysical system. Each system of the kind, in other words, is an attempt to force reality within the confines of some pattern, formed in accordance with the imperfect, limited, relative knowledge and imperfect, limited intellectual powers of some temporal creature. The fundamental trouble with these patterns, moreover, lies not alone in the misunderstood science they embody, but also in the assumption that reality must conform to the demand of the rational intellect for homogeneity, simplicity, and self-sufficiency. This amounts to a claim that the human mind is not merely capable of attaining knowledge, perhaps incomplete, yet absolute; but is also capable, through its logical processes, of determining infallibly the character which reality as a whole must possess.

The mazes of fantastic, tortured, contradictory writing which have appeared to support this claim are themselves convincing testimony to the fact that it is baseless. They need not concern us here; nor need they, indeed, concern any one who cares for truth. They have in our day made philosophy a byword for incomprehensible, pretentious nonsense.[17] They

17 I must refer, for full evidence, to *The Revolt against Dualism,* by Professor Arthur O. Lovejoy (1930). Professor Lovejoy is the most penetrating critic, within the limits of his clearly defined field, who has appeared amongst American philosophers; and he merits unqualified gratitude for his just, patient, and resolute exposure of the absurdities and contradictions inherent in the work of recent and contemporary sufferers from "dyophobia." His book, however, because of its technical nature, is not for everybody. But no intelligent reader will have any difficulty with the first dialogue, "Socrates' Adventures in Wonderland," in Professor James Bissett Pratt's *Adventures in Philosophy and Religion* (1931), where the hollowness of the revolt against dualism is exhibited as amusingly as it is clearly and convincingly. Professor Pratt's book is, I must add, one of the most delightful of its kind, and would by this time be well known throughout the country if we had any critical reviews which were properly performing their office.

represent one of the penalties we have paid for modern science, which is certainly worth a great price, and perhaps all its cost, but which desperately needs—for its own sake and for the sake of humanity—to be separated from its parasitic growth of metaphysics. For science can teach us a very great deal about ourselves and about the possibilities of life, as I scarcely need to insist, and can help us in innumerable ways to realize the purposes for which we live, and can perform its indispensable services because it is knowledge, such as human beings are capable of. It proves, moreover, definitely enough for entire conviction, that though we cannot attain absolute knowledge under earthly conditions, neither are we condemned to absolute ignorance.

A great many people, of course, want everything or nothing. When we encounter this attitude in children we know what to think of it. But we should think no better of it, and much less indulgently, when we discover it in adults. Yet these wilful children of a larger growth are continually imposing on us their mischievous demands:—we must have, they cry, either uncontrolled capitalism or the total abolition of private property, either complete individualism or communism, either superstitious idolatry ("savage and primitive") or atheism, either Chinese stagnation or unceasing change indistinguishable from change-for-its-own-sake—but I need not go on. The list of these unreal and unhuman alternatives is long, but familiar. And it may be said that the strength and solidity of our civilization can be measured by our ability to hold a middle course between them all. In perhaps no instances, moreover, can we do other than hold a middle course, save by grossly deluding ourselves. We have seen that knowledge is a pre-eminent example of this. We are not born with it; we are by no means all equally able to attain it; we have in any event to struggle for it, and though we may gain more or less, no one has ever gained enough; when we do gain it, we find it not all we could desire, since it is not only approximate and incomplete, but is relative and dependent on faith. Nevertheless, no one without an ax to grind professes any doubt concerning the distinction between knowledge and opinion, or knowledge and ignorance;—or any doubt concerning our possession of knowledge which is real, dependable, and sufficient for many of our needs and purposes, even though not absolute and not free from difficulty. In general, moreover, instead of loving ignorance, instead of sitting down in weak despair and declaring that they will have nothing to do with a life not constituted as they might have desired, those who have succeeded in making human existence something other and better than beastly have refused to "indulge in the idle fancy that there is no knowing and no use in searching after what we do not know," have accepted the unalterable conditions of life, and have endeavoured steadily after knowledge such as human beings can attain, and steadily after more knowledge, and after more exact knowledge.

That the search has been greatly rewarded who, after all, can deny? Certainly, however, it has been more successful in the realm of lifeless things and in the realm of sub-human life than in the field of the distinctively human. This was admitted in my first chapter, when it was pointed out that one obstacle to a full scientific knowledge of man lies in the complexity of his organization and in the large element of contingency thus involved. And this, we can now see, is by no means the only or the gravest obstacle to the development of a science of man. Scientific knowledge, to be sure, is a special kind only in its exactness, in the readiness with which it can be verified, and, as a consequence, in the power it confers of accurate prediction. But man is not simply a less predictable creature than a moth or a guinea-pig; he also knows that he is less predictable; and though he is himself an animal, he can distinguish the mere animal as something other than himself. Man, in other words, can detach himself from the stream of phenomena while remaining a part thereof; and in this ability to stand off for analysis and judgement finds, as we have seen, the possibility of attaining objective knowledge, within the field of which his science lies. This means, however, that man stands partly within and partly outside of the realm of scientific knowledge, and that consequently a science of man can never be a practical possibility.

There are further reasons for accepting this conclusion,

arising from man's experience of himself as a responsible being, capable of deliberately chosen or rationally purposive actions; and, as I have tried to make clear, the very possibility of our having any science is not conceivable unless we stand in a real sense beyond its boundaries. Against our conclusion, in addition, there are no facts which can be cited, but only a somewhat miscellaneous collection of passionate prejudices.[18] And it does not follow from this conclusion that man, save in so far as he does stand within the purview of his own science, is condemned to ignorance of himself. For besides objective knowledge, man may achieve, as we have observed, direct self-knowledge, bringing its own verification in experience, and its legitimate sense of certitude. And there are laws for man no less than for things, though man's relationship to the former is different from his relationship to the latter.

The reason for this difference, as well as its nature, will become clear if we consider certain differences between scientific knowledge and self-knowledge. Scientific knowledge is external, concerning sensible appearances; it is fully communicable and verifiable, and thus becomes public property —a possession of society—as rapidly as it is achieved; and it is impersonal. Self-knowledge, on the other hand, is personal, private, and inward. A man may know himself as no one else may know him, and as he may know no one else. Though others may help him, and indeed must if he is to go far in this direction, he alone can discover himself and learn what is to be learned; and he can never directly or fully communicate his self-knowledge, which begins and ends with him, and is, like himself, unique or individual. It has been remarked above that while the life of the race, or more especially of a civilization, is continuous, still, life begins anew in the person of each member of society. Thus a developed, conscious self cannot be passed on to a succeeding generation as science is; though self-knowledge and scientific are both knowledge in the same sense of the word, and the latter is not more genuine or final or trustworthy

18 This is brought out capitally in J. B. Pratt's *Adventures in Philosophy and Religion.*

than the former—perhaps, indeed, is never as real as the former may be. A new human being, then, born to-day, must begin anew, precisely like his ancestors of two hundred or two thousand years ago, the task of self-development and self-discovery, with possibilities not exactly the same as those of any other human being, and under conditions not exactly the same as those confronting any one else, in the past or in the present. This, however, as I have said, does not mean that he is left entirely to shift for himself. Though no one can do his appointed work for him, or compel him to it—any more than the proverbial horse can be compelled to drink—he does have, in records of the past, preserved in history and in institutions, and in the art and literature of former times, an inexhaustible source of help, wherein are shadowed forth, in action, in picture, and in word, the whole life of man in all its variety, and the hidden springs of human felicity—the drama of man's spiritual probation, and the triumph of the liberated soul, winging to eternity from the very midst of earthly defeat.

We have already seen in what fashion the individual finds, or may find, his good as he possesses himself of this his heritage, and we can now see that the fundamental law for man is a law of constructive effort—effort so to use life as to make the most of one's self. This is the character which human life seems everywhere to assume, save when disease supervenes. But, although the form taken by effort is partially conditioned by the individual's native endowment, and by his environment, still, man is finally responsible both for the direction of his own effort and for the persistence, energy, and single-heartedness which may characterize it. A human being tossed from the roof of a lofty building is as helpless in the clutches of physical law as a stone or any other physical object; but the law for man one may obey more or less faithfully, more or less intelligently, more or less fruitfully, depending on one's own choice. Herein, accordingly, lies the difference between a human being's relation to the law for thing and his relation to the law for man. The opportunity for choice given to humanity, limited though it is, makes each man individually responsible for the conduct and quality of his own life. And without this difference between the two laws, man would be merged like any other animal in "the natural order," and would remain the helpless creature of instinct and environment, or the blind victim of an apparently meaningless "life-force." Under such circumstances human life would be, in essence, indistinguishable from that of the moth or the guinea-pig, and man would be as incapable of scientific knowledge and of self-knowledge as are those creatures. This, we have seen, is precisely the conclusion reached by those who have attempted to place man wholly within a mechanistic pattern, or metaphysical system; and a conclusion equally absurd is inevitable on the terms imposed by any philosophical monism, whether idealistic or vitalistic or materialistic.

But, though the pertinent evidence requires only to be understood in order to convince us that there is a law for man, which all men obey according to their abilities, this leaves unanswered the question as to what it means to make the most of one's self. And for a good reason: because the question cannot be answered, when thus asked, save by each man for himself. No one save one's self can really know what one is good for; and certainly not all men are good for the same thing, and not all men are equally good for any even the simplest purpose. No one save one's self, furthermore, can be completely sure whether or not, in all the given circumstances, one is making the most of one's self. Hence no one can determine what is really best for another, and no one can safely judge another, in the sense of deciding that he has or has not failed to do the best with himself that he could do.

Nevertheless, it remains possible to observe men, through records of their lives and especially through their works—of whatever kind, including, of course, their science—and thence to draw general conclusions as to what it *should* mean for men to make the most of themselves. This is as real a possibility as any species of scientific observation, and may be as responsibly carried through, and is by all odds the most important inquiry open to man. Yet it is not the same thing as a scientific inquiry. It is in fact so different that to ape the methods of science in undertaking it is to make failure certain. For what is here wanted is the determination, not of a lowest common denominator, not of some external method of distinguishing man from other animals superficially similar, not even the determination of some external method of dividing men into classes, but the determination of a purpose adequate to engage to the fullest extent the lifelong effort of a man awakened to the distinctively human quality of his nature. By adequate I mean not merely sufficient, in point of difficulty, but worth its cost. And inquiry must take this form, obviously, because effort is not conceivable save in terms of purpose; and because men are actuated by many purposes, some of which conflict with each other, while some are at least seemingly trivial, and some are commonly esteemed important. We are accordingly faced with the question how men should act in order to live the *best* life, and the best *human* life; but a science of human activity would be concerned only with the question how men do act, taking them all together.

And there are other respects in which this inquiry differs from a scientific investigation. In particular, any answer obtained can gain assent only as it may come home with the force of a revelation to the man who has won some measure of real self-knowledge; and it can be verified only as it is tested in the subsequent life of that man. As a consequence, a man may join the ranks of all those from the past whose lives and works bear witness to the answer's truth; but such witness can never have more than presumptive authority. And though the weight of empirical evidence may grow ever more impressive, it cannot ever reach the point of actual proof, compelling assent regardless of the individual's personal trial and verification.

III

THE considerations advanced in this long, yet necessary review of man's position and development in the order of nature should make it clear that the fundamental task of philosophic and literary criticism is the establishment of a comprehensive principle of evaluation, in the light of which human life may at once be understood and judged. Everything else hinges upon this. In some ages, when such a principle has been so established as to have won, for a time, practically universal acceptance, criticism has been able to concentrate its attention upon problems of artistic technique. And, as I have earlier said, such criticism is always a necessity amongst artists themselves, if art is to remain a living and vital activity. But in an age such as ours, which has called everything into question, criticism is forced back to its primary basis in philosophical inquiry;—and no better illustration of the necessity of this return to sources could be found than the muddle-headed anti-criticism and chaotic art of our day. Yet, though philosophic criticism cannot be disregarded by artists without the gradual death of art, it is not directed primarily at artists, nor undertaken for them, but for men— for those whose concern is life, who look, or may or should look, to art as one of the most important means to a fuller and larger life.

This is a distinction which should not be difficult to understand, and which needs no justification. It is simply, as we have earlier seen, a measure of the extent to which education has been displaced by specialized training amongst us, that artists have in recent years been able, even partially, to impose on the public the notion that criticism should be carried on only to enable them to thrive in freedom. This notion embodies the implication that living artists are necessarily more important than their predecessors, that they are really above criticism, and that they require only to be "explained" in order to be admired. That artists should entertain such views of themselves may be "natural"; the abject acceptance they desire is, none the less, perilous to them, ruinous to art, and impossible to an educated public. There is a real sense, as I have said, in which no man can properly be judged by another. If Mr John Dos Passos, for example, whose case has been much discussed, cannot help himself—if, though he unmistakably possesses talent of a high order, and may have noble intentions, he nevertheless is the hopeless victim of "conditions" which compel him to envelop his books in an atmosphere of sickliness, of weak disgust, of prurience— why, he is not personally blameworthy. And no one on earth can determine this question with certainty save the victim himself. But equally no force on earth should prevent the truth from being spoken, so far as it can be known, concerning Mr Dos Passos and his books. And no amount of assurance from the friends of this writer concerning his intentions can or should obscure the fact that he is not, let us say, a man of heroic character, that he has been bowled over by the realities of life, and that he has cast his lot with the enemies of civilized humanity. This is the evident truth, however it is to be accounted for; and though to utter the truth is not to say that Mr Dos Passos is personally culpable, it is in effect to utter a judgement concerning life and his actual relation to it, whatever the reasons; and to form such a judgement is legitimate, necessary, and the very office for which criticism exists. But what has apparently been desired, in this case, is that the writer's alleged intentions should alone be taken into account, while his method of executing them should be laid at the door of the abominable "conditions" which have formed him and which he has depicted vividly in his books. Since, consequently, if you look at him in just the right way he turns out to be a noble fellow, and certainly is a talented one, his novels deserve an enthusiastic welcome and hearty praise.

Obviously this argument is an example of thorough whitewashing—and is the negation of criticism. Few things can be more evident than that the conditions of life on our earth have always been, and still are, difficult. Even should it be granted that every man, as far as we can tell simply from external observation, has always done the best he could under the conditions, inner and outer, which he has encountered, it would still remain true that there are very great differences between men in this as in other respects, and that it contributes most materially to our understanding of life and its possibilities to study these differences, instead of trying childishly to shut our eyes to them. Some men, we know, have faced the most intolerable conditions with dignity and unconquerable courage, though walking towards certain defeat, while others have quailed before the most trifling hardships, or have thought a full belly and a whole skin more important than honour or justice or truth. It is of the very essence of criticism to discern these and the multitude of comparable differences between men, to ask into their significance, and, as clearly as may be, to distinguish those kinds of men who best fulfil the demands and possibilities of a human life under earthly conditions.

The task is one which can never be brought to an end. It must, on the contrary, for ever be renewed. And no conclusions reached can ever be complete, final, or absolute. This undoubtedly is one important reason why the modern world has tended to accept scientific knowledge as our only real knowledge, and has veered uncertainly between the two extremes of attempting to bring man wholly within the sphere of scientific knowledge and of asserting that no human knowledge at all is possible. But both of these extremes have proved themselves equally absurd, while at the same time it has become unmistakably clear that there is no longer any excuse for supposing scientific knowledge to possess absolute or universal validity. It is real enough, and dependable for practical purposes, and invaluable; but, as we now definitely know, it is relative, approximate, limited, and furnishes us with no key to ultimate questions of life and destiny.

Hence, as I have endeavoured to make clear, scientific knowledge is, as knowledge, more different from human knowledge in appearance than in reality. The one kind is, judged by all the tests which serve to distinguish knowledge from belief and opinion, as fully knowledge as the other; and the significant differences between the two arise simply from the fact that their fields are genuinely different. For this reason, we have observed, the methods of inquiry which serve the purposes of science will not serve those of human knowledge; and likewise the results obtainable in the latter field, though they are substantial and are susceptible of trial and verification, cannot be precisely formulated, nor be regarded as exhaustive, nor are they rationally demonstrable. This, of course, is one obvious ground of recurrent difficulties over the question of human knowledge. Because we live in a world of change, because conditions of life sometimes change with great rapidity, because our science changes also, and because our civilization does not merely change, but develops, as man himself has developed—because of evidence, in brief, which no one can deny or think unimportant, men frequently fancy that they must be changing, and improving, too, and that consequently the experience of past generations is no longer pertinent and should be disregarded.

This notion cannot be swiftly or directly combated. It is easy enough to point out that if our human knowledge gathered from past experience is knowledge, it must remain valid and pertinent so long as men do not change into something other than men. But this is precisely what is called into question, on grounds which are always novel and which have every appearance of conclusiveness. And it is a fact, of course, that the experience of any number of men of a thousand years ago is not your experience or my experience, and that if I believe men have genuinely changed in the interval, I will not be inclined to look backward for guidance. This is the more true because there is much in the human knowledge we have which is, to put it mildly, far from flattering, and which men would be exceedingly glad to think not applicable to themselves. Hence, even aside from the stimulus offered by changing conditions—and, too, by sheer indolence—there is a constant tendency to rebel against the law for man, to obey it only in easy ways—to suppose, in particular, that if effort is expended on remaking the earth, and society, it will be unnecessary to undertake the more difficult task of remaking one's self. No one, moreover, would want to contend that attempts to improve the material and social conditions of life have been unfruitful, unimportant, or, indeed, not vitally necessary;—though there is a wealth of evidence, both historical and contemporary, to show that such attempts can have only a limited usefulness, and that these limits cannot be understood by men deficient in human knowledge.

When we are considering these forces which are always making for men's ignorance of human nature, we must, too, remember that knowledge of any kind is only preserved by its being perpetually relearned from the beginning. Science, I believe, is often not easily learned, and it is said that only a couple of hundred men to-day are capable of understanding some of the most recent developments of theoretical science. Nevertheless, scientific knowledge as a whole, even though it is in a constant state of flux, never more marked than at present, becomes, as I have said, a secure possession of society once it is attained. Reasons for valuing it are obvious; while to learn it is a merely intellectual process, with the experimental evidence always available for full presentation. Hence science can be quickly communicated in its entirety, and built on by the proficient learner, so that it is indeed regarded by some rather enthusiastic philosophers as a social achievement. One may suspect that these philosophers are not able clearly to realize the meaning of their words, if they actually intend by them anything more than what has been said in the present chapter concerning the relations to each other of the individual and the race; yet it is a fact deserving of emphasis that science is progressive as human knowledge and the fine arts are not.

And the reason for this difference is simply that human beings are not progressive. A very considerable part of what I have been calling human knowledge is purely empirical, as, indeed, are the basic elements of all our knowledge. It is not given us to know why the facts should be so and not otherwise; but that the facts are so can be learned, and to learn them is the condition of all positive achievement. To say that the fusion of two gases, however, will produce water, and then to exhibit the fusion of the two gases producing water, is one thing; while to say that human beings are not progressive is quite another. There is seemingly conclusive evidence, to be sure, which can be cited, and in this instance biological science supports the historical evidence. Nevertheless, the fact—if it is a fact—cannot be demonstrated experimentally or rationally; and it can only be proved, afresh and separately in the case of each person who may come to accept it, as such persons learn from their own experience that, despite all superficial appearances, and progresses of various kinds for which men are responsible, still, the fact does remain so and not otherwise.

Human knowledge, in other words, may be knowledge in a sense more full and genuine than any scientific knowledge, and yet may in some ages win the assent of only a minority; —and even at the best is not likely to be more than the *belief* of many, who accept it in good faith from the few completely qualified judges in this field. It is merely an indolent failure to inquire into the nature and limits of scientific knowledge which leads some people to suppose, that because the task of the philosophic and literary critic must perpetually be undertaken anew, as conditions change, there is nothing certainly to be known in the realm of human and literary values. The truth rather is that our difficulty in holding and transmitting our human knowledge arises because it is really knowledge, and therefore does not change with the times as scientific knowledge hitherto has changed.

IV

WE have already seen, not only how Mr More became very exceptionally qualified for his critical work by a long, thorough, and comprehensive study of both ancient and modern literatures and thought, but also and especially how he was led into that course of study, and from modern thought was led backward to medieval, and thence to the oldest literature of India and to the philosophy and letters of classical Greece and Rome. A character of Congreve's remarks that "Importance is one thing, and learning's another." Mr More's learning became important, we observed, because it was motivated by a persisting deep personal need. Accepting in good faith the interpretations of life which were closest at hand in his boyhood and youth—Calvinism, and then German Romanticism, and evolutionary Rationalism—he found that he could stop with none of them, for reasons which we have reviewed. And it may be said, summarily, that he was actuated by a profound consciousness of life as a spiritual experience pointed towards a goal beyond itself and beyond the sensible world—a consciousness which could not be stilled, but was only troubled and rendered more explicit by attempts to merge it in the order of nature or to explain it away. Yet at the same time Mr More was not unaffected by modern science and mechanistic thought and efforts to combine spiritual feeling with some brand of naturalism. On the contrary, he was early convinced that scientific knowledge must be accepted and that no interpretation of life which ignored

or contravened it could be legitimate. It was precisely this
contradiction between direct testimony from within—which
stimulated progress in self-knowledge and was in turn clarified and made more insistent by such progress—and, on the
other hand, the apparent teaching of science, which caused
him to pass through a succession of crises, marked by
changes in the direction of his thought and study, and which
finally brought him to see in dualism the one real solution of
his problem.

In undergoing this conflict Mr More was confronted with
the central problem of the modern world, which had begun
to plague men in the sixteenth century, had become acute in
the eighteenth, and in the nineteenth century had sharply
divided society both in Europe and in America. What is remarkable in his experience is the manner in which his spiritual promptings, intense and persistent though he found
them, were balanced by a species of self-distrust which impelled him to look abroad, to accept what the men of his time
thought it necessary or satisfactory to accept, and to try to
accommodate himself to the state of the world as he found it.
This, it may be said, is what every really sensible person does
or attempts to do; and it is also what the mere time-server
does as a matter of course. But in Mr More's case the effort
to find the sensible attitude towards life was markedly differentiated from that of the time-server or the man of the
world, because it was in its turn balanced by his consciousness of spiritual reality—a consciousness comparable for its
steady insistence with Cardinal Newman's, much stronger
and more certain than Arnold's, and, even more, than Pater's, though comparable to his in that there was mingled in
it a vein of aesthetic sensibility which opened him peculiarly
to the appeal of certain romantic writers of the nineteenth
century. And it is just this strong inward opposition, continuing despite all his efforts to resolve it, which distinguishes Mr More alike from men of the world, from the tribe
of metaphysicians, and from great religious leaders of the
last century and of our time with whom he is most closely
allied in feeling and insight.

It is this inward opposition also which accounts, at least

partly, for the seriousness of Mr More's effort to make sense of life. He himself has remarked, of both Cowper and Thoreau, that what other men were merely preaching, or saying, they practised, with consequences which led Cowper to disaster, and Thoreau to a fame still rising and long since secure. Consequences, of course, in such cases, must be as they will. And it was a like intentness which led Mr More to try to *live* by what he accepted, and so led him, for example, into a deeper and more intimate knowledge of the real bearings and nature of Romanticism than he could in any other way have attained, while at the same time this led him many steps along the path towards self-knowledge.

Now I think it was Mr More's unusual knowledge of himself—of a self singularly complete—and consequent vivid understanding of the deepest problems of human existence, which caused him to see in dualism the real object of his striving and search. The fundamental negative condition to be satisfied was that nothing deserving the name of knowledge was to be contradicted. This condition was not satisfied by those teachers or leaders of the nineteenth century who stood on the side either of religion or of science; nor was it satisfied by any metaphysician determined to regard the world as an intelligible unity, and willing to explain away all the evidence from experience that might contradict his ambitious fancy picture. The merit Mr More recognized in dualism, causing this philosophical principle to come home to him as a species of revelation, was that it required no denial of experience, no explaining away of one part in favour of another, but on the contrary offered a simple means of making sense of the whole life of man, including, of course, man's relation to his environment, through the candid recognition that there really was a self standing in a real relation to the phenomenal world.

The trouble with orthodox revealed religion, whether Protestant or Catholic, was that it played fast and loose with the phenomenal world in an attempt to secure for its interpretation of life a basis in absolute certitude. It laid claim, in other words, to a kind of knowledge which we do not have, under earthly conditions, about anything; and in so doing it

opened itself to the most damaging exposure of the hollowness of its claim. By the latter part of the nineteenth century
this exposure, thanks to modern science and historical criticism, seemed complete. But the interpretations of reality put
forward to take the place of what the Church had offered
were themselves hollow affairs, pretending in their turn to a
new basis in absolute certitude, and suffering the fatal disadvantage that they one and all invited man to read himself
out of existence. This they did, most effectually though not
deliberately, by submerging man wholly in the order of nature, or in some vast dialectical process, so that either the
combinations of "matter and energy" or sequences of
"ideas" became the sole realities of our universe. The whole
situation may be summed up briefly—and, of course, very
roughly—by saying that religion endeavoured to secure
man's reality at the expense of the natural world, and that
science and metaphysics endeavoured to hold fast to the
natural world at the expense of man's reality.

These contrary tendencies, though we are accustomed to
think of them as belonging peculiarly to the nineteenth century, when they reached a stage of development which involved their protagonists in bitter open conflict, did in fact
appear plainly as long ago as the age of Socrates; and no attempt to harmonize them has ever been really successful. But
equally no attempt to dispose of one of them in favour of the
other has ever been successful. Consequently the case for accepting dualism as the determining characteristic of human
nature—or even of a universe containing human beings—is
overwhelmingly strong. Dualism, indeed, of some kind is
present wherever we may look in the study of man; we find it
undeniably in his relation to himself, to society, and to the
natural world; and we can understand nothing save as we
contemplate man in these relationships. "Pure man" would
be an object as impenetrable and incomprehensible as is pure
platinum until we begin to define it by studying its relationships—while man cannot be isolated like platinum, even in
imagination, as a measure preliminary to study.

This should all be clear enough from our survey of man's
position as a developing person in the order of nature, and

from our consideration of the problem of knowledge. And we can see equally why, despite the fact that all the evidence points in this one direction, men have persistently rebelled against it, and never more strongly than to-day, even though rebellion has latterly been forced to take some exceedingly odd—not to say ridiculous—forms. The reason is, in itself, not discreditable, but the reverse, and lies simply in the importance to man of knowledge as against belief or mere opinion. What is discreditable, productive of endless conflict and trouble, and always finally self-destructive, is the notion that any knowledge obtained or obtainable by man can be of such a character as to afford an absolute starting-point or basis for secure inference concerning the whole scheme of things of which men themselves are fractional parts. That such absolute knowledge is desirable none would dispute; that it would be marvellously facilitated by such logical coherency in the universe as to justify inferring the nature of the whole from a part is self-evident; but it by no means follows that because something is desirable we have it or can get it, howsoever we may try, or that we are helped by obstinately pretending that we have it, in despite of facts even more obstinate than ourselves. And this is true whether or not we are condemned, as metaphysicians habitually assume, to "discover" that the universe is absolutely self-consistent, or else to admit that it is absolutely chaotic.

If this were our portion, it would still be best, with the fortitude of Bertrand Russell's Free Man, to accept chaos as our home, rather than to join Bertrand Russell or another in building some fool's paradise. But this too has been tried, repeatedly, with consequences so illuminating that only the conditions of human life which have been discussed in this chapter can enable one to understand why anybody should ever insist on trying it again. It was variously tried at the outset of the modern age, and the complexity of the Renaissance was a direct consequence of its being predominantly a revolt of the individual against authority and external compulsions. And when the Newtonian physics inspired in northern Europe a new rationalism, narrow, mechanistic, and tyrannical in its pretensions, which co-operated with neo-

classical criticism to stifle the human spirit, the Romantic
Movement arose as a new and more inward expression of the
spirit of individualism, proclaiming freedom not only as a
social right but also as a right to be accorded all impulses
spontaneously rushing upward from within the individual.
Inevitably this movement was even more protean in its manifestations than the Renaissance, so that it can scarcely be
spoken of as a whole with justice except in its negative aspects. I wish, however, merely to point out that as a protest
against the arrogations of a narrow rationalism the Romantic revolt was fully justified and, indeed, urgently needed.
But it constantly tended to become something quite different; a revolt against reason itself, in favour of impulse and
passion as oracles of absolute truth—or oracles of something
somehow deeper, better, nobler, grander than mere knowledge. And thus it seemed to verify the common belief that
man can only swing helplessly from one extreme of absolutism to another.

This other extreme, of course, continues actively to manifest itself to-day, in educational theory and practice, in philosophy, and in literature. And one pronounced contemporary manifestation of it is the anti-criticism discussed in the
first chapter of this book. It is, moreover, precisely the development of romantic doctrine which strongly influenced
Mr Paul More when he was passing from youth to early
manhood, with the consequences noticed in the preceding
chapter. Those consequences, we observed, were not exceptional; they were in fact just what should have been expected
from handing over the control of life to spontaneous impulse
and feeling. They could be illustrated more strikingly and
fully from the lives and works of very many writers of the
last century, and from the work of some of our contemporaries. Truly exceptional, however, was the clear-sightedness
which enabled Mr More to realize what was happening, and
the resolution with which he set about unbinding the chains
that held him. And this experience taught him that romanticism grossly failed in its effort to vindicate and preserve the
autonomous human spirit by setting free and exalting impulse and feeling; that by this road, on the contrary, man

was submerged in the animal, without having either the animal's instinctive sureness of aim or its simplicity of organization, so that man really sank far lower in the scale of being than the animal, in an effort to reach a goal which was after all no whit different from the goal of any rationalistic naturalism.

Hence Mr More was left with the conviction that the aim which actuated the leaders of the Romantic Movement was entirely sound, but that their execution of it was on the whole an egregious failure. And it was at this juncture that dualism came to him, with an appeal which was irresistible because he had been prepared by disillusioning experience and consequent self-knowledge and development to see it truly in relation to man's real nature and real creaturely position in the world. Had he been less well balanced—in the sense I have indicated above—less disciplined by study and life, less mature, or less reflective, he could not nearly so well have understood its pertinence, nor so readily have given his full assent to it, but would have been inclined to reject it, as others have, precisely because, though it fulfilled its promise, it did not recklessly promise more than is humanly possible.

It is not humanly possible, I should say, to deny the dual character of reality exhibited in various ways and on different levels in the account given, in this chapter, of man and his position in the order of nature. It is only possible, if it be not accepted, to assert that somehow this pervasive duality is an illusion, and to put forward some method of accounting for the data of experience, in terms of which we can imagine that all might be seen as of one kind if seen by a more-than-human, or other-than-human eye; or else to assert that rational knowledge is an illusion, and conscious perception a fraud, and that human beings are the blind, helpless, and ignorant victims of some mysterious "life-force." To become a dualist, then, is simply to give over, once and for all, these futile efforts to imagine ourselves as something other than what we can learn about ourselves from actual experience; to recognize that this for us is ultimate, and that the knowledge, scientific and human, thence gained *is really knowledge*, although limited, approximate, and relative; and to accept the fact that we are limited beings, and that human reason, though real, is limited like everything else about us—normally sufficient, like our eyes and ears and hands, for all practical purposes, especially when trained and aided as these are, but not capable of carrying us into the supernal realm of absolute truth. And these recognitions and admissions are tantamount to acceptance of dualism because it is only required that we should free our minds of certain common prejudices in order to see that human nature is, not simple nor single nor chaotic, but dual.

That human nature is not simple or single has above been shown, and we have noticed the impossible self-contradictions in which every attempt so to conceive it is necessarily involved. That it may indeed be chaotic has been admitted; but we have observed that it becomes beastly or worse than beastly in proportion as man becomes the creature of spontaneous impulse and passion, and that man can and does become human in proportion as he uses the opportunity afforded by earthly existence for constructive effort in the conscious remaking of himself. But such effort can only be understood in the sense that man can attain the power, within limits, of controlling and directing himself; and no one has ever explained how this can be done save by a division within human nature whereby one part directs and the remaining part is directed. Dualism, indeed, of one kind or another, provides the only possible explanation of human nature, from whatever direction the study of man may be undertaken; because, for example, no one has ever really explained how perception is possible unless there is something to be perceived and some person to perceive it, or how knowledge is possible without something to be known and somebody to know it.

It may, of course, be retorted that equally no one can explain how—to use for the moment the familiar language of religion—a soul, by definition immortal and immaterial, can be so united with a mortal and material body as to be capable of acting upon and through it and of being in turn affected by it. To be rationally explicable, genuine interaction would require two bodies, or two souls, for its occurrence, and could not take place between two objects which are totally different from each other, and which consequently could have no single point of actual contact. This celebrated objection, however, though unanswerable if it is valid, is not really relevant; for it depends on the assumption that reason is capable, not merely of sifting, but of transcending experience, and so of explaining away one part in favour of another which is supposed to be absolutely true. This is done, moreover, in the interest of the further assumption that the universe must be self-consistent throughout, whatever the contrary appearances. But we have seen that these assumptions are nothing better than obstinate prejudices. And if, as has been contended, experience is for us ultimate, it may be—and indeed must be—perpetually sifted, criticized, and *understood*, but it must also be accepted in its integrity, as something purely given, as precisely that which we are called on to make sense of, and to live in terms of, as best we may. In so doing it is, at the same time, both legitimate and needful to admit that the familiar language of religion is misleading. From experience we know that "soul" and "body" do interact, and we are entitled to infer that they cannot be wholly disparate. The traditional notions on the subject are, I should desire to insist, perfectly right in their emphasis, because the one essential thing is a clear steadfast realization that human nature is dual, howsoever we are to understand the fact. Yet nothing is gained by gratuitously making difficulties for reason, and this, in their enthusiasm and ignorance, religious leaders of long past ages have done. It is, in truth, as much as we know, and sufficient, to say that somehow there is at once both division and unity within man's nature, as there is both division and union between the individual and the race. And in both cases the important thing, which false philosophers and spinners of social theories and the tribe of popular writers are always smoothing over or forgetting, is that the division is none the less real and paradoxical for not being incomprehensibly absolute.

Mr More, in restating the principles of dualism for our time, has ranged himself, in his critical attitude towards reason, by the side of William James and of Professor Bergson. Like both of these inheritors of the Romantic Movement of the early nineteenth century, he was forced to recognize that rationalism, equally whether idealistic or naturalistic, is a liar and the father of lies, begotten of pride upon self-ignorance, and that truth, so far as it is accessible to us, can only be discovered by the acceptance and examination of what is given in experience. Thus he became, and has consistently remained, a member of that band of philosophers, men of letters, and scholars, most fitly called humanists, who trace their ancestry from Socrates and certain of his contemporaries and who have repeatedly from his day to our own, in varying ways dependent upon circumstances, attempted to preserve the integrity and freedom of the human spirit. We have seen, however, that Mr More went with the earlier romanticists only in sharing their aim, and this is likewise true of his relation to James and Professor Bergson and their followers, save that he has always been, with certain critical reserves, a thorough-going pragmatist.

Reason, then, Mr More has by no means wished to dethrone, but only to confine to its indispensable office of criticism; wherein it remains in a true sense our ultimate and one positive guide through the perplexed maze which we call life. In other words, as we have been at pains most particularly to notice, reason can do no more than faithfully take what is given in experience as matter for analysis, definition, and classification. Performing these offices, it enables us to "perceive sameness and difference." Mr More continues, in his "Definitions of Dualism":

Its effect is to break up the flowing datum of experience into units. By the perception of sameness it combines these units in larger and more comprehensive conceptions; by the perception of difference in smaller and less comprehensive conceptions. Its law is the exclusion of contradictories; that is to say, it holds that if two things are totally different they can have no bond of sameness. It may be designated in accordance with the material in which it works as objective or subjective.

Imagination is the faculty[19] which sensualizes the data of ex-

19 In an earlier section of the "Definitions" (which are to be found at the end of the Eighth Series of *Shelburne Essays*), Mr More says: "The various

perience apart from ourselves as separate existences. It runs
parallel with the reason, and like the reason may be designated
in accordance with the material in which it works as objective
or subjective.

The objective reason deals, not with the whole field of experience, but with the impulses that arise under the immediate im-
pact of impressions from the outer world, by its perception of
sameness and difference conceiving this material as more or less
comprehensive units. The objective imagination projects this
material into the void as discrete phenomena. These phenomena
are seemingly, but not really, made up of the pure matter of impressions, unconnected with our desires; of the actual outer
world from which our impressions flow we can have no unmixed
knowledge.

This is not to say, it must be remarked, that such knowledge is unreal, or that we do not need all of it we can possibly
get, or that self-knowledge alone could suffice for all our
human purposes. It is, on the other hand, to say that all our
knowledge is partially subjective, in the sense that it is an
imaginative construction—based, to be sure, on evidence, but
nevertheless our own construction—of which the ultimate
test is the consequence it turns out to have when we live in
terms of it. But how does reason obtain the opportunity to
perform its work and, in conjunction with memory and
imagination, to bring order out of the chaos which, as some
modern writers have truly enough insisted, is the first condition of man? At least, perhaps I should say, we are bound to
imagine an intolerable chaos as the starting-point of man's
constructive effort; and we can certainly observe, both in very
young children and in idiots, an inability even to distinguish
the inner world from the outer, such as some romantic writers,
and, more recently, the symbolists, managed to acquire by de-

aspects of mental activity we may, without implication of the meaning conveyed in the so-called facultative psychology, designate the faculties of
memory, reason, and imagination. These faculties we can in a way define and
distinguish, but their essential nature and their relation to one another are
probably as impenetrable as self-knowledge itself. Every process of mental
activity appears to implicate all the faculties together, but with varying
degrees of emphasis."

liberately abandoning themselves to it. Mr More opens his
"Definitions" with a brief description of this—I do not say
"natural" condition of man, as would some of our contemporaries—but of this primal or pre-human stage of existence,
true only of those who have never attained or who have
abandoned manhood:

The life of man consists of impulses which spring from the
coming together of inner desires and outer impressions. By the
word desires is here not meant the intelligent want of a definite
object, but the mere outreaching of vital energy. Desires and
impressions, so far as our knowledge attains, cannot exist independently, that is to say, there can be no living organism without the constant interaction of an inner vital energy and an
enveloping world. Impulses tend to pass into mental and physical activities, of the latter of which many belong to our animal
functions and scarcely reach to the senses. Mental activities
react in the form of new desires, physical activities in the form
of new impressions. Certain activities are beneficial to our organization, others are detrimental. The sum of desires and
impressions we call the great self-moving, incessant flux.

Now if this were all, certainly the organism so described
would be neither an animal nor a man, as we know animals
and men in experience. But, Mr More continues, giving the
answer to our question concerning reason's opportunity to
perform its work:

Beside the flux of life there is also that within man which dis-
plays itself intermittently as an inhibition upon this or that
impulse, preventing its prolongation in activity, and making a
pause or eddy, so to speak, in the stream. This negation of the
flux we call the inner check.[20] It is not the mere blocking of one
impulse by another, which is a quality of the confusion of the

20 So far as I know, Mr More first used this phrase in his essay entitled
"Kipling and FitzGerald" in the Second Series of *Shelburne Essays* (1905),
when he wrote (pp. 117–118): "Out of the deliquescence of character and
loosening of the grip on things actual, such as may be seen in Paul Verlaine
and Maeterlinck, springs a sham spirituality that wraps itself in the allure-
ments of the senses. Quite different from this is the mysticism of an Emerson or a Juan de la Cruz or a Plato, where in a strong character the higher

flux itself, but a restraint upon the flux exercised by a force contrary to it.

In the repeated exercise of the inner check we are conscious of two elements of our being—the inner check itself and the stream of impulses—as coexistent and coöperative, yet essentially irreconcilable, forces. What, if anything, lies behind the inner check, what it is, why and how it acts or neglects to act, we cannot express in rational terms. Of the ultimate source of desires and impressions, and of the relation of the resulting flux of impulses to the inner check in that union which we call ourselves, we are darkly ignorant. These are the final elements of self-knowledge—on the one hand multiplicity of impulses, on the other hand unity and *cupiditatum oblivio, alta rerum quies*. Consciousness, the more deeply we look into ourselves, tells us that we are ceaselessly changing, yet tells us also that we are ever the same. This dualism of consciousness, it seems, is the last irrational fact, . . . the reality which only stands out the more clearly the more it is questioned. . . .

Reason . . . is itself an organ of the flux. In endeavouring, therefore, to define the element of our being contrary to its sphere, it can only employ terms which express difference from the qualities of the flux and which must end in pure negation. Thus, in the language of philosophy, absolute unity, or sameness, is merely the complete negation of variety, and conveys no positive meaning; immutability, the negation of change; rest, the negation of motion; eternity, the negation of time; infinity, the negation of all our experience. The error of the reason is to deny the existence of this absolute element because it must be defined in terms of negation. By the use of the term inner check, we accept the inability of the reason to define positively this element of our being, but imply also that it may be the cause of quite positive and definable effects within the flux.

As one impulse is checked, some other impulse may come to the surface and may be permitted to pass into activity. The inner check has thus the semblance of an act of attention or

will to refrain holds the lower will as a slave subservient to its purpose. The one is the defalcation of the will altogether; the other is the subjection of the lower will to the higher, an exercise of the function which Emerson, quoting I know not what Eastern source, calls the 'inner check.' "

choice. Attention, nevertheless, must not be confused with the inner check, which is essentially, in so far as it can be expressed in rational terms, a pure inhibition, having the absence of variety and change which belongs only to absolute negation. Attention is the name of the immediate effect of the inner check in the positive sphere of activities, the last point to which rational analysis and emotional appeal can apply. There is thus in the admonition to attend, that is, deliberately to stay the flux of impulses and exercise an act of choice in activity, an irreducible paradox, similar to the mystery in religion which calls a man to repent yet teaches that repentance is the work of divine grace.

I quote at some length because in these remarkable passages all that is essential in the dualistic philosophy is either stated or distinctly implied, and because Mr More is here concerned scrupulously to keep within the limits of rational knowledge. Hence he not only avoids the language of persuasion, but, for the reason he mentions, confines himself to negative terms in describing that in man which links him with what is unchanging and eternal. And since he wishes to state no more than what we can directly *know*, he admits candidly the darkness surrounding the inner check, save for its restraining command. This peremptory summons has of course been felt—and has been obeyed, too, on occasion, whether or not it has been understood—by every one who will read these pages; and it is safe to say that it would never have been made the base on which so much was to turn, however clearly Mr More supposed he could read his own experience, had it been solely his discovery. The self-distrust of which I have spoken was an effectual safeguard against any weak indulgence in a merely private or "original" reading of life. What Mr More sought he was impelled to seek, as I have tried to make clear, by inward need and inward experience which could not be ignored; but equally what he sought was a way of making sense of life which should be something more and better than just his own way, which should be, not only in harmony with what else is now really known of human nature, and not only susceptible of confirmation from the experience of others, but in a genuine sense an outgrowth, and continuation, of that which had been learned and taught by the great masters of human knowledge, or self-knowledge, throughout the past.

The more closely the passages quoted above are studied, and meditated, the more remarkable will they seem for their success in meeting these stringent, necessary requirements. The dualism there expounded has been attacked as a philosophy of chill negation, fashioned by one who was afraid of reality and could advise nothing better than withdrawal from life—but it has been so attacked only by the youthful, uneducated hack writers who nowadays largely supply our popular periodicals with copy. Actually the inner check is identical with the "voice" of Socrates, and is the foundation upon which the world's mature and still-enduring religions have been erected, and is no less the foundation of all our science, and has been made the cornerstone of Mr More's philosophy only because of its positive effects, by which alone its place and value as an element of human nature can be determined. Its one direct effect is negative, in that it works against hasty conclusions and prevents headlong action, but it thus makes possible the work of reason, and deliberate or responsible decisions, so that its positive effects have a range as wide as human life itself, and an incalculable importance. To heed the inner check, in other words, is simply to take the vital first step towards the development of intelligence, towards self-knowledge, towards a life consciously and consistently directed, and towards an integrated personality. And with each time that the inner check is heeded, it becomes easier to obey its summons, while obedience also is the one possible method of bringing about its increased activity.

To look before you leap, in order that you may be as sure as possible of what you are about to do—the wisdom of that course has become proverbial. And though proverbial sayings sometimes contradict each other, and I have earlier in this book remarked upon one—the man who hesitates is lost—which seems to be an example, the contradiction here is more apparent than real. The man who unhesitatingly does the wrong thing is certainly lost; and only those can follow this advice without disaster who have carefully looked in all

directions, and have taken into account every possible course
of action, long before the occurrence of any emergency. The
inner check, enabling us thus to command situations, progressively enables us also to command ourselves, and so becomes the foundation of everything distinctively human in
our lives.

V

THE dualistic philosophy, accordingly, became Mr More's
criterion, or standard of judgement, in the criticism of literature, and, through literature and men of letters, in the
criticism of life. But when I say that here we have the key
to a right understanding of the *Shelburne Essays*, I do not
mean that they are exclusively directed to the consideration
of a single question, or that Mr More ever conceived himself
to have in dualism a simple or rigid formula, by whose application it was possible summarily to "condemn" or "accept"
authors and their books. The *Essays* are consistently critical, and the vital business of reaching conclusions is never
shirked; but nothing is more surprising, and few things are
more illuminating, in these twelve volumes, than their variety
both of treatment and of matter.

One obvious reason for this is that Mr More has had an
inexhaustible interest in people—though not that idle, undiscriminating curiosity which is practically identical with
the mere love of distraction, nor that gloating malicious interest which motivates many current biographical studies,
nor yet that utterly detached interest which men of science
pretend to, and sometimes really aspire to, in their psychological and sociological investigations. Mr More has, indeed,
in his essay on "The Solitude of Hawthorne," remarked upon
the truth embodied in the story of *Ethan Brand*, who discovered the guilt of the Unpardonable Sin "in his own
wretched heart that had refused to beat in human sympathy,
and had regarded the men about him as so many problems to
be studied." Problems, of course, men are. "The crowning
mystery of life," Professor Warner Fite has said, "is not so
much the mystery of the universe as the mystery of our-

selves."[21] But there is a world of difference between one who
honestly acknowledges the mystery at the centre of human
nature, and one who fancies he can set himself apart from
humanity and can thus, in his isolation, resolve the age-old
problem by a tissue of mingled assumption and external
observation. Proud self-confidence, leading the detached observer to deny to the rest of humanity powers which he expressly claims to possess, may or may not be the Unpardonable Sin; but Emerson was entirely right when he wrote of
certain nineteenth-century ancestors of our present-day
psycho-analysts and other pretenders to scientific knowledge
of what is distinctively human: "The grossest ignorance does
not disgust like this impudent knowingness."

Mr More's interest in people has arisen precisely from his
consciousness of the mystery in the heart of man; and dualism is not an attempt rationally to explain its ultimate
nature, still less to explain it away, but an explicit acknowledgement that man is, in Emerson's phrase, "a golden impossibility"—a living paradox, an incomprehensible union of
opposed forces, neither of which can be denied or ignored
without complete disaster, both somehow working together
to produce intelligence, character, and free responsible personality. Hence the dualistic philosophy does not, like every
system of metaphysics, absorb man, or render him an insignificant particle, in some vast cosmic process. About cosmic
processes we know whatever science can really tell us—and it
is very little, much less than was in the nineteenth century
supposed. From the philosophic point of view, this revelation
of ignorance is the most important outcome of recent "advances" of science. As I have earlier intimated, it is perhaps
too much to hope that the exposure of its vanity will check
the course of metaphysical speculation; but dualism, at any
rate, is guiltless of any contribution to it; for dualism is not
a "system," and makes no pretence of being more than a
statement, sufficiently exact for practical purposes, of what
can be known from experience concerning the distinctively
human elements entering into the constitution of man. And

[21] *Moral Philosophy,* p. 214.

in so doing it emphasizes the significance of human life, not after the fashion of the specialist who magnifies the importance of what he knows, but simply by making clear the dramatic quality of human existence, as an inward conflict between the forces of real good and real evil—a conflict, moreover, which is never in two persons wholly the same, so that every record, every imaginative projection of life, may have its own unique value. And that value is of a kind to come most intimately home to us, because we too are, unescapably, participants in the drama of existence, and stand in need of all we can learn concerning the dangers to which we are exposed, the aid we may look for, and the reward of victory.

No one, in other words, can rise to genuine acceptance of dualism and still cherish, even momentarily, the delusion that he may be able to stand apart, a mere spectator of the ironical comedy and tragedy of life, himself not deeply involved therein. Of this corrupt, dishonest pseudo-detachment we have many examples at present, while there seems to be scarcely any understanding of the kind of detachment described earlier in this chapter, which is not only practicable and genuine, but the necessary condition of full growth. Consequently it is not surprising that Mr More has been stigmatized, freely and often, by our catch-penny journalists, as a "reactionary"—terrible word in the most "progressive" of countries—totally devoid of human sympathy. Yet the charge is simply fantastic; for the *Shelburne Essays*, whatever else may be thought of them, prove beyond dispute that their author has had an endless interest in people, and an interest motivated not by mere intellectual curiosity but by profound fellow-feeling. Not otherwise than through sympathetic insight could any man penetrate to the heart of his subjects as Mr More has done—not always indeed—but again and again, in the cases of men and women most diverse in their circumstances, in their achievements, in the records they have left for interpretation, and, very notably, in their characteristic qualities. How often does one find a man who is able to understand with equal completeness and sympathy persons so diverse as, for example, Sir Thomas Browne, the fourth Earl of Chesterfield, Jonathan Edwards, Horace Walpole, Laurence Sterne, Walt Whitman, and Lafcadio Hearn? The list could be almost indefinitely extended, but is sufficiently remarkable as it stands, being enough in itself to show that the *Essays* possess the utmost variety of human interest.

Their variety, moreover, is not confined to their matter, but extends, as I have said, to Mr More's treatment of his subjects. Arnold's literary method lies on the surface of his work for every casual reader to see, and, to take a formidable American example, so also does that of Brownell. The possession of a formula, of course, may be a resource as well as a liability; and Arnold's use of key-words and phrases, while it condemned him often to over-simplification, and smoothed the way to such insubstantial question-begging verdicts as his famous conclusion that Gray "never spoke out," still served him well, giving him the room he needed for saying easily and comfortably what he could say, with strong emphasis, and with the appearance, at least, of a flexible, sinuous, yet firmly organized advance upon the enemy. By comparison, Brownell's formal, conscientious surveys seem mechanical, laboured, monotonous, like his frigid style, which itself at times conceals vagueness under stiffly heaped-up inkhorn words. But even Brownell's formula takes on the aspect of a strengthening resource when one turns to Lowell or to Coleridge who, for all the solid substance to be found scattered through their prose, were both amongst the most formless and uncontrolled of writers.

Mr More, I should say, is very different in his procedure from all of these fellow-critics. His essays without exception drive steadily to their conclusions, under the impulsion of a controlling purpose never absent from the author's mind, always clearly conceived, and carried out with unfailing vigour. Yet there is no structural pattern, or method similar to Arnold's, which is habitually utilized. Indeed, each essay has its own plan dictated by the particular circumstances calling it forth, or by the nature of its subject, or by the author's intention in the given case. And while this does not mean, of course, that no two essays are at all similar in structure, it is

true that Mr More's aims, though they are related, and in
fact closely coherent, are at the same time as various as his
subjects. For to get the subjects themselves in a clear light,
to see them as they really are, is the first object of the critic,
and is a new and different problem with each new subject.
Moreover, an essay, from its nature, is not exhaustive. I have
mentioned considerations, in this chapter, suggesting that
"the exhaustive thing" is an impossibility where human
knowledge is concerned; and for this reason the essay remains the appropriate and best instrument of the critic of
letters and life. It demands, however, rigorous elimination of
the non-essential, which in turn means that the standard invoked for judgement should not be wider than is needed for
the purpose immediately in hand;—not dualism, in other
words, but that one concrete aspect or implication of it directly suggested by the crucial points emerging from, for
instance, a consideration of Walt Whitman's prose and
poetry—this is the appropriate standard on this occasion.

Thus standards vary with subjects, being in a real sense
determined by them. Byron declared in one of the asides in
Don Juan:

> A panoramic view of Hell's in training,
> After the style of Virgil and of Homer,
> So that my name of Epic's no misnomer.

He also remarked to Medwin: "If you must have an epic,
there's *Don Juan* for you; it is an epic as much in the spirit
of our day as the *Iliad* was in that of Homer." Mr More has
told how the circumstances of his introduction to Byron's
poem raised the question in his mind by what standard it
should be judged, and how the answer came to him only several years later when he returned to it for the purpose of
editing it. He then decided that Byron was to be taken at his
word—that the poem, spite of all appearances to the contrary, was written faithfully in the spirit of epic tradition.
In his essay he shows clearly that it "is something quite different from the mere mock-heroic," and that the tradition of
which it is an outgrowth has nothing necessarily to do with
verse-form, poetic style, or structure, but everything to do

with the reading of human nature and life common to heroic poets. In conclusion he says of Byron:

Out of the bitterness of his soul, out of the wreck of his passions which, though heroic in intensity, had ended in quailing of the heart, he sought what the great makers of epic had sought —a solace and a sense of uplifted freedom. The heroic ideal was gone, the refuge of religion was gone; but, passing to the opposite extreme, by showing the power of the human heart to mock at all things, he would still set forth the possibility of standing above and apart from all things. He, too, went beyond the limitations of destiny by laughter, as Homer and Virgil and Milton had risen by the imagination. And, in doing this, he wrote the modern epic.[22]

The point could be illustrated again and again from the *Shelburne Essays;* and very frequently, as in the present instance, the determination of the appropriate standard has what may be called a liberating effect. The reader's eyes are opened to values which could not be clearly seen or fully appreciated until the poem or novel or, it may be, collection of letters was placed against its right background, or was related effectively to the tradition of which it was, more or less definitely, an outgrowth. This is just what should be expected, from what I have said concerning the character of all our knowledge and the fashion in which meaning becomes attached to objects—and in which, too, people become sig-

[22] Nearly twenty years after the publication of this essay, Professor Grierson, of Edinburgh, independently came to the conclusion that in *Don Juan* Byron "wrote the comic epic of modern Europe." "Byron is in the world and yet not of it." (Pp. 94, 102, *The Background of English Literature,* 1925.) Similarly, it may be noted, Mr T. S. Eliot in a recent essay ("Arnold and Pater," 1930, reprinted in *Selected Essays*) has reached conclusions extremely like some of those in Mr More's essay entitled "Criticism" (1910). These coincidences afford an unusual opportunity for instructive comparison, and place in a clear light Mr More's keener mind, finer and sharper appreciations, and fuller, better balanced scholarship. Professor Grierson, I should add, in revising utterances on Byron for the above-mentioned volume, has partially weakened and obscured, yet not abandoned, the position he had earlier taken as to the epic quality of *Don Juan.* Though he has thus, I think, done himself an injustice, I have felt compelled to cite only his final pronouncements.

nificant. Certainly to place Byron's poem in the direct line
of descent from Homer and Virgil and Milton is to enlarge
and deepen our appreciation of it, by freeing it from the
confinement of relatively trivial associations, and by emphasizing its serious purpose. Nothing in *Don Juan* is taken
from it, but much is added, so that one lays down Mr More's
rather slight "Note," in some respects not one of the happiest
of his compositions, with the feeling that a door has been
opened, looking out upon a novel and inexhaustible vista.
"Byronism," of course, has long since been dead, and is a
good riddance; but the creator of a legend and a pose was
greater than the vast shadow he cast when living, and Mr
More was apparently the earliest of those who have now begun to realize the truth about him and its meaning.[23]

The liberating effect of standards, however, important
though it be, and scarcely understood by any in our generation, is not more worthy of consideration and emphasis than
the office these standards perform collectively. For dualism,
in Mr More's development of it, receives its full meaning,
and at the same time its test, through its concrete applications. It must stand or fall by its uses, its fruits, he would
appear to have said in the beginning; and he did not even
venture to draw up and publish a simple and unpretentious
statement of general principles until seven volumes of the
Shelburne Essays had been completed. This statement,
moreover, is only a framework; it gathers reality, and authority, from the whole body of the *Essays*. Through them

[23] Certain of our anti-critics have complained that though Mr More has
shown himself a gifted and scholarly critic of writers of the eighteenth century and beyond, he has paid no serious attention to contemporaries, and,
when he has had anything to say about them, has written hastily and care-
lessly. With the notion that critics should chiefly discuss their contemporaries I have already dealt; but I may here point out that Mr More himself
has not condemned, as did Arnold, the general tendency to confuse critics
with reviewers, and that he has in fact largely concerned himself with contemporary or recent writers. On one occasion, moreover, he triumphantly
met the severest possible test. Lafcadio Hearn was notoriously sensitive and
quick to take offence; but when he read Mr More's essay on his work, upon
its first appearance in the *Atlantic Monthly,* he recognized it as a remark-
ably just analysis and estimate, and expressed in the strongest terms his
gratefulness for the service thus done him. This case does not stand alone,
though such evidence as it affords concerning the quality of Mr More's work

one comes to see gradually dualism's true character as a practical means of making sense of life—of that part of life which is distinctively human, and which is not positively illuminated by our scientific knowledge of ourselves. And this one sees, not alone from becoming acquainted with dualism's manifold implications brought out in one connexion and then another as need actually arises, but also from its unique serviceableness in the critic's task of separating off what is adventitious, conventional, or commonplace, and turning a clear light on those enduring realities of human nature which can be seen and felt, in the living deed sometimes, through the living word sometimes, but above all in something beyond analysis and beyond the limits of direct expression, in some dim yet vital residuum which, as we say, is just the man himself.

There, in what is recognized as the man himself, we touch human reality; but only its dead husk remains when, howsoever carefully, we attempt to generalize it. This is the rock upon which all abstract theory founders. Dualism, on the other hand, arising from an explicit recognition that each individual is in a real sense unique and that human reality, as a necessary consequence, can be found only in its concrete manifestations, sends the student, not to "man," but to men. The dualist, in other words, is completely estopped from spinning out a fancy picture of "the whole nature of man"; and from supposing that these fancy pictures, which commonly pass for philosophy—and sometimes nowadays for science—really illuminate anything save their own artificers. Hence dualism can never present the trim appearance of a rounded or closed "system." It can only develop through a study which has no end—the study of individuals—and to which any one critical writer, no matter how talented and industrious, can only make fragmentary contributions. For

is seldom received by any writer. I count in all some 36 of Mr More's essays specifically devoted to contemporary men of letters or to contemporary events or conditions; and amongst these are many which incontestably fall within the number of his most careful and most thoughtful pieces. Possibly some of our more boyish journalists fail to realize that Hearn, Tolstoy, George Meredith, William James, and others, not only were Mr More's contemporaries but were still living when he discussed their work.

dualism, I must repeat, is expressly committed to the proposition that something fresh and valuable may be learned from every genuine person with whom we can establish intimate relations on the human level.

This, it may be said, is a romantic view; and it is a fact, as I have tried to make clear, that Mr More's work from first to last has been an attempt to conserve and revivify what some historians and critics regard as the romantic conception of human nature. But that conception happens to be far older than Christianity, older than the age of Socrates, so old, indeed, that we catch sight of one of its forms on the edges of history in central Asia. It differs, moreover, fundamentally from the dualism which arose in Europe in the eighteenth century, and strongly influenced some of the Romantic writers of England and America, and still to-day counts its thousands of adherents throughout the Western world.[24] Everybody knows that the latter was an externalized dualism, opposing man to society and nature to civilization, with the consequence that fantastic notions were spread abroad concerning what was "natural," and what "unnatural," in man. Civilized society was pictured, with much reason, as a corrupt body which depraved its members in constraining them to do its bidding. The individual, that is to say, was "naturally" good, but cursed with a desire to better his condition; —cursed, because this desire it was which led to the attempt to improve on nature, and so to the development of the arts and sciences, and to the organization of civilized society. Hence it was inferred that the life which is subjected to the constraints of social convention, of collectively ordered activity, of reason, is inevitably evil, while the life of spontaneous impulse is good. The guiding principle within man, in other words, according to this familiar view, is not the Inner Check, but the spirit which says Yes, which writes Whim over the door of its dwelling, which goes headlong, just trusting its genius.

This externalized dualism, of which it is impossible to give

24 Its difference from the so-called dualism—or, more accurately, parallelism—of Descartes is so obvious that I have thought it unnecessary even to mention it above.

a consistent account because of the legerdemain whereby the individual's desire to better his condition is transferred to "society," is inseparably connected with the name of Rousseau. And Rousseau was undoubtedly inspired by Plato— particularly by certain passages in the *Republic* and in the earlier books of the *Laws*—and by the *Parallel Lives* of Plutarch, as well as by English philosophers and political theorists of the seventeenth and early eighteenth centuries. So mingled are the currents which form the stream of human thought! So great and constant is our need for critical endeavour, for painstaking incessant effort to pierce through the chaos of mere appearances, and to construct by just discrimination a true image of the past whose children we are. For Rousseau's self-flattering perversion of dualism was motivated not only by generous and indeed Messiah-like feelings, but by a sound evaluation of the tendencies of unchecked rationalism and by a noble indignation against cynical, organized, triumphant injustice. Yet he read Plato as he did everything else, with his "heart," not with his head, which really means that he learned nothing from him save what he wanted to learn; and he remained fundamentally the child of the age he did so much to destroy, so that he did not displace, but merely sentimentalized, the naturalism which he felt, rather than saw, to be the relentless destroyer of humankind. It is quite possible that the Romantic Movement would have run an identical course without him, because he made his own by fiery eloquence what many of his generation were thinking; but, as things were, he and none other did become the fountainhead of a new gospel of "liberation" which quickly spread everywhere and which to-day is still potent, in forms I have dealt with in this volume, and equally in the sphere of politics.

I have endeavoured to show how this gospel is totally, irreconcilably opposed both to the inner dualism of Mr More and to the critical attitude itself, and how it is, consequently, equally opposed to the development both of character and of intelligence. I have also shown how, when Mr More turned away from what he found to be, not freedom, but disintegration, he remained as profoundly convinced as ever that the *intentions* lying behind the Romantic Movement were sound and right. Hence it was that inevitably he had to concern himself with the Romantic writers, making plain the reasons for their failures—for their confused thought, their super-ficiality, their doctrinaire reading of human nature, their earnest self-righteousness and immoralism, and their limp expansiveness; accounting for the way in which the Move-ment dwindled into the encouragement of mere eccentricity, into art for art's sake, and symbolism, and neo-medieval-ism; and explaining at the same time why it could make no effective stand against scientific naturalism, being itself naturalistic at heart, and merely playing—like Mr W. B. Yeats and Miss Townsend Warner and others to-day—with the supernatural as an outlet for irresponsible flights of fancy. But this, of course, was not all. For Mr More was in the field, as I scarcely need say, by no means against all that has ever been called "romantic," but against naturalism, whether sentimental, pantheistic, pan-psychic, or material-istic, and against the malignant absurdities which flow from all metaphysical absolutism. What he opposed, to be sure, he regarded as the dominant note of the Romantic Movement; but he never left the slightest room for doubt as to the real objects of his attack, and took great pains to make it clear that he accounted not a few of the Romantic writers as close allies, with whom he was glad to associate himself in their common struggle to preserve, in our modern world, a living sense of man's spiritual nature, of the mystery surrounding us, and of the transcendent issues involved in those respon-sible choices of ours which daily form us, for better, for worse.

That Mr More was able to take this position exhibits strikingly—I think more strikingly than any other portion of the *Shelburne Essays*—his critical genius. The great ma-jority of men are born partisans. Not many could ever have Mr More's personal experience of the consequences of ro-mantic doctrine—or, for that matter, of rationalism—be-cause very few have either the sensitiveness or the downright seriousness needful to get really inside of any philosophy; and fewer still have eyes clear enough to see where they have really been led.[25] But, granted Mr More's personal experience, most men would have swung violently to the opposed extreme of undiscriminating hostility. Mr More, however, though animated by strong and definite convictions, proceeded, in the very spirit of disinterested critical activity, to collect and set forth the facts, reaching no conclusions without reasons, avoiding unqualified or sweeping judgements, making plain his own standpoint, and determining each question as it arose on its own merits.[26] A single example— the essay entitled "Thoreau's Journal"—must suffice to indicate the quality of the work thus performed. Thoreau's mind, Mr More justly observes, was not fertile in ideas as was Emerson's, so that by comparison he seems thin and derivative; yet his work has both power and distinction, because of his downright though never vulgar assurance and

[25] It has been said of Kingsley, apropos of his attack on Newman, that he seemed to be guided by an imperfect sense of smell rather than by anything recognizable as intelligence. We are loath to admit how often this kind of difficulty influences the course of human affairs. When Mr Wilson, for example, reprobates Mr T. S. Eliot's moral solicitude, he merely betrays his own moral insensibility, but how many stupid people there are whose like insensibility is thereby strengthened! Similarly, much that has been said in praise of the Romantic Movement only reveals, in fact, a failure both of intelligence and of aesthetic sensibility.

[26] Though I make this statement deliberately, because the evidence taken as a whole is entirely conclusive, I have no wish to deny that occasionally, in his treatment of Romantic writers, Mr More exhibits something of the blindness and unfairness of the renegade. This appears, most conspicuously and most unfortunately, in his essay on Wordsworth;—and though this essay may fairly enough be said to err rather in its omissions than in its positive thesis, the impression it gives is confirmed by a number of incidental strictures on Wordsworth scattered through the *Shelburne Essays*. I also think Mr More has betrayed a tendency to lean over backwards in the severe restraint he has imposed on himself in expressing any appreciation of the sheer beauty of the sensuous or moral or spiritual imagination when this conspicuously has shown itself in modern literature. For though abstention from gush is of the very essence of the judging critical spirit, an excessive restraint may sometimes excusably be mistaken for mere dull insensibility. Yet with Mr More—as Dr Lewisohn and other readers have discovered to their uncomprehending astonishment—restraint has been imposed as a defence against what had proved itself to be an excessive sensibility. It is undoubtedly a fact, moreover, that some contemporary writers complain most bitterly against restraint because they know themselves to be imaginatively and emotionally weak, and in constant danger of being overtaken by a benumbing lethargy. It is anaemic people who most admire reckless, impulsive activity, as was abundantly evident during the Great War.

because his thought, as far as it did go, was firmly anchored
to experience. Hence, more easily and more accurately than
through Emerson, one can learn from Thoreau what Concord transcendentalism amounted to in practice, and how far
it was an echo of German Romanticism. There follows a masterly survey of the paths of communication between Germany
and New England, and of the dominant characteristics of
the German movement; after which Mr More says:

Of the systematic romanticism of Fichte and Schelling there
is little or nothing in the writings of our New England tran-
scendentalists. Many of their ideas may be found in Emerson,
but divested of their logical coherence; and as for Thoreau,
"metaphysics was his aversion," says William Ellery Channing;
"speculation on the special faculties of the mind, or whether
the Not-Me comes out of the I or the All out of the infinite
Nothing, he could not entertain." Nevertheless, in its more superficial aspects, almost the whole body of romanticism may be
found reflected, explicitly or implicitly, in his Journal and formal works. He, too, had sat spying in the well of freedom, and
the whole art and practice of his life were a paean of liberty.
. . . Calvinism had been discarded in Concord as Lutheranism
had been by the romanticists at Berlin. There is little concern in
Thoreau with God and the soul, but in its place a sense of individualism, of sublime egotism, reaching out to embrace the
world in ecstatic communion. His religion was on the surface
not dissimilar to Schleiermacher's mystical contemplation of
the universe. . . . This reverie, or contemplation that spurned
at limitations, passed easily into the romantic ideal of music—
and that in a very literal, sometimes ludicrous, sense. A music-
box was for him a means of consolation for the loss of his
brother; a hand-organ was an instrument of the gods; and the
humming wires on a cold day—his telegraph harp he called it
—seemed to him to convey to his soul some secret harmony of
the universe. . . . There is something bordering on the grotesque in this rhapsodical homage to a droning telegraph wire,
but it might be paralleled by many a like enthusiasm of the
German brotherhood. Nor was Thoreau unaware of this intru-
sion of humour into his ecstasy. Like Friedrich Schlegel, he in-

dulges in the romantic irony of smiling down upon himself and walking through life as a *Doppelgänger*. . . . How far this irony carried him in his hatred of Philistinism and his aloofness from society, no reader of his books need be told. The life of the business man he compared to the tortures of an ascetic, and the California gold-fever threw him into a rage of disgust. . . . Nor did the daily commerce of man with man come off much better. He was not one who would "feebly fabulate and paddle in the social slush." . . . Often a passage in the Journal bears the stamp of German romanticism so plainly upon it, that we stop to trace it back in memory to Tieck or Novalis or one of the followers of the earlier Storm and Stress.

One can in fact, Mr More continues, draw out almost indefinitely the closest parallel between Thoreau and the Germans—a parallel which seems not to be a case of deliberate borrowing, but rather of the "larger and vaguer migration of thought from one land to another." Yet, simultaneously, the more fully one sees this all-pervasive relationship, the more definitely one becomes aware of an "underlying difference more easily felt than named." One begins to understand this difference, however, and is enabled finally to name it and, what is more, to determine its meaning, when one examines closely "that free individualism which is the root of all this varied growth." As this is expounded by Schleiermacher, it is something sharply differentiating the German tribe from both Emerson and Thoreau. To Schleiermacher infinity "was only another word for endless variety of particulars, amid which the soul of man, itself a momentary atom in the stream, moves in a state of perpetual wonder." And Schleiermacher, "like the rest of the romantics, when he sought for the basis of a man's nature, turned to pure emotionalism, the very power and faculty by which we are bound within the limits of our individuality." He thus pointed forward to such a development as "the hedonism of Walter Pater as expressed in the *Conclusion* to his Renaissance studies"; and, too, one "cannot sever his unctuous preaching of emotionalism from the actual emotions which ruled among the coterie to whom his discourses were addressed." What

those emotions were Mr More cites examples to show, and
then points out that they had no place whatever in Thoreau's
life, and that individualism with him as with Emerson possessed a very different quality. It may be conceded, he says,
"that the absence of primitive human emotion is so pronounced in Thoreau's diaries as to render them thin and
bloodless"; nevertheless, despite all abatements—and there
are others which must be allowed—these documents have a
real value and interest because, precisely, of the manner in
which they show Thoreau using romantic freedom, not, like
the Germans, to encourage the expansion of his whole emotional nature, but to achieve and develop character through
"a higher self-restraint."

Some there are to-day—Dr Ludwig Lewisohn is amongst
them—whom the bare thought of self-restraint arouses to a
perfect fury of disagreement. They repudiate Thoreau with
loathing, just because of that in him which Mr More singles
out as his truest title to praise. But facts, of course, are not
disputable; and the significant difference between German
romanticism and Concord transcendentalism which Mr
More's analytic comparison brings out, following upon so
much in the way of closest resemblance, is not—and indeed
cannot be—disputed. There it is, make of it what one may.
And in general this is the service performed, not only in that
large group of the *Shelburne Essays* concerned with many
of the Romantic writers of last century and with others, of
that time and of the present, closely related to them, but in
all of the *Essays* The real bearings of modern literature,
and of artistic methods developed in modern times where
these too are significant, are made unmistakably clear; the
issues raised by modern thought are sharply defined; and aid
of inestimable worth is thus given to those who desire human
knowledge, who wish to understand the problems raised in
the conduct of life, and to gain maturity as it alone can be
gained—by making their own the experience of the race and
so entering into that larger continuity of life which I have
discussed in the earlier part of the present chapter.

This great service is, of course, not perfectly or completely
performed, since every man's capacities are limited, and

since, too, at the best only luminous suggestions can be given and useful approaches opened up for the individual's own critical training, which no one can accomplish for him. Nevertheless, as we have seen, what can be done has an incalculable importance; and the *Shelburne Essays*, we are now to observe, share this importance as a direct consequence of the standards achieved and capably used by Mr More. Analysis, selection, and ordination, it must be remembered, are impossible without some point of departure, in relation to which the work is done. And it makes the greatest imaginable difference in the quality of the work and in its usefulness if both the critic and his readers know what that point of departure is. This, moreover, is exactly what our anti-critics to-day do not know; and what, in their reaction from impossible "absolute" standards, they have arrogantly decried, with absurd results. The *Shelburne Essays*, on the other hand, are genuinely and solidly critical, and possess an integrity which has been recognized even when it has not been understood, because of Mr More's realization that there can be no criticism without standards, and because of his successful effort to find a central point of departure, which he has been at pains to define carefully and to use with entire openness.

I do not in the least mean to imply that the critic's standard itself, so long as one is somehow attained and consciously used, is a matter of indifference; but it cannot be too strongly emphasized that some standard, deliberately espoused, really understood, and used with candour is the *sine qua non* of all criticism. Without this, we have the thoughtlessness, the wilfulness, the lack of integrity displayed by our anti-critics in books which, whatever else they may be— propagandistic, self-revealing, self-exploring, self-extolling —are in their total character the negation of the critical spirit. With this, we do have criticism, and have something, by the same token, which serves a useful purpose; because within its limits it is at least soundly informative and a secure basis for thought, whether or not we can accept for our own, or regard as entirely adequate, the standard employed. What this means, we have just noticed in the case of Mr

More's essay on "Thoreau's Journals"; and the same genuinely critical quality characterizes the whole body of *Shelburne Essays*, and by itself gives them a notable value proportionate to their range and variety.

But, though it is much, especially in our time, to have criticism which is criticism, the positive value of the *Shelburne Essays* arises from Mr More's altogether remarkable success in attaining a standard which really does meet the conditions laid down by the present state of our knowledge, which really does make sense of life, and which steadily directs attention to the central aspects of human nature. Dualism as it is propounded by Mr More is at once conservative, contemporary, and constructive. It is not "original"; it rests upon immemorial, constant, unambiguous experience; in times long past it was set up as the one best way of interpreting that experience, of enabling the intellect to grasp the meaning which can be found in life, and so of enabling man to obey the law of his existence consciously and intelligently; it has continued through many vicissitudes and in ever-changing circumstances to hold its place, with the concurrence and support of the most thoughtful, most feeling, and most serious part of mankind; it stands to-day not only untouched but fortified by modern knowledge; and it opens the gates of hope to humanity as does no program or interpretation offered by any of our professional reformers, or pragmatical statesmen, or psychologasters, or anti-critics, or forward-looking pundits. This it does by showing the way to a life of constructive endeavour which makes no demands on others, is equally practicable in bad times and in "good," and is its own reward, while being socially beneficent without qualification. Dualism thus maintains that larger racial continuity with which is bound up the cause of civilization and the possibility of significant individual growth and achievement; while at the same time it meets contemporary problems as if it were made for their solution, and holds out a means of enabling men to command and humanly use those material benefits which have been heaped up by research and invention, but which now threaten to engulf, as they have already in large part enslaved, the race.

As an instrument of criticism, consequently, dualism is fruitful beyond any other criterion with which it can be compared. We have already noticed both the great range of the *Essays*, and the fact that Mr More has found a living interest and significance in the work of the most widely differing kinds of men. A large number of our reviewers and anti-critics nowadays, on the other hand, write as if they were strangers to all humanity save their own immediate circle. When Mr Edmund Wilson mentions Ruskin you might think the poor old fellow had lived five hundred years ago, and had done well enough considering the extraordinary views they held in those dark days. Dryden's tone in speaking of Chaucer is less patronizing, and his understanding of the elder poet is more sympathetic and intimate. And when Mr Wilson goes as far afield as Dr Johnson, or even farther to set the world of scholarship right about Sophocles, he merely makes himself a laughing-stock. Others who could be mentioned, were there space or need, have separated themselves off from humanity much more completely; and in general these writers are at once victims and promoters of the puerile delusion that this present generation stands upon a pinnacle of unique enlightenment, no longer bound to the disgraceful past, but at length free to create, for the first time, by just letting itself out, a real literature and art and a righteous society. Such fellows, alas, somehow carry on, intellectually and artistically, a hand-to-mouth existence amidst a chaos of fevered dreams. By comparison with them, and their sweeping, savage exclusions, their narrowly limited range of appreciation, and their contempt for mere reality, Mr More seems the most catholic of critics and dualism the most liberal of standards, opening up the rich possibilities of our common humanity, enlarging our horizon, extending and deepening our capacity for appreciation, and so making us ourselves more significantly and fully human.

VI

It may be objected, however, that granting what has been set forth in this chapter, still, Mr More has made himself a

philosophic critic—perhaps a philosophic critic of high importance—but not a literary critic. He has, of course, used
literature, but has he not merely used it, as a means to the
criticism of life? This question I have already dealt with, in
showing that literature and life are really inseparable, and
that as soon as you attempt to make literature a thing apart
you produce a mortally diseased or a stillborn art. Our little
theorists who concern themselves with "pure" aesthetics are
the heirs of a sterile tradition;—they are the contemporary
representatives of the neo-classical or, more accurately, rationalistic theorists of the seventeenth and eighteenth centuries who vainly tried to create a science of literary artifice.
Now it is true, as I have said, that there is room, and indeed
the most urgent need, for active discussion of technical artistic problems; and such discussion, accompanied by experimentation, is bound to take place wherever literary crafts-
men are thrown together, unless their craftsmanship has
become wholly stereotyped and they the mere creatures of
tradition.[27] But this, we must recall, is "shop-talk"; it is a
highly specialized form of criticism, which of necessity leaves
out of account certain questions of vital importance—questions, precisely, with which the philosophic critic is directly
concerned.

These, moreover, are by no means exclusively questions
about the nature of man and the significance of the lives
portrayed or the experience or reflections communicated
through literature. These questions become, as I have said,
peculiarly important and insistent in an age so deeply unset-
tled and divided as our own. I have, in addition, discussed
chiefly this aspect of the *Shelburne Essays* because I have
aimed, not to summarize them for the benefit of people in a
hurry, but to give some aid most needed for a right understanding of them. Readers of the *Essays*, however, will find

27 It is a grave misfortune, no less for artists than for a suffering public,
that at a time when the very word "tradition" is ignorantly despised, and
tradition's crucially important good offices are not understood, artists should
engage in experimentation for experimentation's sake, with no conception
of a practicable, desirable goal to be achieved, with the childish notion that
to be "different" is enough, or with the infantile notion that "direct communication" is somehow possible.

that Mr More has well-defined artistic standards, consistent with the principles of dualism or evidently derived from those principles, and that consequently he prefers a closely integrated style, having the intensity which comes of restrained and exact expression, to the loosely flowing numbers and monotonous self-destroying over-emphasis of the impulsive writer who fancies he can "say everything." Correspondingly, he favours selection and simple coherent structure to the vain effort after all-inclusiveness with its resultant blurring of form. In these matters, too, he is a believer —as any one with a genuine social consciousness must be—in the beneficent use of tradition. In general, his artistic standards—of which this brief mention, it must be understood, gives no adequate account—have the sanction expressed in the familiar saying that the style is the man.[28] Hence he has been very ready to agree that, as Ben Jonson put it, tradition should serve as a guide, not as a commander. He has also been very ready to waive, though not to forget, his artistic standards when confronted with the work of a man of true insight.

What Mr More, to his signal credit, has not allowed, but has always strenuously opposed, is the corrupt and, I should say, fundamentally dishonest notion that literature can be judged entirely without regard to that which it expresses. As a consequence, he has been accused of seeking to impose rigid moral rules not only upon all men in their conduct of life, but upon the artist's sacred imagination. This is so flagrant a misrepresentation, however, that it is difficult to take it seriously. Mr More's own public protests against censorship and the mutilation of texts in the supposed interest of morals or decency, in his essay on Horace Walpole and elsewhere, and his belief that freedom, perilous though it may be, is a necessary condition for all true growth, should alone be enough to stamp the accusation as false. It has been levelled

[28] Some of Mr T. S. Eliot's vagaries in criticism have been caused by his recklessness in judging men solely from style—and, of course, from style in its turn judged by Mr Eliot's unexpressed standards. This is a totally different thing from attaining a stylistic standard by determination of that which is consonant with the qualities of a man possessing full self-knowledge and integrated personality.

against him, however, in the face of facts, not because Mr More really has given any ground for the fear that, were it possible, he would limit artists in their choice and treatment of themes, or would forcibly impose strict rules of conduct on anybody, but because our literary titans have wanted much more than the freedom to live and write exactly as they might please—because they have wanted to do as they might please *without being judged*. They have, in other words, perhaps "naturally" enough, as I have earlier said, wanted the public adoringly to fall down before them, without a question, without a single troubling doubt, without a thought of other values than their own.

Obviously, no criticism that is criticism could allow this claim and continue to exist. Intelligence itself, indeed, would have to abdicate in favour of the new dispensation, as it must always abdicate in favour of any really infallible authority. But other cases of the kind recorded in history most strongly suggest that the claim to be above criticism is in fact an acknowledgement of inability to face examination and reasoned judgement. And we to-day, if we can learn at all from history and are not invincibly stupid, should be grateful to any man strong enough and wise enough to stand apart from the swirling currents of contemporary letters and to look critically at the idols of the moment. Whether or not we are prepared fully to accept his standards, Mr More has, in so doing, performed a vital and liberalizing service whose importance is invaluable. Now I have no desire to claim that Mr More's standards cannot be improved on or that his use of them has been flawless; nor would he, who has always made war on absolutes, want any claim of the kind made for him. We have seen why the quest for human knowledge can have no end, and how far this side of what could be desired we are in the whole field of knowledge; but Mr More has at least been on the side of light—as our anti-critics demonstrably are not—in endeavouring steadily after what can be obtained, and honestly forming and using the best standards he could. He has, too, been unassailably in the right of it in aiming to carry on—not without change, but, still, faithfully to carry on—a great tradition; and incidentally he has thereby signified an important truth, that no one man's work in our world stands alone, or can ever be complete in itself. Hence Mr More's significance cannot be grasped until it is realized that, whatever else he has done, he has made his own in our time a cause which has been forlorn, but illustrious and never without its undaunted servants, since the dawn of civilization.

Further, in this ancient and vexed question of the relations between art and morality, it will be found by those who read the *Shelburne Essays* that Mr More's position is substantially this: Morality is a word variously used. To Mr Mencken it seems to denote merely the conventional rules of social behaviour inculcated by Sunday-school teachers and their like when he and Mr Dreiser were rebellious boys. Hence, in carrying on his rebellion long after childish things should have been put away, he thinks himself a convinced and earnest immoralist, entitled to deride indiscriminately all who feel any concern for morality. But, as Dr Lewisohn has pointed out, following a lead given many years ago by Mr Bernard Shaw, this will not do;—because Mr Mencken unescapably is himself a moralist, of a certain kind, though not a very enlightened or thoughtful one. Consequently it is fair to say that Mr Mencken, Dr Lewisohn, Mr Van Wyck Brooks, and Mr More, to name no others, all belong to the same family of critics, in that they are all much concerned with morality, and all recognize that the criticism of literature is inseparable from the criticism of life. Differences, of course, appear as soon as we look beyond this meeting-point; and it is these differences which, inevitably, are foremost in people's minds. Nevertheless, the bond of union just mentioned is significant, and only when it is remembered can we see the fundamental difference which separates Mr More from the others I have named. For these other gentlemen are alike in assuming that there is some absolute rule of conduct with which they have been made acquainted, so that they know exactly what we should approve of or should not approve of, and what we should do or should not do. It is true that each has his own rule, differing more or less from that of the others, but the important fact to be observed is that

each has a sense of perfect certainty concerning what is right
or wrong, extending to specific actions. It is all plain, clear,
simple, self-evident, or a matter of scientific knowledge, and
once the truth is recognized there will be no more moral
problems or controversies.

This may be sufficiently naïve; and Mr More, at any rate,
has been blessed with no comparable revelation. In his *Century of Indian Epigrams* we read:

> One law there is: no deed perform
> To others that to thee were harm;
> And this is all, all laws beside
> With circumstances alter or abide.

Mr More had, in other words, thus early realized that there
cannot be, in the nature of things, any absolute rules for
conduct, and that as a consequence moral problems will always be arising, and pressing for solution, while men live in
a changing world. Hence he turned to the study of the inner
constitution of man, not because he considered practical
questions of conduct unimportant, or was indifferent to them,
but because he saw that light could be shed on the whole
problem of the conduct of life only by proceeding straight
to its centre and origin within man himself. And, as we have
seen, he ended by accepting, restating, and re-interpreting
an ethical dualism as the one adequate and legitimate means
he could discover of making sense of human nature and life.
This meant, moreover, that the conflict of motives or impulses which creates moral problems was seen to be something essential in individuals, really constituting them as we
know them in experience, so that morality is of the inward
essence of human life, and is an unending inner personal
problem before ever it is a social problem. As Mr More put it
long ago in *The Jessica Letters*, at bottom "morality is the
soul's debt to herself." And for this reason the one unvarying positive law for man is the law of obedience to the Inner
Check, since upon this depends even the abiding social law
stated in the above quatrain and the very possibility of determining, with such guidance as can be got from individual
and social experience, the best feasible course of action in

any given specific circumstances. In the criticism of literature, consequently, Mr More has not endeavoured to wall off
any portion of life as "unfit" for artistic uses, but on the
contrary has wisely recognized that rules concerning subject-matter and form, while inevitable and certainly not
without value, can no longer be regarded as seriously as once
they were. At the same time, however, he has insisted that
what can and must be judged explicitly, carefully, strictly,
is the insight into human nature displayed by the literary
artist, and his interpretation of life.

And precisely here, of course, appears the difficulty which
has been acutely felt by certain contemporary writers. The
difficulty does not arise from the contents of, let us say, a
novel, which might conceivably include any incidents whatsoever, delineated with all possible detail and frankness, and
any imaginable characters, howsoever gross, lecherous, or
morbid. At any rate, I suggest an extreme case in order to
make clear the point, that the critical question raised by Mr
More turns, not upon any general rule defining what may be
or may not be represented, but upon the meaning implicit in
the writer's work of selection, emphasis, and construction.
And the objection felt to this is the one discussed in my first
chapter, where it was shown that our "creators" are demanding for themselves a kind of freedom which necessarily involves the denial of freedom to all others—to the reading
public and to critics. This, moreover, is apparently the only
kind of freedom they can or will understand, so that whenever it is infringed they cry out that attempts are being
made wantonly to suppress them.[29] Hence, though it is obvious enough in all conscience, it is none the less necessary to
point out that to utter a reasoned judgement against a book
is not at all the same thing as to suppress it or to move for its
suppression. If, furthermore, such a judgement is faulty,
this can and ought to be shown; and a critical discussion may
thus end, even though it did not begin, with a significant

[29] See, for example, the passage in Dr Lewisohn's *Expression in America*
in which it is pretended that Mr More's criticism leads straight to the
establishment of a ruthless censorship which would infallibly condemn Dr
Lewisohn and his like to proscription, torture, and burning at the stake.

clarification of ideas and standards, and an enhanced appreciation of the book which called forth the exercise of intelligence. Equally, of course, to utter a reasoned judgement against the perfectly unfettered and spontaneous life is not to suppress it or to move for its suppression. If such a life is, as we are nowadays told, the necessary condition of artistic "creation," we may, and indeed should, be grateful to those who voluntarily take up the burdens it entails; but it by no means follows that it would be the best life, or even a practicable, or tolerable, life for everybody, or that the criticism of life can possibly be undertaken in the exclusive interest of these new-fangled "creators."

Yet this, again, appears to be exactly what the "creators" desire, when they come to think of it, because, according to a theory prized especially by demagogues, *everybody* is or should be a "creator"—and everybody would be, too, were it not for the restraints imposed by tradition, government, and the bad men who own property or have amassed wealth. It is not a little curious, at first sight, that Mr More has thus simultaneously been accused of exhibiting lamentably and improperly moral tendencies in the sphere of literary criticism, and properly and lamentably immoral tendencies in the sphere of social criticism. But the latter accusation is, I scarcely need say, as fanciful as the former; and both in fact issue from the same spirit of unscrupulous bigotry. As a social critic Mr More has been accused of defending the rich in their alleged robbery of the poor, and consequently of valuing money more highly than men. He has also been accused of preferring personal security to justice, and, generally, of opposing all efforts to improve the condition of the masses, or of society as a whole, because he feels a "refined contempt for humanity." "Mr More's philosophic conservatism," in short, as "year by year the world has become a more restless and pullulating place," "has forced him gradually into the position of a quarrelsome, one might almost say a febrile, reactionary."

Such accusations as these have been made notably by Mr Van Wyck Brooks[30] and the words I quote are but an echo of

[30] See Appendix B.

that master's voice.[31] The master himself is a talented writer, thoughtful, very much in earnest, fairly well read, with a genuine understanding of the relation of literature to life, and—his friends would add—blessed with a vision of America's future comparable in its assurance only to his contempt for the past and the present. It is just his "vision," however, which has been Mr Brooks's undoing, causing him in practically all he has written to end disastrously, spite of the most promising beginnings. And the trouble with his "vision" is that he has never really seen it, and has not wanted to see it, but has been content simply to feel it intensely. As a consequence, he has supposed himself to be delivering a message when he has merely been engaged in venting his feelings. When, too, a theory has occurred to him, he has allowed his feeling of its truth to take the place of sceptical examination, so that no man in our day has more recklessly overridden mere fact. Scarcely anything else written about Henry James has been so careful, so well based, and so discerning as Mr Brooks's account of his early life and work. But then Theory makes its appearance, and looms ever more formidably as Mr Brooks goes on, till one is forced to recognize that, not James, but the organic relation between literature and the writer's—any writer's—Native Soil, is the subject in hand, and that James was merely seized on as a convenient illustration. Hence it is that the pages which should have prepared the way for an intelligent appreciation of James's mature work, and particularly of the three masterpieces written after 1900, turn out instead to be the prelude to a blind but determined campaign of belittlement. Such a union of critical promise and critical defalcation has to be read in order to be credited; yet Mr Brooks's volume on Mark Twain provoked on all sides, as far as one can tell from a

---

[31] They are taken from a review by Mr Newton Arvin (*The Freeman,* 1 June, 1921, pp. 283–284), who states that Mr More's own voice has become since 1914 "increasingly raucous, splenetic, and vituperative." Another young critic, not indebted to Mr Brooks, but with a gift of his own for distortion, may also be quoted here: "Mr More's economics is very simple. He merely assumes that he who has or gets, deserves. That really is his primary assumption in attacking any and all programs for social change." (Mr Felix Morrow, *The Symposium,* April, 1930.)

large number of reviews, a precisely similar mixture of admiration and of dissent.

As for Mr Brooks's "vision," to which his recipe for successful authorship is somehow related, no one can say what it is. In *Letters and Leadership* he endeavours to set it forth. In an earlier volume, *America's Coming-of-Age*, he had shown how little he could find to approve of in American literature or life, but had hinted that there were vital stirrings here and there, which promised much if only we could forget the past and remake the present—"weed out the incentives to private gain" and simultaneously "build up other incentives to replace them." The later volume is an attempt to advance upon this. But it fails to do so because Mr Brooks merely feels, intensely, that if only everything were different everything would be different. Young Americans everywhere are bursting with creative desire, he says, but unfortunately lack creative power; and for this situation American critics are responsible. So much is clear, and the critics are vehemently execrated, and amongst them Mr More. Beyond this, however, all is confusion. It appears that what is needed is the discovery of "the new faith without which America cannot live." Our critics could make this important discovery if they were willing to interest themselves sympathetically in our young creators and to find out what they are seeking. But admittedly the creators themselves have merely the desire to create something, without knowing what. And though it is the duty of critics to see things as they really are, they are false to their office if they do not see in the creators what the creators cannot find in themselves. The trouble with the critics is that they are not poets, and the trouble with the poets is that they are not critics. And in the end, accordingly, we find that both critics and poets have exactly the same function:—along with novelists they are "the pathfinders of society." Yet none can find a path through the wilderness of the United States because we "possess no cultural tradition filling in the interstices of energy and maintaining a steady current of life over and above the ebb and flow of individual purposes, of individual destinies."

This has, I fear, the appearance of caricature; though in

truth my summary scarcely more than hints at the confusion amidst which Mr Brooks half-conceals the fact that he is straining mightily after he knows not what. He does know that nothing actual is tolerable to him, and he feels confident that if everybody were harnessed to his chariot of progress the earthly paradise could swiftly be approached. But where the road is and whither it leads is more than he can say. Somehow we are all "to love life, to perceive the miraculous beauty of life, and to seek for life, swiftly and effectively, a setting worthy of its beauty." "This is the acme of civilization, to be attained . . . only through a long and arduous process." Well, whatever this mysterious process, at its end we will find ourselves dedicated wholly to one common corporate task: we will all be the servants of the Great Society, working with might and main to keep it going because life itself is so wonderful that nothing less can be a fit setting for it. And our reward will be the wonderful life that can be lived in a fit setting, and only in a fit setting. Everybody's personality will be entirely freed, and everybody will be a significant creator—a part-creator, of course, of the Great Society.

Clearly, a reformer of this stamp is just the kind of person who is sure that any one disagreeing with him must be an anti-social reactionary;—nor is it needful, the reformer argues, to bother one's self with the reactionary's reasons, because they must be corrupt and selfish ones. This, at any rate, is the frame of mind which led Mr Brooks, with a sincerely "good" conscience doubtless, to attribute to Mr More views which the latter has never held, and motives which self-righteous bigots always assume to be the only possible grounds of opposition to themselves, and to give his inventions the appearance of a basis by a single misquotation, which has a different meaning in its context, and with an all-important qualification, silently omitted by our reformer.[32]

I have, however, dwelt upon Mr Brooks's work, not in order to exhibit the real character of his accusations, nor yet because his overstrained doctrinaire volumes give him serious importance as a critic, even though they contain, inciden-

[32] See Appendix B.

tally, much that is sound, acute, and wisely observed. I have dwelt upon his work primarily because it exemplifies in a striking fashion well-nigh all that caused Mr More, at the very outset of his critical career, to reject with unhesitating decision the gospel of the professed humanitarians. His reasons, as they were early set forth in *The Jessica Letters*, we have noticed at the close of the preceding chapter, and they need not be repeated. But it must be recalled that what Mr More objected to was not the compassionate effort to improve conditions of life in so far as they can be improved, and for the greatest possible number of people—not this at all, nor the effort to deepen and render more significant that instinctive fellow-feeling without which the very existence of a real society is inconceivable. He objected to something very different—to the grovelling kind of materialism inseparable from every attempt to convert humanitarian zeal into a species of religion, by exalting its objects as the supreme and sufficient ends of existence, and by setting up "social sympathy" as the sum of all the virtues. He considered that to make just life itself the sole or even first object of life was a patent absurdity—meaningless because it might mean anything one pleased, but could mean nothing until it was translated into terms representing aims or ends which themselves were valuable, or at least seemingly valuable. He also considered that the equalitarianism inherent in humanitarian religion involved not only the denial of an overwhelming body of scientific and human knowledge, but the reduction of life to a lowest common denominator, to a dull and brutal uniformity, practically identical with the merely animal level of existence. And he considered that to externalize and fix upon "society" the responsibility for every base or unlovely human quality, thereby inculcating the notion that social change might bring in an earthly paradise, but thereby destroying at the same time all sense of individual responsibility, was simply to prepare the way for despotism and its corollary, abject slavery—and to fly in the face of what every man capable of honest self-observation and reflection knows about himself, in order to achieve this wonderful object.

Now I do not conceive that Mr Van Wyck Brooks is a materialist, either philosophic or of the grovelling kind whose adherents consider mere animal well-being a more substantial good than honour or integrity or, in general, the most elementary self-respect. Indeed, his understanding of life and evaluation of it is at many points identical with Mr More's, and with the great traditional analyses and valuations by whose light both have profited. And this, in truth, is one cause of Mr Brooks's confusion, because it has impelled him to want something better, deeper, finer than anything he can honestly see in mere social reform, while, nevertheless, he can see nothing that might bring about what he wants except social reform, because he is determined to shift all responsibility for his own failings and for the creative impotence of his contemporaries upon "society." Hence it is impossible to translate his aspiring emotions into practical terms other than those of revolutionary socialism, or communism.

In terms of what is socially feasible under earthly conditions, I should suppose that the new Germany of Herr Hitler illustrates the kind of thing that can be accomplished in pursuit of Mr Brooks's aims. Soviet Russia is of course another practical illustration, but not so complete as the new Germany because of its avowed materialism. Both governments, however, are despotic as probably none in the Western world has been since the dawn of history;—and thus we see demands for absolute freedom translated in practice into the ruthless subjection of whole nations—into abject slavery in fact, by whatever illusions, immemorially known to tyrants, the truth may be veiled.

How could it more plainly be demonstrated that sympathy cannot take the place of judgement? Sympathy is not different from our other feelings—from enthusiasm, for instance, discussed in the first chapter of this book. And like enthusiasm, or like hatred, it may be admirable, or ridiculous, or vicious, depending entirely upon its object. But it is the misfortune of those who imagine external conditions to be the all-determining factors in human life that they are compelled to propagate a cult of indiscriminate sympathy, stultifying alike to intelligence and to character. This cult

undeniably derives no small part of its appeal from the flat-
tery it addresses to the mob, from the stimulus it gives to
envy and greed, and from the sanctifying benediction it be-
stows on our impulses to mind other people's business and so
to regulate our neighbours as to make conditions of life more
favourable to ourselves. It has, of course, other grounds of
appeal as well. But the purest altruism, the noblest indignation, the most tender compassion, are all reduced to a level
with envy and meddlesomeness and self-love when they are
made to feed an indiscriminate social sympathy. And the
reason is not far to seek. For emotion—any emotion—is in
itself a blind force, never at a stand, always growing more
intense or waning, and unstable in proportion as it is keen,
because it exhausts, indeed consumes, its victim. Everybody
knows this; everybody has seen the exhaustion and collapse
following upon waves of intense emotion, and, too, the lightning speed with which emotions may on occasion change into
their seeming opposites.

Hence those who give themselves up to unmeasured sympathy, upon whatever ground, are always in a state of
perturbation, more or less extreme, and inevitably become
unbalanced, nervously irritable, and temperamentally explo-
sive. None of us needs to go far afield nowadays to confirm
the truth of this generalization, or to observe that these unfortunate dupes of feeling invariably consider themselves
most righteous when they are least balanced. Their condition, indeed, verges upon disease, and accounts for the fact,
superficially so odd, that these sufferers from the virus of
social sympathy tend in practice towards a state of chronic
rage against their fellows. Their case may fairly be described
as one of thwarted love, and proves anew what has been
proved a countless number of times in every generation—
that unleashed emotion, equally whether "base" or "beautiful," leads straight to disaster. Nothing is easier than to fill
one's head with a conglutination of desirable reforms and
rosy anticipations—and nothing more certain than the discovery that reforms do not bring the expected results, that
an endless succession is needed, and that after all men remain
under the most diverse conditions much what they were be-

fore. And in these circumstances the blind guidance of emotion tends to confine brotherly love to an abstraction called "humanity," or to some imagined "great society" of the indefinite future, and, in the present, to criminals, imbeciles, ne'er-do-wells, and the like—and above all to the philanthropist's own wronged, unappreciated self—while a venomous hatred is felt against those who play a constructive part in life as it must be lived under existing conditions.

Mr More has earned a large share of this hatred for reasons wholly creditable to him. Sanity and fanaticism are bound to oppose each other, and it is against the brutal extremes into which fanatical "saviours" would lead us that Mr More has directed his attack. His real "crime" has been his respect for reason and for fact. The key-note of his social criticism, on its positive side, is to be found in this sentence:

We are bound, in any clear-sighted view of the larger exigencies of the relations of man with man, to fortify ourselves against such a perversion of the institutions of government as would adapt them to the nature of man as he ought to be, instead of the nature of man as he actually is, and would relax the rigour of law, in pity for the degree of injustice inherent in earthly life.

Looking at man as he actually is, Mr More has understood that we are humanized in proportion as we discover our inward selves and wage there the real conflict of life. It is more important to a man that he should become just than that he should avoid receiving injustice at the hands of others. Each of us can attempt to make himself what he ought to be, but must take others as they are. This corresponds to the fact that each man is at once an individual and a member of society, and so perforce lives out his life on two levels, certainly not unrelated, but certainly different, one being in truth a means to the other. We have no notion what a man in complete isolation would be like. We may suppose, with Aristotle, that he would be either a beast or a god—not a man at all. Hence it may fairly be said that social institutions, and societies themselves, are not man-made, but are slow natural growths, developing in accordance with laws, similar to other laws of nature. To recognize this truth is not to acquiesce resignedly in the doctrine that whatever is is right. On the contrary, it is to take the essential first step towards successful control. For you must obey Nature in order to command her, as Bacon said, and so equally must men obey the unescapable conditions of social life if ever they are to secure the rewards which can really be got from social organization. And this they can only do, not by flying in the face of experience and knowledge, but by submitting themselves to fact—by looking at men, not as it is fancied they may be or ought to be or would be if only they had the zealous reformer's own virtues, but as they actually are.

Men are in fact, as we have seen in the present chapter and as everybody really knows, unequal—no two of them wholly alike, no two of them talented to precisely the same extent, in precisely the same ways. Efforts to legislate them into equality are as little intelligent and as futile as our "noble experiment" with prohibition. Nor is equalitarianism any more desirable than possible. The good we get from social organization arises from the division of labour and of responsibility, by which every member of society benefits. But there can be no organization without order, and no order without subordination, while equally there can be no division of labour without diversity of talent, of training, of station, and of reward. One prime requisite of a justly ordered society, therefore, is the fair division of rewards—not only monetary rewards, but dignities, exemptions, and the like. And a fair division is an unequal division, duly proportioned to the difficulty and importance of the several tasks performed, and to the excellency with which they are performed. We cannot reasonably hope for a perfect division, any more than we can hope for perfection of whatsoever kind within the limits of human life and action; but to do the best we can demands unceasing watchfulness and effort, renewed in every generation, and altering with altered circumstances. This in turn means that we are in constant need of untrammelled, enlightened, honest criticism. It means also, however, that we are constantly in danger of devoting our attention too exclusively to problems of organization, thinking them far more important than they usually are, thinking society more open to change than it really is, and thinking, too often, that men are made for organization, just as certain Jews anciently thought men made for the Sabbath. Hence we have to be always on our guard against a veritable army, or rabble, of zealous bureaucrats, narrowly trained experts, professional reformers, plausible charlatans, flattering demagogues, blackguards of the daily and weekly press, self-appointed censors, and bigots, all of whom would persuade us, for the greatest variety of reasons, to extend without limit the scope and functions of government. It is always pretended, of course, that somebody else will pay the price while we will reap no uncertain benefit, but the consequence is the progressive externalization of life at the expense of personal responsibility, and the relapse of the individual to barbarism.

On the basis of such considerations as these, and of others already sufficiently canvassed in the present chapter, Mr More was strongly impelled towards conservatism—towards acceptance, that is, of the principle of social growth, as against the principle of radical or revolutionary innovation. We can only hope to make approaches to a justly ordered society, he concluded, in so far as we build upon the past, accepting its lessons, and conserving what has been accomplished, instead of repudiating all that is tried in favour of all that is new and strange. And to several of the most vitally important problems which face us to-day Mr More has devoted particular attention, enabling us not only to understand the general character of his conception of society, but to see what it means in practice. He has thus, for example, emphasized the primary place of education in a democratic society, not simply as our one means of opening the door of opportunity equally to all comers, but as our one means of fitting the young to take their places responsibly in the social order and, at the same time, our one means of selecting the right people for those places. Education, in other words, is a discipline and a selective process as well as a method of imparting information and technical skill; and no society can hope to subsist—much less to become justly ordered—whose education is not a rigorous discipline, through which those best able to profit by the fullest and most careful attention are fairly selected for it and really receive it. Technical education, moreover, is one thing, which should be known and valued for what it is, while liberal education should be clearly distinguished from it and should be recognized as something far more valuable to society. For liberal education is *humanizing* education; it is the full development of personality and character through the combined study of exact science, philosophy, history, and literature, and through carefully guided and criticized activity; and by such means alone can we form an *élite*, a "natural aristocracy," without which we have, as Burke said, no nation, no true society, no honest and enlightened government, no directors of our mere technicians, no fair and balanced criticism, no check upon fanatics and charlatans—in a word, no integrity.

Serious defenders of an hereditary aristocracy are scarcely to be found nowadays. Everybody recognizes that though heredity does count for something, still, intolerable abuses flow from fixed divisions in society depending upon the accident of birth. Nevertheless, those who have imagined that a society could be maintained without recognition of the inequalities of men have merely opened the door to plutocracy, a worse evil than that whose place it has taken. Our contemporary demagogues, stubbornly persisting in a course marked out in the eighteenth century, blind to all experience and impervious to reason, tell us that the cure for sick democracy is "more democracy." Mr More is plainly in the right of it when he replies that this is nothing better than a lie, which would plunge us still further in our descent to anarchy and despotism; and when he says that "the cure of democracy is not *more* democracy, but *better* democracy." Submitting ourselves to learn from experience, taking men as they actually are and recognizing their inevitable inequalities, we *could use* these variations for our advantage. Instead of being victimized by the worst men, as now we so largely are, while the best are forced to withdraw themselves from public affairs and the public eye, we could place the latter in all those positions of trust, leadership, and control where we most need character and intelligence. And in the formation, to this end, of a true natural aristocracy, by means of a humanizing education, identical for all those capable of it, there is involved, as Mr More says, "no futile intention of abrogating democracy." He continues:

A natural aristocracy does not demand the restoration of inherited privilege or a relapse into the crude dominion of money; it is not synonymous with oligarchy or plutocracy. It calls rather for some machinery or some social consciousness which shall insure both the selection from among the community at large of the "best" and the bestowal on them of "power"; it is the true consummation of democracy. . . . No one supposes that the "best" are a sharply defined class moving about among their fellows with a visible halo above them and a smile of beatific superiority on their faces. Society is not made of such classifications, and . . . a natural aristocracy signifies a tendency rather than a conclusion. . . . [But] why should there not be an outspoken class consciousness among those who are in the advance of civilization as well as among those who are in the rear? Such a compact of mutual sympathy and encouragement would draw the man of enlightenment out of his sterile seclusion and make him efficient; it would strengthen the sense of obligation among those who hesitate to take sides, and would turn many despondent votaries of fatalism and many amateur dabblers in reform to a realization of the deeper needs of the day.

But if, by recognition and acceptance of human inequality, we can turn it to our advantage, and if, by recognition and acceptance of human interdependence, we can make education a much more valuable and beneficent force, by checking its present atomistic and dispersive tendency, we must also recognize that nothing is possible in the way of development towards a justly ordered society without freedom. This I take to be self-evident, but the meaning of freedom and the conditions irrevocably attached to it are far from obvious. Hence it is that the desire for freedom has been the source of innumerable mistakes and crimes, some of which have been noticed in this volume. We have seen reason to condemn, not

the desire, not freedom, but all attempts to gain absolute
liberty. Everything men can know directly from experience,
we have observed, is conditioned and relative—and so is
everything which men can achieve on earth. Freedom of any
kind is only obtainable at a price, and it behoves us to recognize that the word is empty save when it signifies individual
freedom, and that, inasmuch as men are not disembodied
spirits, the freedom of the individual necessarily has a definite material basis. And this, as Mr More has pointed out, is
the reason why "law is concerned primarily with the rights
of property." Civilization, he has correctly insisted, as the
Western world has known it, has been conditioned by the security of private property. Most of the positive achievements, social and individual, which we account valuable have
had, as their *sine qua non*, the personal independence of our
counsellors and leaders. And personal independence is possible, by and large, with men as we actually find them, only
in so far as private property is secure. The truth of the whole
matter is simply that "if property is secure, it may be the
means to an end, whereas if it is insecure it will be the end
itself." The man, in other words, whose possessions are in
constant danger is a constantly uneasy man; and his energy
and attention and time will unavoidably be consumed by this
one circumstance which should not be the end of all his endeavours, but the means to positively valuable ends. It is, of
course, a too familiar fact that the man made free by the
security of his possessions may misuse his freedom. That is
something to be corrected, as effectively as may be possible;
but the "correction" proposed by those who would transfer
property to the state is worse than even the most serious
abuse of freedom, because it transforms men into slaves, and
either reduces them to hopeless apathy or goads them to des-
perate all-absorbing conflict for the bare means to existence
—conflict precisely such as has taken place in recent years in
the Ukraine.

Mr More has not been primarily a social critic. Some of
his essays in this field have been called forth by disgraceful
events or activities which have more or less unfortunately
coloured his presentation of general principles; and some of

his specific proposals are, it seems to me, clearly impracticable, while others do not fully meet the situations which suggested them. But these are matters of detail, comparatively easy to set right, and they do not really obscure the broad direction and character of his criticism, briefly indicated above. Whether or not this criticism issues out of a "refined contempt for humanity" readers must judge for themselves. Certainly it does issue out of a determined effort to bring intelligence to bear on all aspects of the problem of existence. And certainly not contempt, but true sympathy, as Mr More himself declared at the outset of his literary career, underlies the attempt to show that when critical intelligence is brought to bear on humanitarianism, the cult is seen to be riddled with inconsistencies, to promote self-deception, hypocrisy, hatred, and wholly delusive hopes, and to return no answer at all to the question of questions—for what end do we live? The character of Mr More's social criticism, indeed, has been determined by his realizing sense of the all-important distinctions to be made, between the inner and the outer life of man, between means and ends, between the ideal and the actual, and also by his sane, steady conviction that half a loaf is better than none, that imperfect or imperfectly distributed freedom is better than slavery, that experience is safer than theory, and that peaceful, ordered growth is preferable to revolution. Everywhere, too, Mr More has shown a deeper, truer understanding of what is real in the brotherhood of men, and of the ways in which that real brotherhood may be made socially beneficent, than have our professed humanitarians and reformers and revolutionists, so that on this as well as on other grounds we may fairly denominate his criticism not so much conservative as honestly realistic. And in no direction has his honest realism been more evident than in his treatment of property, for which he deserves the heartfelt gratitude of all who wish to see clearly and to think justly.

IV. THE GREEK TRADITION

I

WHEN Mr More resigned from the editorship of the *Nation*, in 1914, he also left New York, and settled in Princeton, where he has since lived. He had a definite reason for turning away from active journalism as soon as this became practicable: he wished to undertake a connected series of critical studies for which the full command of his own time and energy was essential. The break, however, with his immediate past was by no means so sudden or complete as the bare outward facts might suggest. For, as we have noticed, he maintained some connexion with the *Nation* through the next year or so; and, what is more, he became at this time the leading contributor to the *Unpopular Review*, later the *Unpartizan Review*, which was founded, published, and edited—very badly—by Henry Holt. Six of the pieces included in the Ninth Series of *Shelburne Essays*, and five of those in the Eleventh Series, were originally written for this periodical. During these years, too, Mr More wrote essays on Emerson and on Jonathan Edwards for the *Cambridge History of American Literature*, and a number of articles for the *Atlantic Monthly* and for several other magazines. He had, in addition, begun some years earlier to give occasional lectures before university and college audiences in various parts of the country, and this he continued to do. He had thus delivered, for example, in 1909, the first series of Ropes Lectures at the University of Cincinnati; and after 1914, besides a considerable number calling for no special mention, he delivered the Vanuxem Lectures at Princeton in 1917, a Bross Lecture at Lake Forest College in 1921, and the Turnbull Lectures at Johns Hopkins University, also in 1921. And from 1918 until 1932 he held the post of lecturer, first in philosophy and afterwards in classics, at Princeton, besides holding, during two years late in this period, temporary posts at the University of California and at Harvard.

All of this, without mentioning articles written in recent years for the *Revue de Paris*, the *Criterion*, the American *Bookman*, and other periodicals, might seem conclusively to prove that Mr More was unable to preserve the leisure won from journalism, or to use it as he had planned. But in fact much of the work chronicled above demanded only a fraction of his time, and much of it contributed directly to the execution of the purpose he had formed. The Vanuxem Lectures delivered at Princeton, for instance, consisted of certain parts of a volume entitled *Platonism*, which was published immediately upon the termination of the lectures, and which was designed to lay the foundation for the series of studies since published at intervals under the general title of *The Greek Tradition*. These volumes at present number six. *Platonism*, both because it was originally intended as a general introduction and for other reasons which will presently be discussed, has been placed by Mr More amongst the "complementary volumes" of the series. The core of the work, in which its fundamental thesis is developed, consists of four numbered volumes: I. *The Religion of Plato* (1921), II. *Hellenistic Philosophies* (1923), III. *The Christ of the New Testament* (1924), and IV. *Christ the Word* (1927). In 1931 a second "complementary volume" appeared under the title, *The Catholic Faith*. In the same year the third edition of *Platonism* was published, with a new preface concerning the series as a whole, in which it is stated that "a survey of the Aristotelian philosophy is in active preparation" and that "other complementary volumes are planned but may or may not be achieved."

Those who are familiar with the series will look forward with something more than ordinary eagerness to the promised volume on Aristotle, which it is to be hoped Mr More will not lay aside for any less important tasks, and they will also be glad indeed to see discussed certain other questions raised in the course of the work, or suggested by its implications concerning the development of Christianity since the

fifth century. As it now stands, however, the central portion
of *The Greek Tradition* is complete, and this principal work
of Mr More's later life can be studied and understood without waiting for further additions. We can see, not with perfect certainty but with sufficient clearness, what Mr More's
first design was, how this was modified, or rather trans-
formed, as he went on, and where he has come out. We can
see, too, the extent to which his earlier life and work constituted a preparation for this final achievement, and the sense
in which it completes the great critical task he took in hand
some thirty-five years ago. We can also see that in *The
Greek Tradition*, even more conspicuously than in his earlier
criticism, Mr More's concern has been with the past only for
the sake of the present.

In the beginning what was purposed was "a series of
studies on the origins and early environment of Christianity
and on such more modern movements as the English revival
of philosophic religion in the seventeenth century and the
rise of romanticism in the eighteenth." Mr More's conviction
was, "that behind all these movements the strongest single
influence has been the perilous spirit of liberation brought
into the world by the disciple of Socrates, and that our mental and moral atmosphere, so to speak, is still permeated with
inveterate perversions of Plato's doctrine." His intention,
we thus plainly see, was not that of the antiquarian or mere
historian, but strictly and deliberately that of the critic; and
he was impelled to begin with a new study of Plato, not because he had grown indifferent to contemporary problems
and issues, but precisely because he was convinced that the
pursuit of what I have called human knowledge, and even the
intelligent appreciation of its nature and import, were tending to disappear from the modern world, and that "only
through the centralizing force of religious faith or through
its equivalent in philosophy" can we hope to stay the wave
of decadent barbarism with which we are most gravely
threatened. He went to Plato, in other words, because he felt
assured that the Platonic dialogues are the primal source
in the Western world, "still potent and fresh and salutary,"
still unique and irreplaceable, of "the truth which is in reli-

gion but is not bounded by religious dogma, and which needs no confirmation by miracle or inspired tradition."[1]

II

THIS places Mr More's object in a clear light; but in order to understand the transitional phase of his thought of which it is the outward sign, we must review briefly his development as we have traced its course in the preceding chapters. We have seen that when the dualistic analysis of human nature first presented itself to him as a means of making sense of life he turned to the comparative study of religion, in order to acquaint himself more fully with the significance and possibilities of dualism. We have seen, too, that he was for a time strongly influenced by ancient Hindu religion. He was, indeed, far from being the only student of early Hinduism and Buddhism, a generation ago, to perceive remarkable compatibilities between these ancient interpretations of life and the new conception of the order of nature suggested by scientific discovery in the nineteenth century. And these imperfect yet striking correspondences helped to impress upon his mind the more strongly the relentless logic with which the Hindus drove home their sense of the radical and even deadly opposition between spirit and body. The spirit of man, they believed, was isolated and imprisoned in its earthly vesture, so that man could obtain deliverance from that inner tension and conflict which is at once a perpetual torment and the ground of all hope, only by the denial, as complete as might be consistent with bare self-preservation, of all demands of the body. Undoubtedly abstinence in its Hindu guise made a powerful appeal to Mr More, as the life of renunciation has appealed to great numbers of deeply spiritual people in most ages of the world, because it seems to be a straightforward, uncompromising, honest way of proving that one "means business," and that one cannot for an instant rest content with mere professions.

It is not, therefore, surprising that distinct traces of what

[1] The passages quoted in this paragraph are taken from the Preface to the first edition of *Platonism*.

may a little loosely be called ascetic doctrine are to be found
in some of the earlier *Shelburne Essays*, although by the time
they were written Mr More was swinging free of the Hindus
and had definitely given his allegiance to Plato. There are, of
course, elements of asceticism in Plato's thought, but these
had no part in bringing Mr More under the influence of the
founder of the Academy. Mr More has, indeed, strongly and
rightly protested that the ascetic teaching of Plato is confined to a few passages in a few, probably early, dialogues,
and that it stands there as something which we can, to be
sure, understand, and will regard with sympathy if we do
understand it, but which is plainly inconsistent with Plato's
mature thought. And Mr More obviously has felt concerned
to insist upon this because it is an integral part of the problem upon which all his effort and study has been centred, and
because it goes to the root of the difficulty which sent him
from the Hindus to Plato. He has said, somewhere, that this
change was brought about by a growing conviction that the
Western world could never accept and really assimilate the
Hindu interpretation of life, and by his coincident discovery
that what he took to be true in it was also to be found in
Plato, in a form eminently congenial to the ingrained bent of
the Western mind.

What was the nature of this difference? We can see it
clearly as soon as we recall that Mr More's thought was concentrated upon the problem of human existence, and that
what he wanted was a way of accounting for the nature and
life of the individual in which due heed should be paid to all
the assured evidence from experience. This alone cannot, perhaps, be called the key to every question concerning Mr
More's development, but certainly no understanding of his
work is possible unless we remember why he could not be
satisfied with any of the easy "new" solutions of this problem
put forward with great confidence and recklessness in the
eighteenth and nineteenth centuries, and remember equally
that he could not turn, as so many have done, to other problems or the pursuit of other interests while this central and
profoundest enigma remained unsolved. And evidently what
led him from the Hindus to Plato was the latter's reasoned

assurance that the self, the individual human being, is not, despite all that might suggest it, either a mere illusion or a merely temporary or accidental congeries of sensible elements. For this is the fundamental point of cleavage between East and West. To the teachers of the East as to Socrates and Plato, the life of the individual involved transcendent issues, was directed to an end beyond itself, and was explained in terms of dualism. It was believed, too, in both the East and the West that the spirit or soul inhabiting a perishable earthly body was immortal, and that, for some necessary reason, it underwent a severe probation in our ever-changing sensible world. But to the prophets and teachers of India— and above all to Buddha, in whom Eastern thought reached its culmination—the unchanging, eternal spirit could find deliverance from conflict and mortality and grief only by practices which aimed at and succeeded in achieving the very extinction of selfhood, of all continuing personal identity. Buddha, as Mr More has said in one of the latest, and most masterly, of his essays, appealed to men "with no belief in the human soul or in God, rather with a vehement denial of their existence." And he continues:

Of this as a fact there can be no reasonable doubt. Not once but repeatedly and in every kind of connection Buddha asserted that the last and most fatal illusion is just the clinging to any entity associated with the flux of elements that compose the ephemeral aggregate of body and consciousness; attachment to an illusory Self or Personality or individual Soul is the veritable cause of Sorrow. And so of God. The popular pantheon of deities and spirits and demons he apparently took over without a qualm; but they are all transitory phenomena like ourselves, subject to birth and death and rebirth in the infinite Samsâra, and their heavens and hells are no more than places of temporary reward and punishment for the good and evil of Karma. His universe has no God in the Christian sense; it contains no Creator, no providential Ruler, no Judge, and above all no Saviour.[2]

[2] *The Catholic Faith* ("Buddhism and Christianity"), pp. 38–39.

At the time of which we are speaking, the late eighteen-nineties, Mr More was probably not disturbed by the absence of a personal deity from the Buddhist scheme of things. He had definitely turned away, not only from Calvinism, but from Christianity. He had written, in *The Great Refusal*:

I am not a follower of Jesus. I do not know his God, cannot find him, do not hear his voice. The great self-abnegation and passion of Jesus seem to me often a greater mistake; for what blessing has he brought to the world? To miseries which he cannot alleviate he has added only the further miseries of sympathy. I am not a disciple of Dante. His vision of heaven and hell has passed away for ever. His faith is a thing outworn. The new vision must somehow be a justification and glorification of the life that is bounded by the narrow walls of time.[3]

Substantially the same avowal is made, or distinctly hinted, more than once in the *Shelburne Essays*, and the above passage not unfairly represents, as far as it goes, the attitude Mr More maintained throughout his early manhood and middle life. By "the further miseries of sympathy," he of course meant to signify that which seemed to be left of the gospel of Jesus once it was recognized that miracles, as Arnold said, "do not happen." Such an interpretation of Christian teaching possibly represents an unfortunate side of Professor Babbitt's influence; though the belief was widespread in the late nineteenth century—and still persists in the backwaters of social and religious thought—that the religion of brotherly love, or humanitarianism, was implicit in Christianity from the beginning, and constituted the enduring portion of the Christian "message."

How Mr More evaluated this "message" has earlier been stated; and we have seen reason to conclude that nothing in his career is more creditable, or bears plainer witness at once to his power of intellect, to his integrity, and to his courage, than his unqualified refusal to accept humanitarianism as a religion or as the guiding star of his life. But this refusal only rendered more acute the need of restating and develop-

[3] Pp. 122–123.

ing anew the principles of dualism in such fashion as to make
them really available to men of our time. And in undertaking
the reinterpretation of dualism Mr More accepted the guidance of Plato—or rather, to speak more accurately, of the
Socrates of the earlier Platonic dialogues—because he found
united in Socrates both that which had drawn him to Buddha
and that whose absence had repelled him from Buddha.

To say this, I am aware, is to run a certain risk of false
simplification—a danger not easy for commentators to avoid,
and sometimes the cause of serious misunderstanding. By
way of precaution, in discussing the *Shelburne Essays*, it was
necessary to insist that Mr More had no rigid formula which
could be mechanically applied, that the essays could not be
neatly arranged to exhibit a systematic development of doctrine, and that they fell very loosely and unequally into the
general underlying plan, which, nevertheless, was clearly discernible and sufficed to give them a real unity of spirit and a
formidable cumulative power. It is no less necessary now to
insist that in charting the course of Mr More's thought one
perforce tends to make turning-points sharper than they
really were, and so not to represent adequately the character
of a change which is truly a growth, nor the manner in which
old influences persist, even though more or less weakened and
altered, alongside newer ones. Likewise it is necessary to remember that while certain men are great, and significant too,
because they have exceedingly simple natures which act
themselves out with something of the vividness, directness,
and force of a stroke of lightning, others become significant
in a very different way—because their natures are complex
as well as intense, so that they are capable of true growth and
deep feeling, while actuated by some positive inner power
whose character may be obscure but whose voice is impera-
tive. And Mr More has become significant—the most significant figure amongst American writers to-day—because he
has felt deeply the force of every current entering into the
distinctively modern stream of consciousness, has understood
the inevitableness of certain radical changes in thought
which have taken place, and yet, without any nostalgic longing for an impossible golden age whether of the past or of the

future, has turned uncompromisingly from the all-pervasive naturalism of our age, and thus has opposed himself to the dominant tendencies of the moment in philosophy, literature, politics, education, and religion. But this means that he has been impelled by some power from within, stronger than those outer forces which unintermittently press down upon all of us, bending and twisting us into conformity with the conventions of our time and place.[4] And this in turn means that he has never been a servile follower of those whose guidance he has sought and accepted, but has rather made his own what he has found, out of the past, still valid and pertinent, so that no question concerning his intellectual relationships is susceptible of an easy or unqualified answer.

If, then, it is remembered how complex these questions really are, we may go on to observe that Mr More was drawn to Socrates because both men grew to maturity in ages when naturalistic speculation was in the ascendant, and yet were impelled to react uncompromisingly against it, while nevertheless recognizing that naturalism was built, however ille-

---

[4] I have been told that "modern psychology" has distinguished a definite type of human being so constituted as to enjoy, or at any rate to glory in, opposition and isolation, and that only such men refuse to run with the herd. A few days ago a Jewish barber informed me that members of his race were likely to be objectionably self-assertive and "pushing," simply because every man, by nature, is more concerned over the expansion of his "ego" than over anything else, and because Jews have exceptional difficulties in this matter, on account of an inferiority-complex fastened on them by the gentiles amongst whom they live;—whence he concluded that to dislike a self-assertive "pushing" Jew was to indulge an irrational prejudice. These are examples of what "science" means to an increasing number of people. Those who are not hopelessly befuddled by such naturalistic "explanations" of character will find a clear indication of Mr More's feeling concerning his position, as he then regarded it, at the close of the essay entitled "Victorian Literature" in *Shelburne Essays,* Seventh Series (1910). The passage is too long to quote in its entirety, but the following sentences contain what is most material in the present connexion: "The world is not contradicted with impunity, and he who sets himself against the world's belief will have need of all a man's endurance and all a man's strength. The adventurous soul who to-day against the reigning scientific and pragmatic dogma would maintain no vague and equally one-sided idealism, but the true duality of the one and the many, the absolute and the relative, the permanent and the mutable, will find himself subjected to an intellectual isolation and contempt almost as terrible as the penalties of the inquisition, and quite as effective in producing a silent conformity. If a man doubts this, let him try, and learn."

gitimately, upon a foundation of facts which could not themselves be ignored. Socrates, in other words, had endeavoured
to turn attention away from cosmological theory, which
seemed to him glittering rather than substantial in character,
and towards the study of man, as practically the most important to us of all studies, and one from which we could expect
substantial results, because the fullest and closest examination of the subject was a practicable undertaking. It was,
further, the more necessary because the interpretation of life
which had the sanction of tradition was hopelessly undermined, partly through its connexion with a mythology no
longer credible; and also because various contemporaries
were, in a haphazard, half-conscious way, developing a new
interpretation, or philosophy, in the course of their work as
practical teachers. What these popular and influential lec-
turers taught was "virtue," understood as the knowledge
enabling a man to succeed in politics or the law-courts,
though the word in this sense may be most variously applied.
An accomplished flute-player, for example, would be, as we
say to-day, a *good* flute-player or, as we do not now say, a
virtuous flute-player. These teachers, then—the sophists, or
wisdom-mongers—were making themselves responsible for a
most imperfect, and perhaps equally mischievous, study of
man. For if to be a "virtuous" orator was to be an orator
trained in the use of rhetorical and logical tricks, enabling
one in case of need to make the worse cause seem to the populace the better cause, and enabling one in general to accomplish one's own purposes regardless of what might be "right,"
it was inevitably suggested that a "rightness" going counter
to one's purposes must merely be some one else's "rightness"
advanced to further his purposes, and that consequently
there was nothing which could be called "rightness itself."
And "truth" equally, on this basis, faded out of sight. The
"good" and the "true" were merely names used by those who
were skilful enough or strong enough to impose on the populace standards advantageous to themselves. A classic example
of this dissolving argument, applied to "justice," fills the
early portion of Plato's *Republic*. And taking it as a whole
it comes to this: The decisive factor in life is sheer power.

You must either use other people to further your well-being or submit to be used by them to further their well-being. The wise man, the "good" man, is he who, facing the facts, succeeds by any means in grasping power and so succeeds in imposing his standards—that is, standards calculated to advantage him—on others.

Now Socrates to a certain extent fell in with the sophists —meeting his death, indeed, because the unintelligently conservative people of the time not only mistook him for one, but thought him, in his corrupting, "unsettling" influence, to be the worst of the lot. And except in the light of the sophistic argument outlined above we cannot understand Socrates' famous contention that no man does evil deliberately or willingly, but solely because of ignorance—because he misjudges the consequences of his act, thinking to reap advantage when in reality disadvantages will follow, greater than the "good" he expects and may, indeed, receive. Thus Socrates agreed that every man does seek his own advantage, and that "virtuous" action is action well calculated to this end, and that consequently there can be no unalterable or unchanging rules of conduct, because circumstances, in relation to which conduct must be judged, are in a state of continual flux. He also agreed that tradition carried with it no unquestionable authority, though he thought it entitled to respect, and hence claimed for it much the kind of presumptive authority defined in the preceding chapter. And this brings us to the point where he definitely parted company with the sophists. For he complained that they did not carry their questioning of received beliefs far enough. They appear to have been interested, as a matter of fact, only in justifying what they had to offer. If a young man wanted to succeed, wanted to win influence, and political power, they could teach him how to go about it. But the purpose for which he was to use power, once he had grasped it, was his own affair. It seemed obvious that a man would not covet power for nothing, just as to-day we say a man does not carry on a business for his health's sake.

And, as was just observed, Socrates quite agreed. A man pursues his own advantage. But for that very reason we need

most of all to ask what his advantage really is. Is this the
simple and obvious thing it is supposed to be? The moment
the question is asked one begins to realize that it must be
asked, that men are indeed perpetually deceiving themselves
as to the nature of happiness, and thinking to find it where
it is not, and that goodness or wisdom, accordingly, cannot
after all be defined as a knowledge of the means of grasping
power. Wisdom, however, must be some kind of knowledge;
so that if it does not lie in a knowledge of things, of means,
it must issue from coming to know one's self. Socrates had in
fact been astonished by the declaration of the Delphian oracle, that no man in Athens was wiser than he. Doubtless he
pretended, in his ironical way, to greater astonishment than
he felt; but we need not question his sincerity in asserting
that he did not understand what this could mean, when he
knew himself to be ignorant, and saw on every side men who
appeared to possess useful and even splendid knowledge.
Hence he went about questioning his fellow-citizens concerning their knowledge—with one invariable result, so long as
he continued his interrogations. In every case, he says:

It would soon become apparent that to many people, and
most of all to himself, the man seemed to be wise, whereas in
truth he was not so at all. Thereupon I would try to show him
how he was wise in opinion only and not in reality; but I merely
made myself a nuisance to him and to many of those about him.
So I used to go away reflecting that at least I was wiser than
this man. Neither of us, I would say to myself, knows anything
much worth while, but he in his ignorance thinks he knows,
whereas I neither know nor think I know.[5]

Thus through his unsparing scepticism, or criticism, Socrates learned something of the truth about the inner nature

[5] Socrates wrote nothing. These words are quoted from Plato's *Apology*.
There is excellent reason for believing that Plato's account of Socrates'
trial and last days is substantially accurate. As Mr More has well said,
"It is easier to believe in the power of Nature to create such a character
than in the ability of an author to imagine it." (*Platonism*, p. 4, n. 1.) The
two most recent books I have seen in which this question is considered are
Professor A. E. Taylor's *Socrates*, 1932, and Mr R. Hackforth's *The Com-*

of man, while his contemporaries were, on the whole, content
to study human weaknesses and to devise methods of exploiting them. And what he learned convinced him that in proportion as any man might attain real knowledge of himself,
he must discover a division within his nature, corresponding
to the "body" and "soul" of religious tradition, and accounting for the deceptions which lead men to seek their good
where it is not. For men are continually led on from birth to
death into all their varied activities by a feeling of want
which they hope to satisfy by following the solicitations of
the senses, or of ambition, or of pride; and they make reason
a mere instrument of this passion for absorbing into themselves, as it were, or uniting with themselves, all that attracts
them, or seems good to them; and they find their quest endless and vain, because the satisfaction derived from each successful effort is only momentary, or is mixed with pain, or is
poisoned by fear, arising from the consciousness of insecurity, which is not lessened but heightened by earthly love, by
great possessions or empire, or by glittering fame dependent
on the suffrage of the mob. These are the men wise in opinion
only, who follow after what seems good, and prove to every
one who will stop to examine their lives and characters that

position of Plato's Apology, 1933. Professor Taylor, though he does not consistently write in accordance with his own belief, says (p. 116): "We may be
confident that Plato's version [of Socrates' defence of himself] has reproduced it with close accuracy." And elsewhere (pp. 27–28) he says more
fully: "It is certain that Plato's Apology must have been circulated within
a few years of the trial, and must have been read by many of the actual
judges as well as by many who had been among the audience. A misrepresentation under such conditions would have been suicidal for its author, and
we should infer that the very characteristic 'defence'—in fact, a defiance—
which Plato puts into the mouth of his Master is, in its main features, a
reproduction of what was actually said. So much is, indeed, now admitted
by most of the scholars whose names carry most weight (e.g. Ritter and
Wilamowitz-Moellendorff). But I think, with Burnet, that we are bound in
consistency to go a step further. The same considerations apply with equal
force to the Phaedo." Mr Hackforth believes that Plato invented part of
what he makes Socrates say in answer to his accusers, but that, nevertheless,
"the Socrates of the Apology is true to life" (p. 146). Though there is no
general agreement as to precisely where the line is to be drawn between
Socrates and Plato, I believe the account here given is faithful to what may
safely be regarded as the teaching of Socrates.

they are chasing shadows. And the spectacle caused Socrates to declare roundly that the man who did not examine his own life, so bringing his intelligence to bear first—not upon the acquisition of power to satisfy each impulse as it might arise —but upon the problem created by his own insatiable nature, was not living a *human* life at all. Honest self-questioning, or criticism, experience assured him, would infallibly lead to the discovery that man's sense of want could be satisfied only by participation in real goodness itself—and never by the successful pursuit of ephemeral, imperfect embodiments of what seemed desirable. Such pursuit served its only real purpose if it led a man on—not to mere repetition, which was the road to abject yet restless slavery, and to every enormity of which we are capable as we more and more desperately seek a satisfaction we do not find—it served its purpose only if it led a man on to the discovery of his real want and to knowledge of the real goodness which alone could satisfy him.

Hence Socrates concluded that the happiness men seek is really attainable. But it does not, he showed, consist in the possession and enjoyment of temporal goods, no matter if of every possible kind. It consists in a certain equable and serene condition of inward being, which arises from rationally controlled—as opposed to merely impulsive—activity, directed to the living participation of the individual in goodness itself. And this rationally formed conviction became the foundation of Socrates' life, and withstood its supreme test unshaken when he came to be tried on the trumped-up charges of Meletus. How Socrates lived and how he died has been told once and for all time by Plato, and no summary, or partial quotation, can take the place of that undying record in the pages of the *Apology, Crito,* and *Phaedo.* Yet the picture of this extraordinary man, standing before his five hundred judges, must be recalled. He was seventy years of age. Even those who revered him made a joke of his ugliness, he himself joining in the laughter it caused. There was nothing of the conventional hero about him, and he had no desire to seem other than exactly what he was. He talked to the judges, with his life at stake, precisely as he had talked for many years to all whom he had met, whether in the market-place, or the gymnasium, or the streets of Athens. He tried to tell the plain truth as he knew it, denying nothing, disdaining emotional or rhetorical appeals, giving notice calmly that he would not change his manner of life for any consideration, and, in fine, preferring death to the slightest taint of dishonour. For "you are far from the mark," he said, "if you suppose that a man of any worth in the world ought to reckon on the chances of life and death. Not so; when he acts he has only this one thing to consider—whether he acts righteously or unrighteously, and whether as a good or a bad man." He knew he was different from others, and candidly dwelt upon his excellence, even telling his judges he was concerned to plead his case for their sake rather than his own, lest by condemning him in their ignorance they should throw away a gift from God to the city, the like of which would not soon come to them again. Yet this and more to the same effect he said without effrontery, without seeming to boast, indeed with such evident simple truthfulness, that from his day to ours he has remained the classic embodiment of honesty, fairness, balance, reasonableness, urbanity—of those strictly human virtues which he prized as evidence of inward health. And the wisdom he possessed was, he said, a strictly human wisdom. If he was wiser than others in any one respect it was just in this, that where he had no certain knowledge he pretended to none. "Yet," he declared, "this knowledge I have, and this I know, that it is an evil and shameful thing to do wrong and to disobey our superior, whether human or divine." "Be assured, then," he continued, "that if I am such an one as I said and you put me to death, you will be doing yourselves greater harm than me. Neither Meletus nor Anytus[6] can injure me a whit; there is no power in them to do that; for it is not decreed above that the better man can be injured by the worse. He may inflict death, perhaps, or exile, or civil dishonour; and possibly Meletus and his guild reckon these things to be great calamities; but I for my

6 Anytus and Lycon assisted Meletus in preferring charges against Socrates.

part deem it a far greater calamity to plot unrighteously against a man's life as Meletus is now doing."

I dwell upon the manner in which Socrates endured martyrdom for the sake of honour and freedom—he could undoubtedly have purchased his life with the sacrifice of either —because the man is inseparable from his philosophy, and also because these intangible good things which he held to be more real than any tangible possessions, and more valuable than life, are strictly human and personal in their manifestations within the field of our experience. Hence we can now see clearly this crucial point of difference, with which alone I am at present concerned, between the wisdom of the East and the wisdom of the West. To Buddha, humanity was suspended between a world of illusion and a world of blissful reality; and to secure deliverance from the pain of ceaseless conflict between these two realms within his own person, man was called on to turn away utterly from the world of illusion —this present sensible world, and his own earthly person as a part thereof. More than this, Buddha conceived that illusion obtains its hold upon man by reason of that feeling of want which motivates all human activities, and consequently he centred his attack directly upon it. Desire itself was to be stifled, nay, rooted out, and with its extirpation would disappear loneliness and dread and suffering and all the ills that flesh is heir to, while that which is real in man would be set free in an eternity of inexpressible bliss—in that nirvana which can only be described as a negation of all we know at present from sensible experience.

Now the more we learn to what extent the East and the West have been united in a common perception of the battle-field of life as lying within—the real enemy of man being not his fellow-man, nor the elements, nor anything save only his own inner deficiency, his own baser self—and the more fully we see how identical virtues consequently came to be prized, the more are we struck by the fundamental dissimilarity here under discussion. For the deliverance proposed by Buddhism, no matter what else it is, is self-annihilation, while that proposed by Socrates is self-fulfilment. To Buddha the very sense of personal identity was the last stronghold of illusion and of all misery, whereas to Socrates the soul, or real self, was the ground of hope, its welfare the one true object of endeavour, and obedience to it our one means of piercing through illusion. To Buddha the good way of life was one of complete self-denial, as we have said, and as we can see it must have been; but to Socrates the good way was one of careful tendance of the self, and earthly life not an evil to be shunned but an opportunity of learning through experience, and so of attaining self-command, and thus through right-eous life strengthening the soul and rendering it fit to partici-pate fully in that real goodness which, he was sure, was the eternal, unchanging, one object of its desire. To Socrates, consequently, renunciation was called for only as it is de-manded of all of us, howsoever we may live, simply because we are limited creatures, with small time and small strength at our disposal, able to attend only to one thing at any given moment, and formed, for better, for worse, by that to which we do give our attention. No man can make riches the great object of his life without renouncing whatever would hinder him in that pursuit, and every man in every generation has found that he must similarly pay a price in return for any positive accomplishment. Therefore, though renunciations were demanded of anyone who would follow Socrates, any-thing properly to be called asceticism was not, and, on the contrary, stood unmistakably condemned.

Socrates, however, did not promise those who might fol-low him any reward save only the satisfaction of becoming wise and righteous men. It is impossible for us—impossible for me, at any rate—to see how the Buddhist paradise can appear other than an empty consummation to those who must literally deny their conscious selves in order to gain it. We know that, in fact, to very many Buddhists it has not seemed empty; and we can at least see, whatever we may feel about its character, that Buddhism does set up before its converts a transcendental goal. But Socrates expressly did not. There is ample evidence to show that privately, as one may say, he looked forward to personal immortality with a lively faith; but he did not pretend to have any knowledge

of the matter, and he seems to have felt that it had no bearing on the conduct of earthly life. Here, moreover, we are at
the very centre of the ground on which Socratic teaching—
like Buddhism, yet without Buddhism's fatal program of
self-annihilation—could make a strong appeal to the modern
mind. For Socrates in effect accepted something very like
our modern conception of the order of nature, though in
faithfulness to his scepticism he refused to affirm dogmatically that nothing in the way of real evidence concerning a
possible supernatural order could ever be afforded by legend-
ary tales of divine intervention in human affairs, or of other
miraculous happenings. The consequence was that while he
adopted a respectful attitude towards religious mythology,
he disregarded the claim that it was or could be knowledge
or a means to knowledge; yet simultaneously he rejected the
claims of naturalism—but did so for a reason which any
honest man of science or philosopher was bound to respect.
He appealed simply to actual experience, as affording unambiguous evidence in support of the interpretation of life
which he advanced. And in doing so it was a vital part of his
work to distinguish scrupulously between what could be
called knowledge and anything which might more properly
be called faith, or rational belief, or mere hope. He had his
own serene faith, and he wished to instil it into others;—yet
not by any appeal to authority, or tradition, or alleged supernatural sanction, but only by rational argument from
undisputed experience.

III

It should now be clear to what extent the teaching of Socrates was the inspiration of Mr More's dualism—and equally
of the identical, though less flexible, dualism of Mr More's
closest and oldest friend, Professor Babbitt. It should also be
clear why Professor Babbitt, with complete faithfulness to
the explicit intention of Socrates, has claimed the word "humanism" as the best descriptive name for his philosophy.
And with this Socratic dualism, powerfully used in a very

un-Socratic manner, Professor Babbitt has remained seemingly content.[7] Dualism has, moreover, in the hands of both of its proponents, established itself as an instrument of incontestably sound criticism, arousing anger in various quarters only because the sound criticism of literature and life never has been and never will be popular criticism, and because, short of wrathful misrepresentation, it has been unanswerable. The stupid and angry reaction of a certain part of the populace, in the face of home-truths, has been proved to be little different substantially in our time from the same phenomenon in the age of Socrates—and for the same reason. Socrates, addressing his judges after they had condemned him, told them plainly that they had agreed to put him out of the way because he spoke the truth about them, and because they hoped thus to escape the burden of accounting for their lives.[8] And this—the effort to shirk responsibility—is behind the excited, not to say wild, opposition which has dogged Professor Babbitt and Mr More, as it is likewise the canker perpetually eating at the heart of civilization, and an evil which has grown in the modern age like some malignant disease. I would not dream of saying there are no reasons, in the vast numbers and intricate organization of our modern societies, jerry-built by pusillanimous tradesmen, which explain the ominous growth of irresponsibility; but many hu-

[7] I add the word "seemingly" with some hesitation, but because of a belief that Professor Babbitt has found a congenial resource and support in Buddhism. He is, as he himself has admitted, an individualist to the core, and I do not mean to suggest that he has ever relaxed his jealous independence. I cannot help feeling, however, that he might have held less tenaciously to a very difficult position had he not looked, perhaps with imperfect understanding, to Buddhism as an example of the manner in which the religious implications of his dualism could be satisfied without any taint of doubtful supernaturalism.

[8] I will reproduce the passage as it stands in the *Apology*: "You have committed this crime, thinking to shake off the burden of accounting for your lives; but the result, I tell you now, will be quite the contrary. There are many who will call you to account—men whom I have restrained and whom you have never suspected; younger men who will attack you more savagely and cause you still greater annoyance. You are wide of the mark if you hope by executions to silence all censures of your evil conduct. That way of escape is neither very effective nor very honourable. But there is another way easier and far more noble: do not crush others, but look to the bettering of your own lives." (Here and elsewhere I quote from Mr More's translation of the *Apology, Shelburne Essays,* Sixth Series.)

man phenomena can be explained which nothing can justify, and a malignant disease is no less an evil for being understood, and is no less to be attacked. Hence to say that a man has boldly struck at the irresponsible elements in our society, and at the forces making for their growth, as Professor Babbitt and Mr More have struck at them, is the most honourable thing that can be said of any man who plays any part in our affairs.

Nevertheless, aside from misrepresentation and misunderstanding, there have been persistent complaints against dualism as a philosophy, on the ground that it is seriously incomplete. In ancient Greece this feeling received striking illustration in the course taken by philosophic endeavour after the time of Socrates. Every student of Greek thought is aware that Socrates marks a fateful turning-point in its development, that he concentrated attention upon man and the good way of life for man as "the proper study of mankind," and that subsequently this remained the predominating concern of thinkers until the advent of Christianity, which, of course, as it spread, was accepted as the final answer to the question. And Mr More has clearly shown, in *Platonism, The Religion of Plato*, and *Hellenistic Philosophies*, how Socrates not only marked a turning-point, but gave those who came after him the primary substance so variously and conflictingly elaborated by Cyrenaics, Epicureans, Cynics, Stoics, Sceptics, and Neo-Platonists. These schools, as Mr More says, "are all imperfectly Socratic in the sense that they each laid hold of certain of the Socratic theses to the exclusion of others, while they all aimed at the one common end" which Socrates had in view—the development of self-sufficiency, or of independence of external circumstances, through inward possession of, or union with, real goodness.[9] Of those who were directly or indirectly inspired by Socrates, Plato alone, in his dualism, developed the true philosophy of his great teacher; but even Plato was not content to leave Socratic dualism as he found it, nor was he always, through the whole course of his restless intellectual life, content with dualism itself, making more than one effort to resolve it into unity.

[9] *Hellenistic Philosophies*, pp. 374-375.

This is a fact of the utmost significance. It means that though the work of Socrates was of really unparalleled importance in the ancient world, still, it was essentially transitional in character, so that wherever his philosophy was even partially accepted it served as a groundwork of invaluable criticism, as a stimulus, as a vital directive influence, but never as a possible resting-place for the mind and spirit of man. And this is the conclusion which, in our own time, Mr More has reached, after much experience and reflection. Doubtless, as we say, history never repeats itself; and certainly there is very much to distinguish the time of Socrates from our modern age; yet the more one studies, not superficial appearances, but the real situation of the two ages as reflected in science, religion, and philosophy, and their interrelations, the more one is struck by a close, indeed extraordinary, resemblance. And the sceptical criticism of Socrates, so imperatively demanded in his time, has been even more needed in our day, for essentially the same reasons. Matthew Arnold used to complain against the "licence of affirmation" of which Christians had been guilty, and feared that they had themselves doomed their religion, not only because they had based it upon presumed facts which the progress of knowledge had shown to be not facts at all, but also because they had pretended to an exact knowledge of the divine nature, and of God's relations with humanity, and of the eternal life of the soul, which we do not really have and cannot have. And Arnold was quite right in his complaint; but "licence of affirmation" is a sin of which men have so constantly been guilty—men of all kinds, in our time no less than in the past, basing themselves on scientific knowledge as well as on mere passionate wilfulness or blind hope—that we are absolutely bound to regard it as the expression of something inherent in human nature, of a need which must somehow be satisfied. Affirmation, or, in other words, assent to some positive belief concerning the nature of life and human destiny, seems to be a fundamental condition of human existence;—and agnosticism, the genuine suspension of belief, seems to be, correspondingly, a sheer impossibility. For Huxley, who is responsible for the word, agnosticism was what might be called a talking-point, and it perhaps helped to conceal from him the extent of his own indulgence in the licence of dogmatic affirmation; but beyond that disservice there is not the slightest evidence to show that it represents anything real.

Yet, as was just said, Arnold was in the right of it in complaining against our "licence of affirmation." It is the source of untold evil. In every age of the world it has sanctified delusion and stifled free inquiry. As the very spirit of dogmatism it is the inveterate and implacable enemy of intelligence. It must be fought, and sceptical criticism is our one weapon against it. But scepticism can only play the part which was defined at the outset of this book. We cannot stop with it; we cannot evade the responsibility of reaching positive conclusions, the best we are capable of, even though we know they must fall short of absolute finality and will some day imperatively demand revision. And this responsibility Socratic dualism in a sense fulfilled. Socrates, as we have seen, by no means stopped with scepticism, but went on to lay the foundations of an analysis of human nature which accounts for the facts as does no other advanced before or since, and from this developed a positive and comprehensive rule of life, or law for man, as opposed to the law for things. The very need, however, which he sought to meet, imposed on him the necessity of distinguishing most carefully between knowledge and opinion, or belief, or faith; and, what is more, he felt assured that his positive conclusions needed no support other than that afforded by actual knowledge, or that they were completely demonstrable.

This, it seems to me, is the crux of the matter. I have sought to show in the preceding chapter how faithful to experience, to all of the real factors to be accounted for, dualism is. Nevertheless, the facts thus interpreted not only involve acceptance of a paradox before which reason is brought to a stand, but also point unmistakably to a world of immaterial reality, eternal life in which is the goal we are to aim at during the period of our earthly existence. Hence it is that dualism is really inseparable from religion. It definitely implies a plain and unambiguous religious faith, and really— to repeat the phrase I have already used more than once—

makes sense of life only if that faith is justified. Consequently, to present the dualistic philosophy without supernatural reference, as if the deliverance from evil to which it
opens the way might be fully achieved, and perfect happiness
enjoyed, during man's present earthly life, is to go counter
to well-nigh universal testimony from the days of Job and
indeed from the beginnings of history until this present moment. And even were this not so, the mere fact of man's mortality would be sufficient, for beings capable of looking before
and after, to render all talk of perfect happiness on earth an
idle vanity. There are, I am aware, buzzing creatures who
have a different notion, who tell us that everything "natural"
is lovely, that death is as natural as life, and, presumably,
that therefore a dead man is as happy in the processes of dissolution as a living man in the processes of life. But in an age
such as ours we may expect every kind of notion to be advanced, as Professor Whitehead has warned us, and as we can
see from certain of his own writings, which nobody professes
to understand. For several excellent reasons, we may regard
anything coming from Professor Whitehead with respect,
being sure, for example, of finding in all his work gleams of
true wisdom; but we are not called upon to pay serious heed
to any crack-brained enthusiast who imagines that felicity
"must" result from the development of an attitude of co-
operation with "the system of things." We know, on the contrary, if we know anything at all, that the law of life is a law
of conflict aimed at mastery for the satisfaction of the organism's needs, and that the whole story of developing civilization is a story of successful interference with "the system
of things."

And the facts of observation, which only the dualistic
philosophy can account for completely, suggest with a plain-
ness beyond mistake that man's life is a search for a happiness which cannot be fully attained on earth. Again and
again within history, moreover, in proportion as men capable
of learning from experience have grown disillusioned, yet not
utterly defeated, they have begun to perceive that the human
law, the law for man as opposed to the law for beast, is one of
conflict, not against others, and not against things, but

against a man's own self. The law of human life, in other
words, as I have earlier said, is one of effort directed towards
the remaking of one's self, or the fulfilment of one's better
self—but to what end? This is the all-important question,
and there is only one answer: to the end that we may enjoy
perfect, therefore eternal, happiness in complete union with
goodness itself, and truth itself, and beauty itself, in the unchanging world of immaterial reality. How this may be, what
this would actually mean, we cannot, alas, know. There sur-
vive from the past many attempts to picture the things of
eternity in the guise of the things of time and space—and
they are all, to tell the truth, if we take them literally, more
or less ridiculous. But they have, again and again, been taken
literally, only to become incredible and empty with the passage of time, with changing circumstances, and with the
growth of scientific knowledge. Thus not only has the medieval Christian heaven disappeared with the progress of as-
tronomy, not only has the heavenly life pictured by Milton
seemed anything but felicitous to Taine and to many another; thus too the gods have one after another become incredible, and their trappings of divinity a subject for scoffing
laughter.

It was this outworn husk of Christianity—its story of
creation, its miracles and the rest, once appropriate, convincing, and a resource, but now become a grievous burden
and a standing invitation to disbelief—this it was, we have
seen, which drove away Paul More when a young man. And
he had at hand abundant evidence from the accumulated
stores of history to show how inevitably a symbolic mythology
becomes confounded with the reality it is intended to shadow
forth, and how consequently religious belief itself, instead of
developing with the prolonged experience and growing scientific knowledge of men, becomes discredited and is abandoned.
Hence we can understand, and indeed heartily second, his
resolve to follow the example of Socrates, to study men, to
try to make sense of life as it is here and now, without re-
liance upon anything beyond the bounds of present experience, to confine himself to what we can really know, to avoid
metaphysics and all other ambitious pretence to more than

human knowledge, and to indulge as little as might be in abstract generalization, allowing men themselves, when interrogated critically, to show forth the substance and meaning and worth of our humanity.

Substantially this was accomplished in the *Shelburne Essays,* and the trouble with it, as Mr More came gradually to realize, was on the whole similar to the difficulty anciently felt over the teaching of Socrates. It was not enough. The religious faith so plainly and deeply implicated in dualism should be, in fact must be, set forth positively. Mr More was now no less concerned than in the beginning to avoid "licence of affirmation." He remained as anxious as ever to distinguish knowledge from faith, and to repudiate any faith or belief contradicted by our knowledge or arising simply from the wish to believe. But he himself, like Socrates, like Plato, actually had the faith implicated in dualism. It rested upon a basis of certitude which had been the inspiration of all his work; and experience had taught him that it was—not a leap into darkness—but the indispensable *completion* of knowledge. It was impossible, moreover, after all these centuries, not to recognize that Socrates' happy confidence in man's reasonableness, and in the certain outcome of free discussion, was by no means justified. We keep supposing that all men are like ourselves. Socrates was plainly aware of that which differentiated him from others, yet still believed, even when his wisdom had brought upon him a sentence of death, that the mere force of free and reasonable discussion would suffice to wean men from delusion and to put them in the way of learning for themselves the truth he had learned.

But, in fact, the average human being is not reasonable, and an appeal to reason is one of the last things he can learn to appreciate. You can more successfully appeal to his imagination, to his feelings, and, of course, to his senses. And it was shown in the last chapter that without an initial act of sheer faith a man cannot come to learn anything at all, and that to learn much we need every possible kind of help from our fellows, and must perforce acknowledge the authority of masters from whom alone aid can come. Faith, in other words, is inseparable from life; and its place in life grows, not smaller, but greater, as man becomes more civilized, and learns more about his relation to his environment, and organizes larger and larger communities. To contrast faith and knowledge, as if the latter could ever displace the former, or as if we should labour to increase knowledge in order to discredit and banish faith, is hopelessly to misunderstand both. And so too with authority; it is absurdly and often said that men in the modern age have completely repudiated all authority, that they will accept nothing on trust, or because they are told to, or without full evidence, and that this unprecedented freedom from bondage is at once the sign and seal of the progress of humanity. But men to-day are, in fact, more dependent upon authority than their fathers were in any earlier age; and bare existence would be impossible within forty-eight hours in any of our large cities if men really began acting as their unscrupulous flatterers pretend they act. What is taking place to-day is that men are accepting blindly any authority clothed in the garb of "science," and cherishing an empty faith in "progress" or mere expansion. To invite men to repudiate authority is really to hand them over, ignorant and unaware, to the next authority able plausibly to disguise itself or otherwise to recommend itself by popular promises. In the field of politics we have had in recent years illustrations of this process convincing enough to dishearten and sicken everyone who cares even lightly for the welfare of mankind. Yet too often those who protest most loudly against Fascism in Italy and Hitlerism in Germany are the warmest friends and defenders of the much more cruel, ruthless, and bloody dictators of Russia.

What is wanted, of course, is a crusade, not against faith and authority, but against empty unfounded faith, against stubborn prejudice or wilfulness disguised as faith, and against merely arbitrary authority. This is one of the unending tasks of criticism. And it can only prosper in so far as the critic understands, and constantly helps his readers to understand, the true and necessary place of faith in life, and of authority; and in so far as we come to understand what knowledge is, and what its limitations are, and its kinds. These questions were all discussed in the last chapter, so that we may go on at once to observe that it was a largely practical problem with which Mr More was faced—the problem of assent. There are, of course, all degrees of assent, and many ways of obtaining it, some of which have above been mentioned or alluded to. But Mr More was interested only in real and full assent, which cannot be obtained by force, or deception, or "suggestion." His has at no time been a practical problem, then, in a sense with which we are but too familiar, from the practices of dictators and advertisers. What he desired has been finely expressed by Benjamin Whichcote, in a sentence deserving of remembrance: "That which doth not proceed from the judgement of the mind, and the choice of the will, is not an *human* act, though the act of a man."[10] Mr More had come to realize, however, that though real and full assent is of necessity something voluntary, individual, and, so to say, private, still, the method of bringing a man to the point where it is possible for him to make his own intelligent decision must vary both with varying men and, no less, with varying questions which men have to resolve. Thus it comes to the same thing whether one says, as I have said above, that Socrates had an undue confidence in the reasonableness of men, or that he had an unwarranted confidence in reason itself. All kinds of men may *become* reasonable, given a sufficient stimulus, within whatever limited field they may acquire some real knowledge, and so attain standards which can be used critically. But, as Socrates himself discovered, this does not mean that a carpenter, reasonable, "virtuous," and wise within the field of his competence, can be argued thence into self-knowledge, or from self-knowledge can discover unaided the faith which is its completion, and in whose light self-knowledge may become fruitful.

Things with us are not, unfortunately, so simple as this. The interaction of faith and scepticism in the field of human knowledge is not essentially different from the same process in the field of scientific knowledge. But men do not pursue any kind of inquiry without motive; and while motives for acquiring scientific knowledge, both of things and of ways

10 This is quoted by Mr More in "With the Wits" (*Shelburne Essays, Tenth Series*), p. 304.

of *using* men, are exceedingly prominent and strong in well-nigh every person, those for attaining self-knowledge are not. The latter usually require awakening, by experience and reflection upon experience, and very often the discontent in which they express themselves even then remains fumbling or blind, unless there is aid at hand, to afford wise direction. It is, moreover, incalculably important that men should be enabled, as far as possible, to anticipate the slow, painful lessons of experience; and the uses of civilization are largely summed up in its available accumulations—before which, however, the unaided individual would stand as helpless and confused as an Australian aboriginal suddenly transported to Times Square or to Piccadilly Circus. On this account education grows more and more elaborate, and absorbs more and more time, thought, and energy, as civilization grows older and more complex. I need scarcely remind the reader that it does not, however, constantly become more successful; and indeed the very causes which drove Mr More away from Christianity have been powerfully instrumental in turning the attention of men more and more exclusively outward, and in giving them the notion, inspired by uncritical, superstitious faith in "science," that a "science of humanity" is being born as a consequence of the united generative efforts of biologists, sociologists, economists, political scientists, psychologists, and anthropologists. No one would wish to seem ungrateful for these gallant efforts, which certainly have their usefulness; but we know definitely and finally, from evidence canvassed in the present volume, that they cannot take the place of human knowledge, and that there is not the slightest possibility of creating a "science of humanity."

Hence it is not an exaggeration to say that the whole trend of our education at present is calculated to promote ignorance of that which most concerns us. And it was, one may judge from the Preface to the first edition of *Platonism*, Mr More's keen sense of the magnitude of this calamity which brought him to a realization of man's abiding need for an active, organized centre, for a society or church, devoted to the faith implicit in dualism and employing every possible means, by appeals directed through the senses, the feelings, and the imagination, to awaken us from our fevered dreams of outward conquest.[11] I do not believe Mr More was at this time any nearer Christianity than he had been since early youth. But he was forced to recognize as he grew older that the cause he stood for needed organization on a positive basis, no less than any other cause in whose success men have, or can be made to believe they have, an interest, and perhaps even more urgently than any other cause, on account of the implacable, ruthless nature of the opposed spirit of worldliness, with its universal appeal to the inexperienced, the immature, the slothful, and the dull-witted, and its myriad disguises and traps for capturing and enslaving them. This was tantamount to a recognition that the manner in which, historically, religious faith has always assumed institutional form was no accident, no result of temporary or special conditions, but a development necessary to the life of faith. The reasons might be strictly practical, but, in any case, the facts simply corresponded with all that we have learned concerning man's nature, at once social and individual, dependent and independent, formed only through submission and discipline and only thus winning freedom and becoming capable of judgement. And to realize this was also to realize that one's own faith imperatively demanded something more than

[11] Inasmuch as only the last sentence of the passage to which I refer appears in the Preface to the current (third) edition of *Platonism,* I reproduce it here: "I know that the current of thought to-day runs against me and not with me. . . . My hope would be with those who are still searching —particularly if I might touch the minds of a few of our generous college youth who, finding the intellectual life deprived of centre or significance, drift through the supposedly utilitarian courses of economics and biology, and so enter the world with no better preparation against its distractions than a vague and soon-spent yearning for social service and a benumbing trust in mechanical progress. I can foresee no restoration of humane studies to their lost position of leadership until they are felt once more to radiate from some central spiritual truth. I do not believe that the aesthetic charms of literature can supply this want, nor is it clear to me that a purely scientific analysis of the facts of moral experience can furnish the needed motive; the former is too apt to run into dilettantism, and the latter appeals too little to the imagination and the springs of enthusiasm. Only through the centralizing force of religious faith or through its equivalent in philosophy can the intellectual life regain its meaning and authority for earnest men." (It will be noticed that I have quoted a part of the last sentence earlier in the present chapter.)

the author of the *Shelburne Essays* had given. It demanded, in other words, either public adherence to Christianity, as the faith's authoritative guardian in the Western world, or, if that was impossible, a loyal effort to build up a society capable of performing the offices which Christianity was no longer fitted to perform.

The Greek Tradition is Mr More's answer to this demand. And evidently what he at first aimed at was a critical restatement of the dualism implicit and explicit in the Platonic dialogues, because this was, he believed, the primal and still unique and inexhaustible source of all that is philosophically true in Christianity. Hence on this basis he hoped to disentangle and so to give aid in saving what is genuine and valid in Christian belief, while relieving the faith of its burden of falsehood, the consequence simply of deficient natural knowledge in a long past age and of that "licence of affirmation" of which something has been said above. He hoped also, by examining and making clear their real relationship to Plato, to show that the metaphysical speculations of Plotinus and Aristotle—both of whom exerted at different times the strongest possible influence on the development of Christianity—were not fulfilments, but perversions of Platonism. Thus his design was to bring about a renewal of faith in the Platonic world of immaterial or spiritual reality, on the ground that this faith alone answers to our direct knowledge of human nature and life, summed up in the dualistic philosophy, and that it completes our knowledge in a manner open to none of the decisive objections felt to orthodox, historical Christianity.

Obviously this design indicates a change, of the kind I have sought to define in the preceding pages, from the position, reflected in the *Shelburne Essays*, which Mr More took in earlier life; yet it is a change which can only be described as a *completion* of his earlier thought. In a word, he was now convinced that the faith implicated in dualism is by no means necessarily, or even usually, summoned forth through the mere attainment of human knowledge, that religious faith cannot be trusted to take care of itself, any more than any other valuable element in our lives, that an undefined faith is in practice impossible—a mere standing invitation to charlatans, fanatics, and people with axes to grind—and that "independent faith" is inconsistent with our responsibilities as social beings, and almost certainly indicative of a condemnable pride. It is equally obvious, however, that Mr More at this time still felt unable to identify himself with any existing religion, and that he thought an "equivalent" of religion, more suitable to our present intellectual situation, could be found in philosophy.

IV

IN *Platonism* Mr More proceeded to set forth the philosophy in question. He prefixed to the first edition an acknowledgement that the book gave a very incomplete account of Plato's thought, explaining that its scope was controlled by his special purpose, which was to write, not an historical work, but "what a Greek Platonist would have called a *Protrepticus*, an invitation, that is, to the practice of philosophy." Nevertheless, the invitation was to be Plato's, so that, as he said, "historical accuracy must be the first requisite." Now there was nothing necessarily inconsistent between this aim and this requirement, nor would their conjunction have invited comment, had not Mr More failed, unhappily, to make a necessary distinction demanded by his program. For his purpose, as he was fully aware, was strictly critical, yet he went about its execution in a manner suggesting that it was simply historical. He had certain reasons; but these were, I conceive, mixed, and some of them likely rather to cloud than to clear the mind. He felt, of course, a debt to Plato, which he wished fully to acknowledge. And what is more, he felt anxious to show that his own philosophy was deeply rooted in the past, was supported by a formidable weight of testimony, and was true, not merely to the ephemeral circumstances of our own time, but to constant elements in the experience of the race, long since perceived and made the basis of enduring constructive thought. In this, I think, he should have his readers' sympathy; and he deserves their gratitude for the light he has certainly shed on Plato, however inadequate, or

even misleading, his *Platonism* may be from the purely historical point of view.

Coleridge once remarked of the Cambridge Platonists of
the seventeenth century that they should really be called
Plotinists. He was, of course, right, but his remark would
have been equally appropriate to the great majority of so-
called Platonists from ancient times to ours. From Plotinus,
and indeed from Aristotle, to the tribe of modern German
philologers and to the English Hegelians of the nineteenth
century and to Dean Inge, the usual opinion has been that
Plato was a struggling pioneer, endeavouring with imperfect
success to construct a system of idealistic metaphysics. Dean
Inge has given typical expression to this opinion, and simultaneously has shown how it straightway carries us beyond
Plato:

The great constructive effort of Neoplatonism [he writes],
in which the speculations of seven hundred years are summed
up, and after which the longest period of unimpeded thinking
which the human race has yet been permitted to enjoy soon
reached its end, is of very great importance in the history both
of philosophy and of theology. Historically, this is what Platonism came to be; this is the point at which it reached its full
growth—its τέλος or φύσις, as Aristotle would say, and then
stopped. The Neoplatonic philosophy underwent no further
development of importance after Plotinus, but it absorbed into
itself most of the rival theories which had flourished alongside
of it, so that it seemed to later students to have unified Plato
and Aristotle, and the Stoics to boot. But its later history, from
an earlier date than the closing of the Athenian schools of philosophy by Justinian in 529, must be sought not among the
crumbling ruins of Hellenism, but within the Christian Church.
If it be true, as Eunapius said, that "the fire still burns on the
altars of Plotinus," it is because Christian theology became
Neoplatonic. This involved no violent changes.[12]

The most celebrated and familiar testimony to the accuracy of Dean Inge's final statement is that of St Augustine,

[12] *The Philosophy of Plotinus,* 3rd ed., 1929, Vol. I, pp. 10–11.

in his *Confessions,* where he tells how he had learned from the
Neoplatonists, before his conversion, the whole sum of Christian doctrine, the historical incarnation of our Lord in Jesus
Christ alone excepted.[13] But it is precisely this development
of Platonism, important and influential from ancient times
to the present day, which Mr More has sought to discredit.
And thus he has performed an invaluable service; for I think
Mr More has conclusively shown that Plato really was a
thorough-going dualist, and that, just because of his persistent dualism, he was never able to enter the promised land
of idealistic monism. It has been the well-nigh universal fashion, however, to regard this failure as a crucial defect, which
Aristotle, Plotinus, and many others, each in his own way,
have endeavoured to repair; whereas Mr More boldly stig-
matizes all these efforts as perversions of true Platonism, and
sees in Plato's failure to "transcend" dualism his real claim
to greatness and his enduring significance. Herein, it seems
to me, Mr More has shown a critical power not short of
genius, and has produced the most useful commentary on his
author that has been written in modern times. With the sure
grasp of the master, he gathers, marshals, and integrates the
evidence showing the nature, development, and meaning of
Plato's dualism; and thus lays bare the steady drive of ordered thought and feeling which holds the dialogues together
and gives them an undying power and value so great as to
leave Plato still unequalled, still unrivalled, still an unique
source of human wisdom.

This is a brilliant achievement, at once the most difficult
undertaking and the most successful amongst all Mr More's
critical essays. But it is *criticism,* and it will be misunderstood and misjudged whenever it is read as though it were
anything else. Plato was not in fact less subject to the common limitations of humanity than are we. There is a quantity
of perishable matter in his dialogues, significant of the time
and the place of their composition, but now only a hindrance
to those who would learn from him what he still has to teach.
On occasion, too, he could be as wrong-headed, as careless,
and even, some would insist, as wilful as any of ourselves.

13 Bk VII, especially Chaps ix, xx, and xxi.

His work, moreover, like ours to-day, was cut out for him by
his predecessors, and no one familiar with the history of
Greek thought should be surprised by the fact that his conscious aims were not different from those of Thales, or Heracleitus, or Parmenides, or Anaxagoras. His problem was different from theirs because he came after them and others,
after Pythagoras, and above all after Socrates; but his aim
was bequeathed him, and was simply to describe the absolutely Real in such terms as to account for all observed phenomena, in all their aspects and relations; and he never
doubted the fitness of human reason for this task. The scepticism of Socrates, though genuine enough, had been merely
implicit, expressing itself in a form of abstinence; and Plato,
as I have earlier said, was closer to mankind than his teacher,
in being unable to content himself with the Socratic profession of ignorance. What he learned from Socrates, consequently, sharpened his critical powers and, it may be supposed, opened his eyes to the opposition between materialism
and the spiritual nature of man, and indelibly impressed
upon him the necessity of reconstructing, by rational demonstration, the spiritual view of reality which hitherto had depended on the sanction of tradition. But in this Plato was
not conscious of bringing to light an issue between monism
and dualism, nor did the full meaning and importance of this
issue become clear until modern times. Plato, in fact, was a
dualist only in spite of himself, and, so far as conscious intention and effort went, was on the side of rationalism and of
absolute, idealistic monism.

Mr More understands this as well as anyone else, and in
Platonism he has not ignored it. But he has persuaded himself that Plato was "really" a dualist, that since he wrote one
thing at one time he "could not" have meant something different at some other time, that occasionally he lost his way
or forgot what he was doing, that in old age he wandered into
speculations "for which enigmatic is a mild word," and that
consequently the ordered exposition of doctrine in *Platonism*
is the result of nothing other than historical fidelity.[14] For

14 See especially pp. 305 and 234 of *Platonism* (3rd ed., 1931). It may be
noted here that though this edition contains a new Preface, its text is iden-

this kind of self-deception there was a special reason, besides those already mentioned. Mr More realized that in this book he was setting forth his own dualistic philosophy, implicit throughout the *Shelburne Essays*, but not hitherto given systematic form save briefly and more tentatively in the "Definitions of Dualism," cited in my preceding chapter. In the Preface to the first edition of *Platonism* he wrote:

To one criticism I should be sensitive. Those who have read the eighth volume of my *Shelburne Essays* will recognize that the present work is virtually an expansion of the views there summed up in the "Definitions of Dualism," and they may think that I have tried to impose my own theories on Plato, to measure him in my pint cup. In a way every interpreter of a great author must be open to such a charge; he has no other measure than his own capacity. But at least I am not guilty of attempting to force Plato into conformity with a preconceived system; the "Definitions of Dualism" were themselves the result of my study of the Dialogues, and avowedly rejected any pretensions to originality.

Mr More, in other words, very properly wanted to make clear the full extent of his indebtedness to Plato, and here took steps to guard against a misunderstanding all the more likely because of the novel character of his interpretation. But at the same time he desired something further. He had come to the conclusion, as we have seen, that the "spirit of liberation" raised up by Plato was the strongest force, not only in the early development of Christianity, but in various modern movements, religious, philosophical, and literary; and he now wanted to brand, and discredit, these movements as "perversions of Plato's doctrine." Thus he was allowing himself to be drawn into the position of resting his case on

tical with that of the second (1926), when it was thoroughly revised. About 135 alterations were then made, chiefly in the interest of clarity. In the Preface to this edition Mr More expressly stated that he had not attempted to bring the book into conformity with his later conclusions. It was, he thought, "less confusing and more honest" to allow the work to stand substantially "as it was originally conceived."

Plato—of appealing to Plato, when "correctly" interpreted, as a final authority.

Evil consequences were bound to issue from this false step, and not the least of them was its effect on Mr More himself, who has since tended on more than one occasion to appeal to Plato rather than to experience, and so to evade certain inconvenient questions concerning authority and assent. In addition, by this step he has seemed, at least, to justify an old and often repeated charge—that he merely wishes to turn back the clock. No wish, of course, could be more vain, and were it really his, there could be no serious reason for further discussion of *The Greek Tradition*. In fact, however, Mr More does not propose to the modern world a return to Plato any more than he would propose a return to Greek dress, or to Greek slave-labour, or to Greek methods of lighting, heating, and sanitation; and the difficulty we have encountered, though it is real enough to necessitate warning and explanation, is rather one of appearances and of method than anything else. For in substance *Platonism* is exactly what it appears not to be, and exactly what its author's true purpose demanded.

In substance, *Platonism* is a clear-sighted, rigorous, and extraordinarily successful attempt to distinguish what is ephemeral in Plato, concerning human nature, the conduct of life, and man's ultimate goal, from that which, so far as we can yet see, is perennially true to experience. The book is, then, as I have been concerned to insist, a critical review of the Dialogues, in which, with sure discrimination and great constructive skill, Mr More brings together and arranges what Plato, better than anyone who has come after him, still can teach us. The general character of the dualism which thus emerges has been sufficiently indicated, for our purpose, in the third chapter of the present book. What we are now concerned to notice is the manner in which the transcendental or religious implications of dualism took form under Plato's hands. Doubtless the curious fact will have been observed, in what is said above concerning the teaching of Socrates, that he met the central issue raised between himself and the sophists by a mere affirmation. It was positive enough in all conscience, and unqualified; nevertheless, in answer to whatever plausible reasons advanced for regarding man as the measure of all things, Socrates merely affirmed that, on the contrary, by honour and truth and goodness man is measured. He did not profess to know how or why it is so—he simply *knew* that the just and good man is happy, and that the evil and unjust man is miserable. By this conviction he lived, and for it he died. And those who were closest to him knew, as Mr More says, that in his death no less than in his life,

What all the world desired, yet threw away, he had. For, however we may calculate the sum of pleasures and pains in such an existence as that of Socrates, the records, if words have any meaning, leave us in no uncertainty as to his happiness. At the end of the account of his last day in gaol the reporter of the scene declares that to his friends he seemed in death the best and wisest and most just of all men they had known. To these epithets the reporter might well have added "the happiest." That, indeed, is the strongest and most enduring impression we get of the man, his peculiar testimony to the reality of the spirit and to the value of philosophy—his happiness.

And elsewhere Mr More adds that no reasoning can be strong enough to persuade us that the life of Socrates was based on a delusion.[15] Certainly this was the position taken by Plato himself, and is that taken by many another in modern as in ancient times. No one, indeed, has ever doubted the depth and strength of the impression received by Plato from Socrates, or has thought it other than just and inevitable, and therein lies the problem which Plato exerted all his powers to resolve: How could the faith so uncompromisingly affirmed by his Master be rationally demonstrated, or explained, or even defended?

Now Socrates had had, beyond his own felt happiness, a certain mysterious ground of assurance that he was—shall we say?—on the right track. He had possessed a Spirit, or inner Voice, which never bade him do anything, but which, on

15 *The Religion of Plato,* 2d ed., p. 67.

occasion, commanded him *not* to do this or that or another thing, in order that he might pause, reflect, and come to an intelligent decision. And because of the fruits of obedience to this Voice, Socrates considered it to be one of divine guidance. It led him safely past what *seemed* good to what, he found, *was* good. The Voice, as I have earlier said, is in Mr More's language the Inner Check; and Mr More gives it, very rightly, a crucial place in his account of human nature. Plato, however, appears to have taken the Voice much as Socrates did, as something peculiar to him, not to be hoped for by others, and therefore of little or no usefulness for his purposes. His endeavour, indeed, was precisely to motivate the Socratic conduct of life in such fashion as to make it not only desirable but possible for those who must find their way on earth without direct supernatural aid.

Hence Plato turned to problems of the Real and of knowledge. It may suffice here to recall that he saw the world around him, and equally the people around him, as composed of two evidently, or even essentially, different elements. On the one hand, every object apprehended through the senses—save, as he thought, the stars—is continually changing; so that everywhere we seem to find things in the midst of a process of becoming, and nowhere anything we can see or touch or smell or hear or taste which is constant. But on the other hand we discover, all about us, evidences of a constant order governing the processes of change, and the relations of things with each other. And this order is intelligible, as things in themselves are not. Obviously that which changes under our eyes into something else cannot be grasped by the understanding, because each moment we find ourselves contemplating something different; and though rapidity of alteration varies indefinitely from one object to another, we find mutability the universal characteristic of earthly things, of our earth itself and of all that it inhabit. What we can understand, and increasingly have come to understand, is the constant order perceivable in, or through, the mutable objects of our sensible world. And this we can understand just because it is constant. Hence our world is intelligible in so far as, by the means it affords, we are able to construct an unseen world of ideas corresponding, imperfectly but genuinely, with the invisible realities which mould and govern sensible appearances. These are not subject to change, are simple or unmixed in nature, and for this reason are real as sensible objects are not. We may find, or we may bring about, for example, a momentary approximation, exceedingly close, to complete equality between two sensible objects; but equality itself, absolute and for ever the same, we know only as a standard by which we measure imperfect concrete instances. Yet this standard, or pattern, or idea of equality is more real than any examples in our world brought to us through our senses. So too in the case of "man": we can see men everywhere embodying more or less imperfectly the characteristics which enter into the pattern or standard by whose means we do not only identify but measure them; yet not one of them, not one man from all who have lived, has ever embodied completely for a moment the "idea" of "man." Nor is this "idea" merely a composite picture, an imaginary "typical" man. It is a norm, man in his perfection; and while this idea is much more difficult to possess one's self of than the idea of equality—so that, indeed, it cannot become known in all its fulness by earthly creatures—still, we can all grasp it sufficiently to *use* it. And this is equally true of the idea of "goodness," which as an absolute is not really definable by us at all.

So it was that Plato developed, upon a basis laid down by Socrates, the famous doctrine of ideas, or forms, which was promptly misunderstood by Aristotle—as it has been by many others since—but which has persisted to this day with undiminished vitality as the source of all later effort to bring out the meaning of the spiritual hope which burns in the heart of man. It was inevitable that critics should object that Plato, by giving free rein to his wishes, had merely projected into some realm of his own imagining our subjective concepts; yet it would have been strange indeed had he fallen into such a trap, when he was most of all concerned with precisely this question, and was passionately in earnest in his attempt to demonstrate conclusively the objective reality of the ideas. He knew, of course, as well as anyone else, that

we do form concepts which may be termed subjective, or
which may indeed be subjective, but the whole importance
of the doctrine of ideas lies in the fact that these concepts,
in so far as they represent truth, must correspond with objective reality. And it is no small part of Plato's greatness
that he saw and, as one of the most eminent of contemporary
Platonists says, "with irrefutable logic" showed that the
ideas or patterns or forms must be objective and immutable
—or, in other words, absolutely real—if any of our conceptions are true. The ideas, that is to say, are necessary postu-
lates, exactly as a real correspondence between sense-impres-
sions and objective phenomena is a necessary postulate in the
realm of physical science. Professor Ritter, whom I have
just quoted, continues:

Everyone understands the word "true" as expressing a definite relation of our ideas and assertions to reality. That thing
is true which is as we conceive and predicate it. As Plato weighs
the objections which were destroying this conception of truth,
he finds that the Heracliteans are right as far as the physical
objects, the things perceived by our senses, are concerned. The
concepts and terms which we employ when predicating something permanently retain the meanings attributed to them and
are, therefore, only adapted to designate the permanent characteristics or the essences determined by them. From this Plato
concludes: *If there are true predications and a correct naming
of things, this truth and correctness can only be grounded in a
reality which is also immutable. Our thoughts and words must
refer to this reality.* In fact, in our predications concerning any
individual object, we refer to something universal which that object has in common with many other individual things. The
word used when designating these things subsumes them or their
characteristics under a general concept. The characteristics of
this general concept must be objectively based in nature if our
ideas are correctly formed. This, it seems to me, is the basic
thought of the doctrine of ideas, which is very explicitly expressed in the *Cratylus* without even using the words εἶδος and
ἰδέα in the decisive passages. The same view is expressed in the
Phaedo. It is also at the basis of the exposition of 102B

[*Phaedo*] where εἴδη is used to designate the objectively real species. *I am convinced that all these propositions of Plato are absolutely correct,* and every one has to admit as much, unless he is willing to be engulfed by Protagorean subjectivism which, as Plato shows in the *Theaetetus,* permits no difference between truth and falsehood. This subjectivism would preclude all understanding or rational interchange of thought and only idle babbling would remain.[16]

Mr More's treatment of the doctrine of ideas is incomplete and seriously imperfect; yet it is enlightening just where light is most needed. Even from the little here said, one can see that the ideas are not all of a kind, that they form, indeed, an organized spiritual world, and that this world is diametrically opposed in nature to our present sensible world, which, nevertheless, is penetrated through and through by the ideas. Here is the paradox of dualism confronting us in a new form, and accompanied by the apparent paradox that we are able to know only ideas, but cannot truly know them save as we become disembodied souls rightly prepared for eternal happiness. To put it differently, we can only know what we cannot see, and can only see what we cannot know. Plato honestly faced the difficulties of his doctrine, acknowledging that there were perplexing problems concerning the range of the ideas, concerning differences between them, and above all concerning their presence and influence in our sensible world where nothing truly is, but all things are constantly changing or becoming; yet he held tenaciously to the doctrine despite objections which he could not answer, because its acceptance raised fewer difficulties than its rejection. The plain fact is, of course, that we are not, while on earth, in direct contact with the world of ideas. Its existence is not directly experienced, but inferred. This inference, however, is not merely legitimate; it is *necessary* if our experience, of whatever kind, is to have any objective meaning.

And here is where Mr More's exposition is specially useful. For he makes it clear that a resolution of the problems

16 *The Essence of Plato's Philosophy,* translated by A. Alles, pp. 112–113.

raised by the doctrine of ideas is not only impossible but unimportant. The realm of ideas is by definition essentially different from our present sensible world, so that, knowing it only by inference, we can only describe it in negative terms. We can know that it *is;* we can know in part what it is, or what it must be like; we can know it as the goal towards which our own lives should be directed; we can discover something in ourselves which holds us apart from the phenomenal world even while we are immersed in it, and which seems to be identical in nature with that other world of the spirit;— all this we can know, and we can be sure that if perfect knowledge of the Real is possible for us, it can only come when we are no longer mixed beings, but have left the sensible world behind us, at death. Hence, though fulness of knowledge, which would resolve all problems, is withheld from us now, what we can know is sufficient. Yet this present knowledge itself impels us to try to give it living positive form which may aid us to envisage it, to grasp it, to hold fast to the saving truth. And for this Plato turned, as humanity has turned before and since, to the imagination.

Plato's glowing pictures of the world of ideas are to be understood, then, as imaginative constructions, while they are to be felt as the embodied truth in its majesty and beauty. They are at once illusion and reality—ultimate eternal reality clothed in an earthly vesture that it may be seen by the weak eyes of temporal creatures. Thus the ideal philosophy joins hands with poetry, and the poet whom the world has recognized in Plato gives form and life and power to the divine world of the spirit in his doctrine of ideas equally as in his myths. The ideas and the myths are not the truth itself, they are something like the truth. They are not arbitrary symbols, but they are symbols. "Hence," Mr More points out, speaking only of the moral ideas, "the varying terms which Plato gives to their operation":

They are always, as products of the imagination, objective entities, separate from the world of phenomena and from the soul itself, but at one time he may speak of them as patterns, laid up in heaven or in some undefined region, to which we look as models to mould our conduct by, or, at another time, he may speak of them as visitants to the soul, neither exactly corporeal nor yet incorporeal, by whose presence we possess the qualities of which they are the substance, or, more vaguely still, as mere forces that play upon us and make us what we are. The looseness of Plato's terminology would indicate that, to him at least, it is of relatively slight importance how we take them to be, so long as we accept their being and bow to their authority.

But why, we may ask with many others, did Plato, himself a poet and one who still best enables us to understand the noble and indeed divine offices of the highest poetic art—why did Plato nevertheless condemn the poets of his land and time, and banish all wandering artists from his ideal society of good men? The answer is after all not far to seek, and leads us to the heart of what Mr More rightly calls true Platonism. For Plato profoundly distrusted mere "inspiration," and thought it the more dangerous when it was united with powers of expression which might be turned to the highest and most beneficent uses, because such powers might equally be turned to the basest uses. And the "inspired" poet was in effect the man who trusted his spontaneous impulses, who just let himself go, who spoke, or acted, at random, who was a kind of natural force—but who, being also a poet, clothed his vision with beauty, rendering it fatally persuasive to his fellows and giving it an authority which only wisdom deserves. Such freedom of the imagination is indistinguishable from the play of irresponsible fancy, and Plato was bound to discredit it unless he was willing to acknowledge that man is the measure of all things, or, in other words, that objective, universal truth is inaccessible to us. But this, of course, is exactly what he was not willing to do. He was confident that there is a certitude grounded in truth, which men can distinguish from the false certitude arising from obstinate self-will or obstinate self-deception; and the freedom he wanted to establish was the freedom born of knowledge, so that he unqualifiedly condemned the imagination save as it might become the servant of known truth.

Truth, moreover, is not to be discovered by consulting the

utterances of "inspired" men, who speak at random and, if
they speak truth, do so by accident; it is to be discovered by
critical observation, by consultation of experience sifted and
clarified through the processes of dialectic. Here, unfortunately, Mr More does both Plato and himself an injustice,
when he insists that the moral ideas occupied an essentially
different place in Plato's thought from all other ideas, and
when, as a direct consequence, he quite fails to show how the
moral ideas are discovered.[17]

Mr More is certainly right in holding that Plato was pre-
eminently a moralist, and most deeply concerned to establish
the objective reality of the moral ideas; and he is equally
correct in distinguishing moral knowledge from what we now
call scientific knowledge; but the process of discovery is the
same in nature for both kinds, differing only as the kinds
themselves are different, requiring, as I have said, identically
the same postulate and the same faith in ourselves for identically the same reason, and yielding results of the same validity in both cases.

And the question to be asked in searching for moral knowledge is simply this: What conduct, what way of life, will
bring a man secure happiness, or will bring him that imperturbable happy serenity sometimes called the peace which
passeth understanding? This is something vitally different,
it need scarcely be said, from any question concerning immediately pleasurable acts. Yet, even so, it may be asked, and
often has been asked, with what right do we assume that true
happiness cannot be based upon sheer delusion? Has it not,
so far as we can judge, frequently been so based? Do we not
see instances around us? The only answer to these questions
is that if a man be indeed happy, possessed of the peace
which passeth understanding, he has evidence which for human beings is ultimate, and in that sense absolute, like any-

---

[17] Indeed, by his use of such phrases as "the pure intuitions of consciousness" (as on p. 202 of *Platonism*) he practically opens the door to a mysticism of which Plato himself was an energetic and unceasing foe. But Mr
More has since repudiated mysticism of this kind (*The Catholic Faith*, pp.
206–312, *passim*), and I am able to say that he would now wish to repudiate
the implication that men have somehow within themselves any absolute
direct positive knowledge of, for example, justice.

thing else directly experienced. We do not, it is true, implicitly trust our eyes; we have learned certain mistakes to which the eye is liable, and limits beyond which it cannot perform its tasks, and we know that some eyes fail to distinguish certain colours, but, correcting the mistakes and deficiencies of the eye as far as possible, and making sure that a "normal" eye is used where colours are concerned, we then do accept the evidence of our eyes. If we could not do so, we would be completely helpless. But in fact we are not; we prosper by trusting our eyes, and court disaster if we refuse to use them. And this pragmatic criterion, which we may express by some such phrase as "results favourable to our well-being," is the fundamental ground of all our rational convictions.

Hence when critical observation convinces us that a given course of action truly brings with it secure happiness, we have a reason behind which we cannot go for concluding that this course of action does participate in real goodness. There is every reason for defining happiness most carefully; there is every reason for a searching examination into any claim that so and not otherwise true happiness will come to men; there is every reason to remember constantly that we cannot here hope to discover "pure" goodness save in the sense in which, much earlier in this book, we spoke of "pure" water; but at the same time we do have full rational assurance that the happiness of a Socrates can only result from the active participation of real goodness in his nature. Such a man, in other words, may not be, indeed cannot be, wholly free from illusion; nor can we, howsoever critically we may analyse our evidence, discern absolute or unmixed goodness present in him; yet we can be certain that the justice, the temperance, the fortitude, which the Socrates of history made so indubitably real to himself, are absolute realities, and unfailing sources of happiness, equally accessible to us.

V

WHAT is here said by no means exhausts the scope or the value of Mr More's *Platonism*; it merely shows why Plato, as

Mr More understood him when the book was written, seemed to him to have given men for all time a valid philosophical equivalent of the promises of religion. But in fact Mr More at this time felt that the Platonic philosophy was definitely superior to religion, as one can see from several passages in *Platonism*, and in particular from one which I shall quote:

Religion, though like philosophy it is really based on the Socratic affirmation [that it is better to be just than to be unjust], is yet too fearful to rest on this truth alone, and will seek another foundation for its faith in some miraculous event of history or in some revelation from above. So St Paul argued to the Corinthians:

"Now if Christ be preached that He rose from the dead, how say some among you that there is no resurrection of the dead?

"And if Christ be not risen, then is our preaching vain, and your faith is also vain.

"If in this life only we have hope in Christ, we are of all men most miserable."

We are of all men most miserable—is not this the very reverse of what Plato thought philosophy was to teach when he set forth on his great search in *The Republic?* I have not in mind to speak slightingly of the Christian faith, or of any genuine faith; I know the sources of religious conviction; but when I see the perplexity into which even St Paul could be thrown by the fear of losing his belief in a particular miraculous event, I appreciate the force of Plato's boast that he alone, with his master, had the courage to rest his faith on the simple common sense of mankind. This is philosophy. Having expounded the meaning of the commonplace that it is better to be just than to be unjust, and having thus given authority to the affirmation of the spirit, philosophy does not seek for extraneous proofs of this truth, but proceeds to use it as a principle for investigating the manifold life and activities of the soul.

Philosophy, that is to say, asks for no evidence not equally at hand in all times and in all places, pretends to no knowledge of the destiny of the soul, makes no promises of heavenly reward in a city paved with gold and encrusted with

jewels, but takes her stand simply on her ability rationally
to vindicate the proposition that the good man is the only
happy man, here and now, regardless of accident, misfortune, or persecution. And Mr More, believing that philosophy in Plato's hands was successful in taking this stand,
seemed clearly headed in 1917 for a series of essays or books
which should show the failure of later Greek philosophy to
maintain the truth set forth by Plato, and the perversions
of Platonism which thus came into currency and were taken
up and preserved in early Christianity, and so were handed
down even to our day to plague successive generations. But
four years went by before another volume appeared—years
devoted to a study of the origin and early development of
Christianity, which had been planned, indeed, but not carried out before the writing of *Platonism*, and also to a renewed study of Plato suggested by what was learned from
the Greek fathers of the Church—and when the next volume
of *The Greek Tradition* was published it was, significantly,
another book concerning Plato, *The Religion of Plato*. A
new start, in fact, was being made, as Mr More frankly
enough confessed in the Preface to this book, and was necessitated by a pronounced change of mind brought about by
the studies of these years and by further thought. He now
recognized that Plato had tacitly repudiated, as inadequate,
the philosophical stand taken in the *Republic*, and had in the
Timaeus and the *Laws* developed a mythology and a theology which, together with the philosophy embodied in the doctrine of ideas, constituted a full-fledged religion. Nor did he
stop here, as we can see from the following passage in which
he stated the thesis he proposed to develop and maintain in
The Religion of Plato and in the volumes which were to follow:

My belief is that Greek literature, philosophic and religious,
pagan and Christian, from Plato to St Chrysostom and beyond
that to the Council of Chalcedon in 451 A.D., is essentially a
unit and follows at the centre a straight line. This body of
thought I call the Greek Tradition, since the main force in pre-
serving it intact while assimilating large accretions of foreign

matter was the extraordinary genius of the Greek speech. The initial impulse to the movement was given by a peculiar form of dualism developed by Plato from the teaching of his master Socrates. The great Hellenistic philosophies—Epicurean, Stoic, and Neoplatonic—were attempts, each on a different line, to reconcile the dualistic inconsistency in the nature of things, as we know them, by forcing our experience into the Procrustean bed of reason. And each of these philosophies, it may be said here, by its rationalistic rejection of the paradox in the nature of things only succeeded at the last in falling into grosser paradoxes of logic and ethics. Christianity, on the contrary, notwithstanding its importation of a powerful foreign element into the tradition, and despite the disturbance of its metaphysical theology, was the true heir and developer of Platonism, truer than any of the pagan philosophies. And by the side of the orthodox dogma, as set forth in the Faith of Nicea and the Definition of Chalcedon, there ran a succession of heresies which endeavoured, each again on its own line, to reconcile the paradox of the two natures and one person of Christ by methods curiously resembling the monistic rationalism of the heretical philosophies, if I may so call them.

It is this tradition, Platonic and Christian at the centre, this realization of an immaterial life, once felt by the Greek soul and wrought into the texture of the Greek language, that lies behind all our western philosophy and religion. Without it, so far as I can see, we should have remained barbarians; and, losing it, so far as I can see, we are in peril of sinking back into barbarism. Unfortunately the direct tradition passed in the East into the keeping of a people who had no strength of heart and mind to maintain it, and, roughly speaking, with the death of Chrysostom, the virtue had at last gone out of it; then Greece came to an end. But in the West the tradition met a different fate. There it was taken up by a people of stronger nerve, who showed in religion the same faculty of assimilation as they had shown in pure literature, and who passed the inheritance on to the vigorous young races of the North.

Yet if the Latin genius assimilated much, it also adapted; and the tradition, as it comes to us through this medium, assumed a new *Ethos* at the first, and in the centuries since the separation of East and West it has received accretions which threaten the integrity of its foundation. I do not mean that religion has gained nothing by its transmission through the Latin mind; a certain note of character and worldly wisdom it wanted; and these Rome and her heirs could give. Nor would I belittle the intellectual achievement of the great doctors of the western Church and the western schools in the Middle Ages and since the Renaissance. But withal I am convinced that in certain important matters the Latin, and I may add the Teutonic, mode of thought has perverted the stream of philosophy and religion, and that the need of the modern world becomes daily more urgent to make a return to the purer source of our spiritual life. This does not imply that we should forget all the secular learning of the intervening ages, or that we should cease to be ourselves, if that were possible; but it does recognize in the Greek Tradition something which we must recover if religion is not to disappear and leave our existence dismally impoverished, something without which our wisdom may become vanity and our science a bondage. "We now are turning," says Dr Foakes Jackson in his *History of the Christian Church*, "from the great men whose writings made the Christianity of the Middle Ages and of the Reformation, from St Augustine and St Thomas Aquinas, from Luther and Calvin, to the Greek thinkers, St Athanasius, St Gregory of Nyssa, and St Cyril, to help the religious difficulties of a scientific age." I would broaden Dr Jackson's statement by regarding this eastward movement as the culmination of a half-conscious tendency of the English Church from the time of the Reformation; and I should like to modify it by including Plato with the masters of eastern theology.

I quote this passage in its entirety, despite its length, because here Mr More sets forth, better than could anyone for him, the aim which he has carried out in *The Religion of Plato, Hellenistic Philosophies, The Christ of the New Testament, Christ the Word*, and *The Catholic Faith*. His attitude towards Christianity has, indeed, undergone a very important further development during the writing of these volumes, as we shall notice, but this has not caused him to alter the conclusion stated in the above words in 1921. And

these words announce what is hardly less than a reversal of
the position he had held throughout middle life. He was still
writing, to be sure, as a Platonist, interested in separating
off true Platonism from its perversions, whether rationalistic
or, in his sense of the word, romantic; and interested in early
Christianity as the "heir and developer" of true Platonism;
but evidently his conception of Platonism, or of what is still
valid and significant in Plato's work, had changed, and with
this change had come a measure of genuine acceptance of
Christianity. This remarkable alteration did not bring him,
it may be said once and for all, within speaking distance of
Roman Catholicism. He has briefly indicated the reasons in
the above passage; and elsewhere he has made it abundantly
clear that he feels compelled, however regretfully and even
sorrowfully, in effect to denounce Rome for a betrayal of
Christianity in her philosophy, in her theology, and in her
mythology—in all the components of religion as he has defined it in the opening chapter of *The Religion of Plato*. The
Christianity to which he was drawing close in 1921 was, as
he tells us, Eastern Christianity; and that which he has since
accepted more unreservedly is modern Anglo-Catholicism,
the legitimate descendant, as he believes, of the Orthodox
Church.

Now if we ask what brought about Mr More's decisive
change of mind, surprising and indeed shocking as it was to
some of his friends, the answer is, up to a certain point,
simple enough and easy to give. The attempt made by Socrates, and by Plato after him, to show that it is better for a
man, while here on earth and regardless of the possibility of
an eternal unearthly life, under all circumstances to be just
rather than to be unjust—this noble and heroic effort unescapably depended on the proposition that justice does actually prevail on our earth. That justice should have objective
reality, and should enter into and participate in earthly
events, would not be enough. The whole argument of the
Republic hangs upon the question whether justice is not
merely real and productive of happiness, but, more than this,
actually unfailing here on earth. And Plato tacitly gave the
argument up, as Mr More perceived only after *Platonism*

had been completed,[18] when he failed to demonstrate "his
hypothetical thesis that the just man under torture with no
expectation of a future life is happy." Yet in this our life
just men are the victims of cruel misfortune equally with unjust men, and just men are very often the victims of relentless persecution which others escape by very reason of their
injustice. The fact is so familiar that it would not be worth
mentioning did anything less than the issue between philosophy and religion depend upon it. The fact unequivocally and
emphatically means, however, that unless earthly life is directed towards a goal beyond its confines, where justice does
prevail, no adequate reason can be found why men should
invariably seek justice and try to make it a reality of their
being.

Nor is this all; for though Plato sought to disregard the
daemonic voice, or inner check, of Socrates, he never succeeded in dispensing with it, but merely smuggled it into his
psychology under the cloak of "reason." There can, it seems
to me, be no doubt of this, and consequently no question of
Mr More's correctness in giving the inner check the place he
does in his version of Platonism. But the result is that the
soul of man cannot be regarded as a particle of simple, unmixed Being, immortal by definition, yet devoid of individuality when severed from its temporal vesture. Plato, truly
enough, argued for immortality on this basis; but an immortality which is nobody's eternal life, which means that your
personality and mine perish with bodily death, is the empti-
est of mockeries; and in his maturity and older age Plato
tacitly ignored his early, probably Socratic conjecture, and
wrote, as Mr More has made clear, in terms of a dualism extending to the soul, which in turn permitted him to accept a
doctrine of true personal immortality. For personality, so
far as we can see, lies in the nexus of the dual elements composing the soul, one of which, howsoever Plato writes of it or
names it, remains indistinguishable from the daemonic voice
of Socrates. And the background of Plato's religion, Mr
More believes, is his "sense of the daemonic lying everywhere

18 See the foot-note on pp. 90–91 of *Platonism,* 3rd ed.

half-concealed and half-revealed behind the material phenomena of the world."

We may sum the whole matter up by saying that Plato
went beyond philosophy to religion because he found philosophy radically incomplete without it, or, in other words, found
a definite religious faith clearly implicated in his reading of
life. The law for man, as was said in the third chapter of this
book, is a law of self-fulfilment which can be understood only
as a preparation for the soul's eternal life. Thus Mr More
can say that Plato's theology is "an extension of his 'philosophy of the soul.' " It is a body of rational and, we will say,
unescapable inference from philosophy, which itself is simply
the analysis of direct experience. Mr More traces Plato's
progress through philosophy to theology and mythology in
a paragraph in *The Religion of Plato* which I will quote:

If we have been right in our interpretation, Plato's philosophy grows out of a sense of dualism as the central fact of man's
ethical experience. As he says in the first book of the *Laws*, all
cities are by nature in a state of continual warfare with all
other cities, and this warfare extends to the citizens of the same
city, and further to the internal life of the individual man. "And
that is the first and greatest victory when a man is victor over
himself, as that is the basest and most evil condition when a man
is defeated by himself." We are still within the bounds of philosophy when the object of this victory is made the Idea of the
Good, regarded as an entity outside of the soul, which plays a
dominant part in our moral life as the final cause of our being.
We pass to theology when, as in the preamble to the *Laws*, the
gods are brought into the warfare as personifications, or ma-
nipulators it might better be said, of the Good: "The heavens
are filled with powers of good, many in number, and with contrary powers, more numerous still than the good; and now we
say that we are involved with these in a deathless battle needing
a marvellous guard, and that the gods and daemons are our
allies." The further step to mythology is taken when the procedure of the divine Providence is described in detail as preparing for men a judgement seat and as guiding men upwards, so
far as they suffer themselves to be guided, by the pathway of

birth and rebirth. In this last stage the essential truth of philosophy as a concern of the individual soul, is rendered vivid and convincing by clothing it in the imaginative garb of fiction—fiction which yet may be only a veil, more or less transparent, through which we behold the actual events of the spirit world; and this aid of the imagination is needed just because the dualism of consciousness cannot be grasped by the reason, demands indeed a certain abatement of that rationalizing tendency of the mind which, if left to itself, inevitably seeks its satisfaction in one or the other form of monism.

Evidently the motivating force behind Mr More's renewed study of Plato, and behind his recognition that Plato's philosophy was really an integral part of his religion and inseparable from it, was his discovery that this was the Platonism which maintained its vitality, without essential perversion, until it was taken up and incorporated into Christianity by the Greek fathers of the early Church. The *philosophy* of Plato passed through the hands of Aristotle, finally reached its conclusion in Neoplatonism, and was then taken into Latin Christianity, to become the basis, with aid later derived from the Aristotelian writings themselves, of that metaphysical theology which has decisively repelled Mr More from Roman Catholicism. Metaphysical theology he has steadfastly regarded as a hollow pretence, and as a perversion of true Platonism—of the Platonism, let us say, which has not been undermined by the passage of time, because it is true to constant experience. And this Platonism, ethical and spiritual, Mr More found at the centre of the early development of Christianity, altered by its new relationship but not twisted, not falsified—rather, as he came to recognize, improved and deepened. The union, indeed, between Christ and religious Platonism made the difference between theory and achievement;—and from the moment when he saw this truth may be dated Mr More's "conversion," if the word may fairly be used to designate a change, profound and even startling, yet not without ambiguity and certainly not a contradiction, but an unexpected fulfilment, of earlier thought.

The difference between theory and achievement of which I speak is simply this: Plato was not himself the founder of a religion, whereas Jesus Christ was. All that enters essentially into the religion of the Western world Plato gave, except just that unmistakable divine confirmation which was needed to raise belief into certitude, or to convert a doctrine of the schools into a conquering faith. And this Jesus Christ alone gave, alone could give, as history very plainly teaches; so that in the fortunes of Platonism we have a conclusive demonstration that we of the Western world can have no philosophical equivalent of religion, and no living religion without divine intervention, supernatural, miraculous, and compelling. Whether or not this demonstration holds only for the Western world is more than doubtful, and it would be curious, to say the least, were it really so limited; but I put the matter thus in order to raise no question with which we are not here concerned.

To Mr More, indeed, the demonstration was so far conclusive that he was presently content to rest the case, not only for Christianity, but for religion itself, upon acceptance of Christ as the Incarnate Word.[19] But first he went on to show how the spirit of rationalism had led the ancient world astray, in the centuries after Plato, causing the several philosophical schools to offer "meaningless answers to impossible questions raised by gratuitous hypotheses."[20] His condemnation of Epicureans, Cynics, Stoics, Neoplatonists, and Sceptics is not, of course, so sweeping as this quotation would imply; it is, on the contrary, temperate and qualified; and though *Hellenistic Philosophies* was written, as I have earlier intimated, to show how Plato alone of all those who followed after Socrates was true to the teaching of the Master, the book nevertheless has positive value, as a piece of critical exposition, so great as to make it, in my opinion, the best of all Mr More's many volumes. I do not know, indeed, of any other modern work of scholarship so nearly perfect in both form and substance; and the essays on Plotinus and Scepticism are specially remarkable for their insight and grasp, the

[19] See *The Christ of the New Testament,* p. 293.
[20] *Hellenistic Philosophies,* p. 223.

former dealing with the most difficult of all philosophic writers, and the latter with the most neglected and yet the greatest of the Hellenistic philosophical schools. At the end of his essay on Scepticism Mr More wrote:

So far I have endeavoured to show how the philosophy of Plato embraces both scepticism and the spiritual affirmation, and how by virtue of this inclusiveness it proves itself more thoroughly positive than the materialistic exclusiveness of Pyrrho. For the relation of theology and mythology to philosophy in such a scheme I must refer the reader to the appropriate chapters in my *Religion of Plato*. The problem of philosophy is to ascertain what spiritual knowledge is consistent with a legitimate enlargement of Pyrrhonic scepticism; with theology and mythology, so far as we remain true to our Platonism, we pass from the assurance of knowledge to that land of varying probability which was discovered, but never occupied, by the great explorers of the Middle Academy. If there is any escape from the restrictions of probability in the religious sphere of theology and mythology, it cannot be achieved by the guidance of unassisted reason, but must wait on a revelation which comes with its own authority of immediate conviction. Such a revelation the Christian theologian found in the life and words of the historic Jesus, and this belief will be the theme of our next two volumes in the Greek Tradition.

The first of these volumes was *The Christ of the New Testament*, in which Mr More, making full use of what seemed to him "the solid results of the past century of German investigation," surveyed the life and teaching of Jesus and the earliest presentations of Christian belief, contained in the New Testament. In this his endeavour was "to show how the achievements of the higher criticism may be accepted without succumbing to a purely humanitarian view of Christianity." And of the success of the endeavour there can be no doubt. The book is a brilliant vindication of the position suggested alike by the fortunes of Platonism in the ancient world and by the efforts of so-called modernists to "save" Christianity while discarding traditional faith in the mysterious union of divinity and humanity in the person of Jesus. "Most of the reasoning of the liberal and semi-sceptical school" of modern theologians, Mr More says, "seems harder to accept than the difficulties it undertakes to explain." Mr More discards a great deal once thought essential in Christian belief; he is "sceptical of miracles"; he rejects the virgin birth of Jesus, the objective reality of the resurrection, and the doctrine of the personality of the Holy Ghost; he grants, too, only a symbolic value to a not inconsiderable portion of the Apostles' Creed;[21] and in general his realization of what is implied by the humanity of Jesus is keen and full, so that his presentation of the life and inner development of the Saviour includes several courageous admissions and reminders impossible of acceptance either by the Fundamentalist brethren or by Roman Catholics. What then would he preserve? Just that which we have marked as the one essential difference between Platonism and Christianity. At one time he had considered that Platonism was strongest, was indeed impregnable, where Christianity was weakest—Platonism being founded upon philosophy, and Christian faith only upon mythology. To Mr More, we must realize, mythology is not fiction, but genuinely symbolic of truths which are beyond our full comprehension. It is the fruit of an effort to portray or represent the things of eternity in terms of our present world of time and space. Hence the Incarnation of the Word of God in the person of Jesus, the historic man of Nazareth, corresponds to that which we call mythology in Platonism. It is an *accommodation* of divinity to the conditions of humanity. And Mr More makes it clear beyond question that the Christian religion was founded solely on the conviction that this accommodation had actually occurred within history, at a definite time and place, so that it was not an imaginative vision of "something like the truth," but the saving truth itself appearing as a visible sign from above to prove once and for all that the transcendental goal of life postulated by the dualistic philosophy was not an empty dream, but completely real.

[21] See his essay on "The Creeds" in *The Catholic Faith*, pp. 76–121.

It is evident upon the most casual reading of *The Christ
of the New Testament* that by the time Mr More wrote it he
had reversed his earlier position. He now considered it the
weakness of the Platonic religion that it was based upon
philosophy, and the peculiar strength of Christianity that it
rested squarely and solely upon "belief in Christ as a person
manifesting in himself both the nature of God and the nature
of man."[22] Yet neither in *The Christ of the New Testament*
nor in any later volume does he profess to debate the truth or
error of this belief. He simply shows that by it, by the doctrine of the Incarnation, Christianity stands or falls, now
no less than in the earliest years of our era. And in *Christ the
Word* he goes on to show how the Incarnation was a stone of
stumbling to many early Christians, who attempted in various ways to rationalize it, with one invariable result. They all
ended by denying either the divinity or the humanity of Jesus.
This was steadily recognized, moreover, by the Church of the
first centuries as equivalent to the destruction of Christianity,
with the consequence that the history of Christian doctrine
during these years is largely the history of repeated attempts
to safeguard the doctrine of the Incarnation against attack
and misunderstanding, until finally this "fundamental dogma
of the Catholic Faith," as Mr More calls it, was formulated
"at Nicea in 325 and more precisely defined at Chalcedon in
451."

VI

WE now see the road Mr More has travelled and where he
has ended. There is in his final position, as I have said, an
element of ambiguity. His youthful rejection of Christianity, as he then knew it, and his effort, prolonged through the
greater part of his life, to find his own way through the maze
of experience, has left a mark upon him which cannot be
erased. He still maintains a certain detachment from the
faith he has at length embraced, speaking as a convert only
to draw back the next moment in a kind of uneasy alarm, as-
suring us that after all he is only a student of history, seeking to discover what we should mean by Christianity, and

22 *The Catholic Faith,* p. 76.

leaving us to decide, once our minds are cleared and we have
before us the real alternatives, whether or no we would be or
can be Christians. Thus *The Christ of the New Testament*
gives us the same problem over again that we faced when we
encountered *Platonism*, and we are tempted to say in this
instance that Mr More has dealt with every question raised
by Christianity except the very one upon which all others
hang. For why should we at all concern ourselves, save as
mere antiquarians, with the problem of Christianity, if Jesus
was after all essentially a man like the rest of us, or if we
can never know what he was, while we do know thoroughly
the mountainous difficulties in the way of supposing that he
and his disciples were not deluded? The crux of the whole
matter lies just there. If Jesus was the Christ, the early
Church was perfectly right in holding tenaciously to its
doctrine of the two natures joined in one person, in resolutely fighting heresy, and in pushing the effort as far as
language can be stretched to define exactly the Incarnation.
That doctrine, moreover, if Jesus was the Christ, is precious
to us beyond words, as the perpetual charter of our liberty,
of our humanity, of our hopes. It must then be disengaged
from the masses of incredible legend, of superstition, of discredited thought, of outworn moral dogmatism, which have
come to surround it, so that it can be seen anew for what it
really is, and can be made the cornerstone of a religious life
and development fully appropriate to our own contemporary
civilization and knowledge.

All this we can admit, indeed must admit, I should say, in
so far as we understand what the Christian religion has been,
and may be; and in so far as we judge it—not, as its cheaper
opponents habitually do, by the failures of some of its guardians and of their followers—but by its success, where it has
succeeded, in liberating and deepening our humanity, in giving substance to our hope, and in bringing to birth that happiness which issues only from true self-fulfilment. But is its
foundation real? Can we still believe that Jesus was the
Christ? The Platonic doctrine of ideas, it has always seemed
to me, requires only to be understood in order to command
our assent. It has frequently been misunderstood, from the

time of Aristotle, we have earlier noticed, until the present
day; yet there it stands, untouched by time, more firm and
solid than any rock, demanding, as Mr. More says, no evidence which lies not ready to hand in every generation. With
Christianity, however, the case is far different. Here everything depends upon a single questionable event in history,
ever receding from our view;—and precisely here Mr More
has drawn back, refusing to ask whether or not this event did
actually take place, saying only that if it did not take place
we have no religion, no basis for that which religion professes
to give.

Some six or seven years ago Mr Lewis Mumford accused
Mr More of leaving him and other very righteous young men
"in the lurch."[23] The charge was worse than frivolous, as its
author made sufficiently evident when he explained that what
he sought was, not guidance, but support—and support in
humanitarian endeavours, to which he found Mr More's
criticism "mainly irrelevant." Well, Mr Mumford is "mainly" insignificant; but has not Mr More, at the culminating
point of his most serious and mature work, indeed left his
readers in the lurch? Certainly to more than one reader of
The Christ of the New Testament the following words have
come as a chilling anti-climax, marring almost fatally a
sound and beautiful book:

It does not fall within my design to debate the truth or error
of Christianity. I have argued that the dualism of faith cannot
on any sound philosophical basis be rejected out of hand as incredible because it is incomprehensible. I have tried to show that
the belief of the Church corresponds with the deeper self-con-
sciousness of Jesus himself; that is a problem of historic evidence. But as for the simple fact, whether Jesus was deceived or
not in his claims, that is a question of a different sort, to be
answered individually by each man as the voice of conscience
responds to the words spoken so many ages since by the lake of
Galilee. Only, thus much I would urge: if the supposition of

[23] The essay containing this accusation appeared in *Books* (Vol. 4, No.
11), and was answered by Mr More in the Preface to *The Demon of the
Absolute.*

Christianity be not true, then we have no sure hope of religion. The Ideal philosophy of Plato waits for its verification upon no belief in anything outside of what we can test and know in our immediate experience, and he to whom the other-world of Ideas is a reality possesses a spiritual comfort beyond which it may be presumptuous to search—I do not say. But the full scope of religion requires a theology and a mythology as well as a philosophy, and if the crowning element of religion is to be more than a reasonable conjecture, as ultimately it was to Plato, if it is to be confirmed by the certainty of revelation, then I see not whither we are to turn save to Christianity. For mythology, the crown of religion, is just the coming together of the human and the divine, the descent of God to man and the consequent elevation of man to God. In this sense all religions have their myths, and might be regarded as the groping of men in the darkness, "if haply they might feel after him, and find him, though he be not far from every one of us." . . . In contrast with all other religions the peculiar strength of Christianity is that in the Incarnation it reduces mythology to the simplest possible terms; every extravagance, every overgrowth of fancy, is swept away for the bare fact that God in Jesus appeared among men. Indeed, of all arguments for the supernatural origin of the Christian faith the most convincing is a frank comparison of its superb simplicity with the wild tumult of Hellenistic superstitions through which it cut its way by what has the semblance of providential direction. . . . To say that the dogma of Christianity is endangered by the comparative study of religions implies a gross ignorance of facts or a wilful misapprehension of values. If there be any true myth, if the divine nature has at any time in any wise directly revealed itself to man, if any voice shall ever reach us out of the infinite circle of silence, where else shall we look but to the words of the gospel? Not Christianity alone is at stake in our acceptance or rejection of the Incarnation, but religion itself.

There we are. Some of these words could only have been written by one who had himself embraced Christianity; yet what he can say for it comes down to this, that because our loss would be so grievous, were we deprived of religion, we should accept the Incarnation, even though we can never know whether or not we are deluded in so doing. But before we conclude that Mr More has really ended by throwing up his own cause, there are several questions to be asked. May not Mr More simply have been guided, after all, by the desire to play fairly? How can we possibly have direct or full *knowledge* of the Incarnation as an historical event? How can anything of the kind ever be rationally *proved?* Is not the determining question concerning Christianity one of a different order? Do we not have here a question of probabilities to be balanced? How could we have anything else? Why else have Christians from the beginning exhorted those outside the fold to believe, to have faith?

The truth is, we want an unmistakable sign, a proof, because an historical incarnation seems to us extremely improbable. Many to-day would say flatly it is ridiculous, because they are believers in some dogmatic naturalism. But Mr More's criticism has made it clear, like that of Plato and the Sceptics in the ancient world, like that of many sceptics and pragmatists in the modern world, how vain, under earthly conditions, is our longing for absolute knowledge. We have earlier seen how deluded are those who fancy they have it in some form of naturalism; and we have seen that direct experience is the only absolute we do really have in this world, and that dualism, though not free from difficulties and perhaps itself a kind of mythological construction, still is uniquely serviceable in enabling us to make sense of life. To the dualist, moreover, there can be nothing incredible in the doctrine of the Incarnation. It does no violence to modern knowledge; it is strictly analogous to what we know, from direct experience, about the constitution of human nature. It can be accepted to-day without reservations, without allowances for the time or place of its origination. It must, however, be accepted or rejected as a "supposition," as an hypothesis, and not as a doctrine which can be proved or disproved. An historical incarnation, in other words, cannot from the nature of things be made a matter of knowledge, but is necessarily a demand upon our faith.

We all know reasons why the doctrine of the Incarnation should be rejected; against these what reasons can be advanced for its acceptance? It is here, I think, and not in his scrupulous insistence upon the suppositional character of the Incarnation, that Mr More is guilty of a certain confusion of language, if not of thought, which might open him to the charge of defalcation. For he simply tells us that we cannot have religion without assent to the doctrine of the Incarnation. And this is, to say the least, a very dubious assertion, besides being one which seems to beg the real question. What is religion? Is it something we must have whether true or false? Is it indistinguishable from superstition? Can we gain its benefits by acting "as if" it were true, putting to one side the troublesome problem of objective reality? Mr More means nothing of the sort. His whole critical career has been a fight against sham and delusion, against the easy substitution of make-believe for reality, against the credulous acceptance of dogmatic philosophies. And the progressive change of belief whose course we have followed in the present chapter has not ended in a repudiation of rigorous criticism or dulled Mr More's power to distinguish superstition from truth. What then does Mr More mean? He means only, I think, to place before us as impressively as possible the full scope and weight of the issue raised by the doctrine of the Incarnation, leaving each of us to answer the call for faith as we may or can, but doing everything in his power to awaken us to the momentous character of our decision.

It is a misfortune that Mr More was not able, at the crucial point, to accomplish this great object without ambiguity, without in fact opening himself to serious misunderstanding. It is a misfortune, too, that he has not been able, in direct and outright fashion, to tell the story of his own personal acceptance of the doctrine of the Incarnation. Yet after all we are not left in much doubt concerning his reasons. For all the volumes making up *The Greek Tradition* are, like *Platonism*, critical and constructive in purpose, rather than historical; and the whole body of Mr More's criticism, late as well as early, springs vitally from deep personal conviction.

His fundamental conclusion, born of developed self-knowledge and tested by the most searching examination, may be
expressed very simply: Life is an opportunity for self-fulfilment; but man is a creaturely being, born into a world not of
his own making or choosing, endowed with capacities which
it rests with him to develop and integrate in accordance with
laws not of his own contrivance; so that self-fulfilment depends upon the discovery, through reflection upon experience, of the "law for man," and upon obedience to it. Life,
then, it may be said, is an opportunity for the ordered construction of a self, in harmony with an objective, unchanging reality which lies behind and imperfectly penetrates our
world of shifting phenomena, giving that world such semblance of order, of integration, of partial reality, as we find
it possesses. The grounds and implications of this conclusion
we have examined at length, and we have seen how, step by
step, Mr More was brought to accept what may be called the
philosophy of Christianity. Further, we have noticed the
close and constant interdependence of human beings, and the
fact that, though human knowledge must begin and develop
afresh within each individual, and is a process of inner discovery, still, we are all aided incalculably in attaining human
knowledge by intimate acquaintance with our fellows—and
with those, most especially, whose lives, or whose imaginative
representations of life, have been recognized as classic embodiments of perennial human truth. I have dwelt in the
present chapter on the life of Socrates as one of the best of
all examples of what is here meant, and as one wherein we
see clearly the fulness of human development issuing from
obedience to the "law for man." The memory of Socrates is
kept alive, and continues, unimpaired after many centuries,
to exert an irresistible influence upon us, because of his obedience to the inner check, and because of his success, consequent on that obedience, in achieving a justly ordered personality. Socrates, not directly by talking about it, but by
the quality of his life, by what he became, made justice itself
something present in this world as an objective reality, and
at the same time demonstrated conclusively that through

such participation as his in the realm of ideas we become most fully human.

And we are entitled to infer from the later volumes of *The Greek Tradition* that Mr More came to accept the doctrine of the Incarnation because it finally seemed to him, after long study and in the light of all the evidence, that Jesus made divinity itself something present in this world as an objective reality. No man knows better than Mr More the difficulties of this conclusion. His whole life, from the time of his youthful revolt against the Calvinism of his parents, has borne witness to that. In the end, however, he has simply become convinced that the difficulties involved in a rejection of the doctrine of the Incarnation are far greater than those involved in its acceptance. For his position, moreover, there is this to be said: It is the outcome of critical inquiry, and of a profound knowledge of human nature. As an act of faith it is no way different from other acts of faith which, as we have seen, we all make, and are compelled to make, in our age no less than men in any earlier age, as a condition of existence. The only differences there are between acts of reasonable faith are differences discernible from their consequences. We accept favourable consequences as definitive verifications in every field of experience. Bigoted dogmatists alone, imagining they can gain the kingdom of truth by force, deny some kinds of real experience in order to exalt other kinds. The world has always been full of them, and Europe and America are crawling with them to-day, but they remain in the long run insignificant, and are nothing better than troublesome insects. We can in fact be sure that in religion as elsewhere a venture of faith is legitimately converted into knowledge by favourable consequences. "How," Mr More asks in *Platonism*, "do we know that which surpasses knowing? The answer was given by Plato in the argument of *The Republic;* it may be found summarily stated in an early Christian theologian who was often a better Academician than were the Pagans who usurped the name: 'Plato himself says that happiness (*eudaimonia*) is the well-being of the daemon, and that by the daemon is meant the governing element of our soul, and that the most perfect and fullest Good is this happiness.' " There, within, as Mr More truly says, lies the final test which the doctrine of the Incarnation has to encounter; and in the fact that Paul More, travelling the road he has travelled, has found his goal in its acceptance, we have, I cannot but think, the weightiest reason given in our time for stopping to search our own hearts.

V. CONCLUSION

I

THERE is probably no better summary statement of the meaning and worth of Mr More's criticism than one written several years ago by Mr Walter Lippmann: "Mr More, besides being a scholar of extraordinary attainments, is by way of being an adept in the mysteries of faith and in his own right something of a spiritual genius. The *Shelburne Essays* and the five volumes of *The Greek Tradition* are more than the monumental work of a literary critic. They are a record of continuous religious discovery within a nature that combines in exquisite proportions a delicate sensibility with a hard-headed instinct for reality. It makes no particular difference whether one agrees with all his particular judgements; to read him is to enter an austere and elevated realm of ideas and to know a man who, in the guise of a critic, is authentically concerned with the first and last things of human experience."[1]

I have taken a view of criticism in the present volume which is more inclusive and less depreciatory than Mr Lippmann's, so that I do not feel called on to agree that in the *Shelburne Essays* and *The Greek Tradition* we have something more, and better, than criticism; but, with this reservation, I am content to accept Mr Lippmann's words for my text in these last pages.

We need not agree with all of Mr More's particular judgements. He does not agree with all of them himself. His writings are a record of growth and development. No one understands better than he that criticism is a process of inquiry which can have no end; and no one has been readier than he to admit mistakes, to refuse to be bound by them, and to go forward as new knowledge and further reflection have

[1] *Saturday Review of Literature,* 15 March, 1930, p. 817.

pointed the way. He has indeed thus traversed the whole tangled field of modern thought; and if his passage has left ineffaceable marks upon him, this does not really lessen the greatness of his achievement. Rather, we may say, these are marks of honourable combat, proving that Mr More speaks to us, not from some retired and peaceful corner of our mad world, not from some ivory tower of dreamy or desirous speculation, but from our midst, standing shoulder to shoulder with us, knowing all our doubts and waverings, knowing the full force of that whirlwind of change which has bewildered us and twisted our lives, and simply realizing more keenly and deeply than we the meaning of our common experience. This realization did not come suddenly, as a gift from heaven, nor has it ever been perfect and complete. It has, on the contrary, been won gradually, through faithful perseverance in true critical inquiry, motivated by a constant sense of the emptiness of life not directed to an end beyond itself. And this motive, at work "within a nature that combines in exquisite proportions a delicate sensibility with a hard-headed instinct for reality," has concentrated his attention upon the great questions, on our answers to which depends everything we may do or become; and has kept him from resting content with any specious half-truths, or bold dogmatism, or superficial answers suggested merely by what is new in our own time and circumstances.

Mr More, in other words, has been *authentically concerned with the first and last things of human experience*—with that which has been constant and central in human life in all ages, in all places, in all circumstances—and he has approached the great problems, not with his own already formulated answers, not attempting wilfully to impose himself on the world, not as a self-appointed prophet or lawgiver, but modestly as an inquirer, anxious to follow the evidence wherever it might lead, anxious to learn the truth whatever it might be. And thus he has come to speak with an authority which has been felt—and, of course, often resented —wherever he is known. And his authority is unimpeachable, within the field of what I have called human knowledge, because it is conferred upon him alike by friends and enemies,

who perforce recognize that what he tells us strikes home.
Authority is given him, that is to say, exactly as, in their
field of competence, we confer it upon men of science. Hence
it behoves us to distinguish carefully the grounds of our disagreement, when we find ourselves unable to go with him.
We are dealing, as Knut Hagberg has written, "with one of
the most learned and keen-minded thinkers of our time, in
whose work is exhibited a rare combination of profound
spiritual insight with penetrating analytical powers." "An
author of his dimensions and depth," the same critic adds,
"America has scarcely had since Emerson and Thoreau."[2]
And this is what Mr Gorham Munson felt when he wrote,
a few years ago, that Mr More "is a force that has not been
encountered on its own plane"; for our journalists, by and
large, have revealed their own limitations rather than Mr
More's when they have tried to attack him.[3] They have by no
means always been wholly in the wrong of it, yet too many
of them have written, not as critics, not as fellow-inquirers
taking up and continuing a discussion, but at once irrele-
vantly and abusively, as if they cared neither for truth nor
for honour, but only at whatever cost to prejudice all issues
in the minds of their readers. This is called, in another field,
dirty politics; and the opportunities opened up by mass cir-
culation have been used in our day to extend the methods of
dirty politics into well-nigh every field of discussion and activity. The self-righteous, we know, are as open to this temptation as the most corrupt devotees of self-expansion, and
have always been; but undoubtedly, along with an enlarged
field for the exhibition of anti-criticism, there has arisen in
our time a new reason for it. The vulgar inference from the
doctrine of progress is that novelty is another word for
truth, and that to float with the oncoming current is the
highest wisdom; and our cheap propagandists have encouraged and capitalized this notion until, in many quarters, it

[2] I quote from an article in *Nya Dagligt Allehanda*, Stockholm, 16 November, 1930.

[3] Mr Munson's statement occurs in his *Destinations*, 1928, p. 21. Those
who care to notice what some journalists have been capable of writing may
turn to Appendix B.

seems to be assumed that the one real critical problem is the determination of "the coming thing," and that the touchstone of excellence is "newness" or "modernity."

Doubtless one should not blame our anti-critics too harshly. Democracy itself promoted, indeed almost enforced, this grovelling attitude, before the doctrine of progress was ever heard of in America. Everywhere, too, as Byron observed,

> Men are the sport of circumstances, when
> The circumstances seem the sport of men;

and nothing could be more evident than that these anti-critics are simply the creatures of the age, or of some part of it, as fully as the "creative" writers whose newness they love to celebrate. We should blame ourselves, rather, for our dislike of criticism, which is a dislike of intelligence, and for our readiness to accept in its place without discrimination the work of time-servers or of fanatical "reformers" or of propagandists. For "the spirit of inquiry," as Principal Tulloch wrote more than half a century ago, "in every age springs, by way of reaction, from the prevailing dogmatism with which it comes in contact."[4] And in this sense every true critic is a "reactionary" force and a challenge to self-righteousness and complacency.

In proportion as his work is understood, moreover, I think it will be found that where we cannot go with Mr More he himself has not been entirely true to his own critical principles. We will not, for example, join any thoughtless anti-critic in censuring Mr More for being a moralist. Every significant critic of literature must be also a critic of life, and therefore a moralist. It does not follow, of course, that literature shall be expected specifically to teach moral lessons or to illustrate established rules of conduct. It is the critic, not the literary artist, who comes before us as a moralist; and the critic asks only, in this connexion, that literature should be a faithful reflection of life, and judges it as best he may in accordance with this standard. Everything has been

---

[4] *Rational Theology and Christian Philosophy in England in the Seventeenth Century,* 2d ed., 1874, Vol. II, p. 8.

done that can be done to cloud the issue between art and morality, but through these treacherous currents Mr More has steered a straight course. He has certainly been correct in refusing to be swept off his feet by our modern philosophers of change, and by the evidence of change which has multiplied on every side in our time. He has been fully alive to the significance of this evidence. He has fully recognized that our circumstances are always changing, more or less rapidly, that we ourselves inwardly are always changing, that our creaturely knowledge is relative and imperfect, and consequently that we can never establish any absolutely fixed rules of conduct, or of manners. But he has steadily seen, too, that this is not the whole truth; and, by way of reaction from the dogmatism of our apostles of the flux, he has been impelled to examine anew all that other body of evidence which shows that constancy as well as change characterizes our world and ourselves, because it is the abiding which we can understand, and in terms of which alone we can bring at least partial order out of the chaos of our unformed selves. Thus, moreover, he has sought to ground us afresh in those elements, or constant principles, which lie behind our rules of conduct and of manners, and towards which, as ends, those rules are framed. These constant elements are the standards which suffice for the criticism alike of literature and of life.

But practical moral and social codes are framed relatively to ever-changing circumstances as well as to unvarying ends, and it is to this vexed question of adaptation that Mr More has given small attention and jejune answers. While no one else in our day—certainly not even Professor Babbitt—has seen so clearly and dealt so effectively with the fundamental questions concerning human nature which are always being raised anew by changing circumstances, still, in the field of our more immediate practical problems Mr More has largely confined himself to the needed though ungrateful task of showing that sympathy, or fellow-feeling, cannot be made the basis of a new morality; and, for the rest, he has tended to remain seemingly content with the practical rules which were good enough in the last century for Howells and Longfellow and Lowell and Holmes. I should not wish to be num-

bered amongst those who fancy there is nothing to be said
for such moral cautiousness. "Live by old Ethicks and the
classical Rules of Honesty," wrote Sir Thomas Browne;—
"Think not that Morality is Ambulatory; that Vices in one
age are not Vices in another; or that Virtues, which are under the everlasting Seal of Right Reason, may be Stamped
by Opinion." Such advice, though unduly simplified and not
very practical for us, is safer than that given by cocksure
enthusiasts of the daily and weekly press, to whom the formu-
lation of new rules of honesty seems mere child's play.

Certainly, however, many new rules are needed to-day,
and some of Mr More's particular judgements, born of his
failure to see this need, merit the hostility they have aroused.
But the failure only proves, after all, that Mr More has not
succeeded in wholly freeing himself from provincialism, and
that he has remained in some ways the child of his generation. And what man at any time, in any place, has ever succeeded in completely emancipating himself from the influences of his early environment and upbringing? What man,
in addition, has ever done all that others can see he might
have done? It is of the very essence of our humanity that
none of us lives alone, develops alone, or works alone. We are
links in a continuing chain. We do not choose our place
therein. We take up a station appointed for us, and work
loyally for causes which we did not originate and which we
cannot bring to full consummation. In no field is this more
true than in criticism, for reasons which I have attempted to
make clear in these pages; and I now emphasize the fact
that criticism is a process of inquiry, never completed, but
handed on from one man to another and from one generation
to another, in a continuing effort to bring intelligence to
bear on life and to keep attention fixed on the masters of
human knowledge, because it is not Mr More's partial failure, but his heartening and real success, which is remarkable,
and significant.

II

SEVERAL years ago a rather fumbling kind of book, entitled
The Reinterpretation of American Literature, fell dead
from the press, killed by too many doctors, some of whom

had been allowed to drift into the wrong profession. Both
Professor Foerster and the other professors who wrote his
book talked a great deal about the frontier as an important
continuing influence upon our literature, following, like well-
nigh all subsequent historical writers, the famous hint
dropped in 1893 by Turner. But what the literary historian
really should make of the frontier they tacitly confessed, by
their hesitations, their vagueness, their differing opinions,
that they did not know. It does not say much for them that
their opinions were on the whole more sensible than those
ventilated by Mr V. F. Calverton in his windy, pretentious,
muddle-headed book, *The Liberation of American Literature*. Yet only one of Professor Foerster's learned gentlemen, Professor Murdock, even approached the understanding of this pervasive influence which has been displayed, underneath his characteristic prejudices and distortions, by
Mr Van Wyck Brooks, in *The Ordeal of Mark Twain* and
elsewhere; and not one of our contemporary critics or professors has shed as much light on the subject as did Harriet
Martineau in the 1830's when she wrote, after a stay of
nearly two years in the United States:

The pioneers of civilization, as the settlers in these new dis-
tricts may be regarded, care for other things more than for
education; or they would not come. They are, from whatever
motive, money-getters; and few but money-getting qualifications are to be looked for in them. . . . They are doomed to the
lowest office of social beings; to be the mechanical, unintelligent
pioneers of man in the wilderness. . . . I suppose there must be
such pioneers; but the result is a society which it is a punishment to its best members to live in. There is pedantry in those
who read; prejudice in those who do not; coxcombry among
the young gentlemen; bad manners among the young ladies;
and an absence of all reference to the higher, the real objects
of life.[5]

This is not the place in which to discuss generally a large
question. I speak of it, however, because it must be taken
into account when we consider and try to evaluate the

[5] *Society in America*, Vol. I (2d ed., 1837), pp. 298, 299.

achievement of an Emerson, of a Thoreau, of a Paul More. "How shall we sing the Lord's song in a strange land?" cried the psalmist; and that really is the question which American men of letters in every generation to our own day have had to attempt to answer—and have answered, taking them by and large, after a fashion which conclusively demonstrates the impossibility of bringing a great literature to birth in a new country. Uprooted, transplanted, man becomes something less than man; clings fanatically to those shreds of old religion, old culture, old far-off humanity, which he can bring with him; at the same time develops a new individuality both irritable and vacuous, and loses himself between two worlds, one of which he imagines he should put behind him, while the other remains a tantalizing dream of the future. For the literary historian, moreover, the influence of the geographical frontier merges into that of the intellectual and technological frontier created in the middle years of the last century by scientific discovery and by the new inventions and new speculative thought following thereupon. In the realm of the mind both frontiers have acted identically, and have given us a long succession of bewildered and frustrate lives, mirrored in imaginative literature, in thought, in action, and in education. I have earlier spoken of some part of this palsying influence, and of *The Education of Henry Adams* as a classic picture of a mind rendered helpless and hopeless by kaleidoscopic change with which it could never come to terms fast enough. Adams, his readers will recall, concluded that he loved change and motion, but found little satisfaction in it for all that, and never ceased trying to find an anchorage beyond it, in something that would at least look like, though it would not be, scientific law.

The conditions requisite for the development of our full humanity, in other words, are also those requisite for a great literature. And the whole history of America proves that a perpetual round of novelty is merely what, in daily life, we recognize it to be—a means of giving empty pleasure to children and to childish men and women. To overcome childishness, to attain maturity, to discover our full humanity, we need above all things stability in our surroundings, fixed

points by which to steer our course, foundations accepted
and established on which something can be built, and a line
of communication constantly open between ourselves and
those, of whatever generation or place, who have seen most
clearly and deeply the meaning of life, or who have so pictured it as to lead us below the changing surface to the constant elements of experience and to a vision of that ideal
Being which everywhere penetrates and gives form to our
world of Becoming. Yet the influence of continuing frontier
conditions has been, all along the line, of a directly contrary
sort. The disastrous notion has been implanted in us, and
has been every way encouraged, that we can somehow make
the United States an earthly paradise for everybody by de-
structive activity, by obliterating fixed points, by overturn-
ing everything accepted and established, by cutting lines of
communication with the past, by emptying our minds and
hearts and lives, in short, for a brand-new start. This process
of repudiation and reversion has, of course, provoked resistance—but prevailingly the fanatical resistance of lonely
outcasts clinging desperately to some "one thing necessary"
for salvation, and closing their minds obdurately to those
ever-changing factors in life which render their position
hopeless and ridiculous. Thus we see one impossible extreme
bringing to birth another, and nothing really to distinguish
the tone and attitude of a Harry Elmer Barnes from that
of a William Jennings Bryan, while an atmosphere of un-
reality equally surrounds both noisy contenders. For meanwhile the United States has been filled with money-getters,
assembled from all the world, whose values are completely
expressed in terms of cash and the things that cash will buy.
And when in 1929 the crazy pedestal toppled upon which
they had placed their god—whose name is Prosperity—and
the rock upon which they had founded themselves turned to
water and oozed away over-night, they were left suspended,
utterly without resource, and helplessly open to blank, para-
lysing doubt. This widespread *mood* of depression in 1932
seemed to an acute English observer the really significant
outcome of the great crash of material values. And her way
of accounting for it shows equally why we have always been

much more at the mercy of every chance new wind than the peoples of Europe upon whom we have tried to turn our backs:

Extroversion—that is a major characteristic of daily existence in the States. Of course, I am entirely aware and fully admit that any and every phase of American life, including this, finds itself repeated in Europe. It is not the American type of building, nor the American system of plumbing, . . . nor American methods of business, publicity, advertising, finance and so on that are invading us most seriously; it is the American outlook, of which all these things are but external symbols. To that outlook, with its purely material standards of value, corresponds a technique of life. My point is that the outlook and its technique are now exacting their penalty. That penalty, in the United States, is a general alarm, a general sense of insecurity, a general feeling of having no firm ground under the feet and no clear sky above the head, which, though insubstantial, and therefore difficult to describe, is the grimmest and by far the most serious aspect of their depression, as it is the basic explanation of that moral defeatism that is causing so many thoughtful people to look out on to the future with a dread that the present facts do not justify. And we need to understand this, just because, while the danger is there for us, for us there are factors and forces that counteract it: factors and forces that we can either strengthen or weaken, according as we choose to "Americanize" our civilization or to transform it in an antithetical direction. One feels them, those factors and forces, when one visits the U. S. A., because they are not there; it is awareness of them that makes one, there, a European in a foreign land. It is they, weak as they may be against the immense pressure of the money-values standard of Capitalist society, that have, up to date, enabled European nations, so much harder pressed materially, to resist with more of vital moral force and more of living self-respect than are to-day to be found in the United States.

  Take a small but significant point. In Europe, in any country in Europe, persons who are poor, even very poor, may still feel themselves and be accepted by others, as gentlefolk, if they either possess by inheritance, or have achieved by self-discipline, what is known and recognized as "breeding." This mysterious "breeding," which may, and often has, nothing to do with birth, and not very much to do with education in a formal sense, is a factor that, in a period of economic depression, counts power-fully in holding minds steady. It is a factor rarely met with, and practically never mentioned, in the U. S. A. There, money lost, all is lost. Again, in those societies, however overlaid, vulgar-ized, and commercialized their life may be, . . . other values still contend for recognition with the pecuniary, material ones. Europe, little as it may honour them, still has in its bones and blood, in the life cells that make its inhabitants, the Classical and the Medieval traditions; is still interpenetrated by an out-look upon life that, however crudely rejected in much of its action, deeply colours and conditions its thought. The age-old dispensations live on, and exert a sustaining authority.[6]

The age-old dispensations live, obviously, because they still have meaning and value, because without their light and guidance we are doomed to remain something less than men. And Professor Babbitt and Mr More in our day have at-tained pre-eminence and authority because they almost alone have seen not only that we must recover and conserve the past if we are to save ourselves from sheer barbarism, but also that for this task neither the antiquarian nor the pure traditionalist is in any way adequate. "The scholar," Mr T. R. Glover has wittily remarked, "for whom all facts are of significance and all of equal significance, never under-stands anything, though Nature is kind to him and conceals from him that there is anything to understand."[7] Men of this stamp, industrious, complacent, and jealous, we have in shoals, accumulating in our libraries vast masses of undi-gested fact and of learned comment, which nobody knows or ever will know how to use, and proving the truth of the an-cient saying recorded by Bacon, "that there is no great con-currence between learning and wisdom."[8] Yet without learn-

[6] *In America To-day,* by Mary Agnes Hamilton, 1932, pp. 163–165.
[7] *The Influence of Christ in the Ancient World,* 1929, p. 2.
[8] *Advancement of Learning,* Bk. II, xxiii, 4.

ing we cannot have wisdom; and the rare man whose learning issues in wisdom is he whom we should most especially and most gratefully honour. For what is needed anew in every generation is, as we have seen, re-interpretation and reconstruction; and it is in this sense, and because we have been cut loose from all moorings and been set adrift, that Lowell's often-quoted declaration—"Before we can have an American literature, we must have an American criticism"—is profoundly true, though, even so, much less than the whole truth. We must have an American criticism before we can have American men, with emphasis upon men, not upon "American"; and this criticism must penetrate and inform our higher education and, generally, our institutional life, so that, regaining our heritage of conserved human experience and reflection, we may come to recognize that which is constant in life amidst that which is changing, and may thus achieve stability and depth—may even bring forth a literature not merely reflecting "the times," like so much from Mather to Masters which is precious only to the social historian, but reflecting the timeless or universal elements of life which distinguish us from other animals and render us capable of rational morality, rational knowledge, and rational devotion to ideal ends.

And it is because of Mr More's success in breaking through the barriers set up by a "strange land," and by "the times," in overriding American isolation, or provincialism, and in making himself at home in the larger world of immemorial human experience; because of his success, too, in distinguishing the real problems raised by new knowledge and by changed conditions, and in reaching a solution which does violence to no part of our experience, which truly makes sense of life, and which is in harmony alike with ancient and with modern thought; and because, again, of his success in exhibiting the continuity of life, in opening up lines of communication with the past, and in establishing principles which have endless possibilities of further development and extension;—it is, in a word, because of the high value of his positive achievement that we do ourselves a wrong when we concentrate our gaze censoriously upon things he has failed to see or to accomplish, or upon particular judgements from which we feel bound, for reasons, to dissent. No critic's work, no man's work, is ever perfect or complete. The significance of a man's failures depends upon what else besides failure there is to record of him. And Mr More in his concern for principles, for that which is fundamental and primary, has blazed a pathway certain to be widened, paved, and pushed forward by others coming after him.

III

WE do ourselves a grievous wrong, moreover, if we fail to recognize that the most important and significant evidence we have of Mr More's success in critical endeavour lies in the development of his attitude towards Christianity, even though here, again, I do not think we can or should go entirely with him in his conclusion.

In general, however, Mr More's religious history—if I may so term it—accurately reflects an extraordinary change which has taken place during the last seventy-five years or thereabouts. During the second half of the nineteenth century it was believed by an ever-increasing number of thoughtful and educated people that Christianity was finally dead. The combined force of historical criticism and of scientific discovery had at last made the old fairy-tale completely incredible. Religion was simply, as Comte had declared, a relic from the race's childhood—and it was high time to put away childish things. Some there were to whom the disappearance of religion seemed simply a good riddance, bringing up no problem; but most realized that a substitute for religious belief must be found, and looked for it in philosophy, though Comte himself had ended his career as the inventor and high priest of a new religion—the religion of humanity. In one of these ways or the other the attempt to make good the alleged loss of Christianity has continued, and everybody knows something of its history, and of its ineffectiveness, save as it has degenerated into gross, though often sentimentalized, materialism.

Viewed broadly, the work of Professor Babbitt and the

earlier criticism of Mr More form one chapter in the history of the effort to find a philosophic substitute, not only for Christianity, but for religion. Both men were so impressed by the "advance of knowledge," by the independent critical methods responsible for it, and by the profoundly altered outlook attendant upon it, that they did not think of denying the new dispensation, but only of trying, by a more rigorous and consistent application of accepted critical methods, to find a place under it for responsible human life. And their success, as far as it went, seems to me incontestable. With this effort, furthermore, Professor Babbitt has remained content. Early defining his purpose, and its limits, he has used his massive powers rather as a faithful soldier fighting the good fight than as an alert and anxious inquirer. Thus he appears fully formed in his earliest essays; and his later books exhibit no further personal or philosophic development, but merely fortify his original position, or illustrate its applications, or restate his conclusions and admonitions. Thus too he has shown a forthright directness, a primitive integrity almost Homeric, which has enabled him to hew his way through complexities, through conflicting or doubtful evidence, sure of his object, and strangely sure that his bold simplifications laid bare, rather than sacrificed, the truth. This indeed has been his most unfortunate weakness, justly opening him to attack; though it has also been his strength, as a teacher and, if one may say so, as a party-leader. For he has been able, by his singleness of purpose and his directness, to inspire the confidence he himself has so obviously felt and, concurrently, to make a definite unmistakable impression in which the man himself and his convictions have seemed organically to be combined.

Nevertheless, spite of his penetration and the essential rightness of his reading of human nature, Professor Babbitt has rather intensified than solved the greatest of our problems. He arouses in one the same feeling of mingled admiration and dissatisfaction that Socrates arouses, and the same conviction that one cannot go with him at all unless one is prepared to go further than he himself thought necessary or, it may be, possible. This, as we have seen, is the conclusion to which Mr More came, after standing many years shoulder to shoulder with Professor Babbitt; and I believe it is the conclusion to which every student of Professor Babbitt's writings must come, in proportion as he understands them and reflects seriously upon their constant implication.

Nor is this the whole story; for it has become as clear as anything can be in our world that those eminent men of the nineteenth century who believed they were witnessing the death of religion were fantastically wrong. They were, like Professor Babbitt, like Mr More himself, dazzled by the growth of knowledge, and, howsoever they differed from each other, were alike in their confidence that men could at length live on the basis of what they positively knew, or were certainly coming to know. But even while this confidence was rising to its height, warning signs were multiplying to disturb it; and by now it is so obvious that it was founded on misunderstandings of more than one kind that I shall not waste words in arguing the matter. Man is as truly a religious animal as he is a social animal, and the only question which really arises at any time concerns the kind of religion he is to have.

Mr More's realization that there can be no substitute for religion and his consequent activity thus make him, not simply one representative of a transient though inevitable phase of thought, but a significant leader through the several phases of the whole troubled movement of reconstruction which the times demand. For Christian faith is not incompatible with any scientific knowledge we now have or are likely to have; nor is it incompatible with any human knowledge we now have or are likely to have; on the contrary, it is so completely consonant with our human knowledge that the Jesus of history may properly be said, as we have seen, to have confirmed religious faith rather than to have implanted it in us. And that which new knowledge and changed conditions have caused to die is simply a mass of legend and of symbolism and of moral legislation which gradually had come to surround Christianity, until the faith itself was obscured, and then transferred to its perishable integuments; so that from the sixteenth century to the present time Christianity has seemed again and again to be discredited by scientific discoveries and by increased historical knowledge. But during these centuries a great deal outside of Christianity has also been discredited for good and all—a great deal which once passed for science, a great deal which once passed for history —while Christianity itself has continued to live, successfully defying every learned or insolent pronouncement that its day was over. Obviously, it continues to live because it has within it, like certain other age-old dispensations, an unexhausted vitality, not touched, not susceptible of being touched, by enemies. And only the very ignorant can be deceived by the claim that Christianity no longer appeals to any save themselves. Mr Edwyn Bevan, one of the most learned of contemporary English scholars and Christians, has pointed out that to-day no less than in the past we find within the Christian fold men as learned and as able as any outside it;[9] and he has admirably stated the real point of cleavage between the contemporary Christian and non-Christians:

That Jesus was the Divine Son who existed before His incarnation with God and who retained in His incarnate state knowledge of His heavenly state, which enabled Him to speak with authority of the things beyond man's ken—there is no question that this is the teaching of the Fourth Gospel, as it had been the teaching of St Paul. It is not found explicitly in the earlier Gospels, the Synoptics. . . . If therefore our view of what Jesus Himself taught is limited to the sayings attributed to Him by the Synoptists, it is hard to show that He Himself ever claimed what He is represented as claiming in the Fourth Gospel. That does not mean that the claim is not true. That it *was* true, was certainly the belief of the Christian community many years before the first generation of disciples had passed away. Whether we to-day regard it as true is no longer a question of historical criticism, but of the philosophy of religion. One may say, indeed, that the real battlefield between the Christian tradition and non-Christian views of the universe in coming days will be in the region of philosophy, not of literary and historical

[9] *Hellenism and Christianity*, 1921, p. 265.

criticism. Conclusions in the field of literary and historical criticism can never be anything but conclusions of greater or less probability; but what we judge to be probable and improbable depends upon our general view of the universe; that is, upon our philosophy. To anyone who sees ground for accepting the Christian view of the universe, many things stated in the ancient documents will seem probable, which must needs be improbable for those who cannot accept that view. It is in the field of philosophy that the issues are really determined.[10]

This does not mean, of course, that to Mr Bevan *everything* "stated in the ancient documents" seems either true or probably true. Nor does it mean that Mr Bevan is a Christian believing everything, in exactly the same way, that was believed by some member of the earliest Christian community, or everything that was believed by some orthodox contemporary of St Thomas, or everything that was believed by some reformed churchman, Anglican or Calvinistic or Wesleyan, of the early nineteenth century. It means that he has determined for himself what is essential in the way of belief if one is to be properly a Christian, and has discovered for himself that the real conflict which we are all aware of to-day is not one between Christianity and knowledge, but one between two perennial types of people—between the kind of man who feels that we are all creaturely beings, able to accomplish nothing without supernatural aid, and in need most of self-reformation, and the kind of man who feels that we are all "lords of creation," able to discover for ourselves the absolute truth of things and able to act perfectly in accordance therewith.

I believe this conclusion to be substantially correct, and it suggests, amongst other things, that neither the Christian view of life *nor any other* will ever be accepted by all men. But the point with which I am here specially concerned is that no one to-day can reach the above conclusion without effecting a radical re-interpretation or reconstruction of traditional Christianity, and that unless such a reconstruction

[10] *Sibyls and Seers,* 1928, pp. 90–91.

can be and is effected—not privately and by a few, here and there, for themselves, but officially and institutionally—the Christian view of man and the world really is doomed to a long period of eclipse, and the western hemisphere to a long period of progressive barbarization. It is true enough, as I have already said, that historic Christianity has weathered many crises; but it has not done so without being itself changed with changing conditions. There is a natural tendency to forget this, because in modern times change has come principally through the multiplication of sects, while each church or sect has hardened itself in opposition to others as a means of self-preservation. The resultant confusion is now almost inexpressible. At one extreme the dead weight of illegitimate metaphysical speculation, exploded science, discredited legend, and traditional absolutism which the Roman Catholic Church has come to carry is notorious and suicidal; but, at the other, many recently formed groups seem to carry no weight of tradition at all, dead or alive, being only nominally Christian and actually devoted to "ethical culture" or to humanitarianism or, more specifically, to political reform or to social revolution.[11]

Hence arises the importance of the great work of reconstruction carried out by Mr More in *The Greek Tradition*. For Mr More does not hold on to the mere name, or to traditional usages, of Christianity, while divesting them of all reality; he does not sacrifice either the substance or the spirit of the Christian tradition, which he rightly regards as having

[11] No one can understand the contemporary situation of Christianity who wilfully closes his eyes to the fact that Protestantism, spite of one concession after another, is rapidly declining. Many so-called Protestant sects are no longer Christian in fact, and their members do not even understand what Christianity is. Roman Catholicism, on the other hand, spite of all that is noted above, is growing in strength. Only Rome, in other words, and the American Fundamentalists are in the Western world securely holding on to that which gives Christianity its vitality;—and both present religion to us in a form not even remotely credible, I should say, to anyone who is at once educated, honest, and reflective. Hence I cannot help thinking that Rome's present appearance of strength is deceptive; that the true custodians of Christianity to-day are a few scattered individuals; and that the future of organized Christianity depends upon, and must await, the construction of a new Christian Church, at once modern and genuine.

its centre in the doctrine of the Incarnation; yet he does sacrifice without hesitation the dead weight carried by Roman
Catholicism and by various Protestant bodies; so that he
really succeeds in building up, on a solid foundation of Platonism, a structure which enables us to see why the Christian
religion does have an inexhaustible vitality. Professor A. C.
McGiffert has said that *Christ the Word* is written "by a
Platonist not a theologian."[12] In these words he has stated
one reason for Mr More's success, as we can see by looking
at the principal work of Bishop Gore's later years, which in
its collective form is entitled *The Reconstruction of Belief*.
The two series of books are the more readily comparable because they not only have the same general purpose but come
to some identical conclusions. But the theologian's appeal is
to "reason," whereas Mr More's is to experience; and Bishop
Gore's "reason" leads him triumphantly to one fore-ordained
conclusion after another, in a manner only too familiar after
all these years, and now at length perfectly unconvincing.
Further differences there are, all of them, I believe, to Mr
More's advantage, and suggesting most strongly that the
fate of Christianity to-day lies in the hands of those who have
felt the pressure of the modern age sufficiently to compel
them, for the present, though reluctantly, to stand outside of
the Church.

And this precisely is the cause of my conviction that we
neither can nor should go the whole way with Mr More. No
one, I will venture to say, could have a more unqualified admiration than mine, or a deeper gratitude, for the fine
achievement, at once critical and constructive, represented
by *The Greek Tradition*. This work contributes far more
than any other I know of to the formation of a new Christianity, authentic, solid, and fully consonant with experience
and knowledge. But when Mr More had completed his long
journey from the Athens of Socrates and Plato to Chalcedon,
he apparently thought he had found a way of acceptance of
Christianity as it is understood by the Catholic party within
the Episcopal Church, and he then began to write, in *The*

---

[12] *History of Christian Thought,* Vol. I, 1932, p. 343.

Catholic Faith, rather as an apologist for orthodoxy than as an independent critic. The distinction I would make is by no means absolute, and the volume in question contains several essays very remarkable for penetration, vigour, formal beauty, and sane convincing thoughtfulness. But one of these, the essay on "The Church," perfectly illustrates the difficulty I speak of. Here Mr More argues, unanswerably I believe, that

Religion can be neither purely individualistic nor purely determined. In one sense individualistic, yes, in so far as the ultimate responsibility of choice cannot be withdrawn from the conscience of each man, whether he shall accept this dogma and this form as complying with what seems to him the verity of his own inner life, or shall reject them as expansions in a false direction; but determined also to this degree, that he will be extremely hesitant to set up his private judgement against a formulated tradition, and will prefer to abide in humble, yet not abject, submission to the authority of a wider experience than his own.

It follows that, even at the best, religion must be seriously imperfect unless it is guarded and conserved by an authoritative Church; but it also follows that the Church's authority, though real and sufficient, cannot be absolute. The whole discussion could scarcely be bettered, and in the course of a few pages Mr More draws out a picture of the Church as it should be, and perhaps might be, which leaves one feeling that the judicial habit of mind has in this essay one of its surest and most admirable vindications. Yet where is such a Church to be found? Mr More writes as if we had only to open our eyes in order to discover it, or as if he himself had become hopelessly submerged in that atmosphere of determined and bold pretence which unfortunately characterizes "Catholic" Episcopalians in the United States and in England. Had he stopped to ask himself how legitimate authority—authority not "sanctioned" by sheer physical force or by trickery—is ever won or preserved, he must have seen that a hundred problems, besides those fundamental questions which he has sought to answer in the earlier volumes of *The*

Greek Tradition, remain to be faced and resolved before any Church can attain that position of authority in the modern world so excellently defined in his essay. At its close, to suggest what may be said for authority acknowledged to be sufficient yet not absolute, he quotes a sentence by Emerson: "God offers to every mind its choice between truth and repose; take which you please, you can never have both." Had Mr More not finally sought repose, he could never have imagined that the crisis which now faces Christianity could be met by tinkering with the Apostles' Creed, after the fashion which he illustrates in another essay in *The Catholic Faith.*

No, the hard necessity which drove Mr More as a youth into lonely ways, apart from Christians no less than from the self-satisfied yet discontented children of this world, and which has made his writings from early manhood to elder age "a record of continuous religious discovery"—discovery, be it marked, not reconciliation, not submission—that hard necessity still exists, and still calls for heroic resolution equally with "spiritual genius." No specious compromises, no careful patching of outworn garments, no union of existing sects or groups, no exercise of "ecclesiastical statesmanship," will now suffice to "save" organized or institutional Christianity. There are times when a ship must be stripped bare, when precious cargo must be thrown overboard, when everything must be sacrificed to the one end of riding out a storm, in order that at least the ship herself and her crew may be saved. Historic Christianity has encountered a storm of unparalleled magnitude, and it is nothing short of folly to suppose that any half-way measures will keep the ship afloat. Mr More has shown, better than anyone else, as I believe, what must be saved, and he has courageously thrown overboard much that we should not try to save. He and others with him in England have thus made an honest and good beginning, which can be taken up hopefully and carried further;—but only on the condition that we refuse unqualifiedly to follow his guidance when he begins to intimate that Anglo-Catholicism is our promised land.

IV

Though we cannot, then, agree with all of Mr More's "particular judgements," we can never forget either that he "is authentically concerned with the first and last things of human experience." For the stamp of a high seriousness is impressed upon all his work, and through his pages we everywhere feel that we are in the presence of a man of character who is devoted singly to the cause of truth, and who brings to his search a mind at once incisive and informed, and an extraordinary determination to follow the evidence at whatever cost. This is conclusively attested by his readiness to change when he has found himself on the wrong path. We have seen him alter his course more than once, where any smaller man would have hesitated long, preferring above most things to save his own face, as we say. And while it is a fact, alas, that a man may be utterly sincere and wrong, still, in a world where such knowledge as we can have is relative, our knowledge must often await our own development and accumulation of experience, so that without a sincerity like Mr More's no significant critical inquiry is possible. And with it, Mr More through his very changes has preserved an enviable and rare integrity. Hence it is that as we come to know him from the pages of his books we discover a man who renews our confidence in the dignity and worth of human nature, a man who rewards acquaintance in other ways also as few in any generation can, a man too whose judgements are always significant and stimulating, whether or not we think them always right. Clarendon tells us of himself that,

Next the immediate blessing and providence of God Almighty, which had preserved him throughout the whole course of his life (less strict than it ought to have been) from many dangers and disadvantages, in which many other young men were lost; he owed all the little he knew, and the little good that was in him, to the friendships and conversation he had still been used to, of the most excellent men in their several kinds that lived in that age; by whose learning, and information, and instruction, he formed his studies, and mended his understanding; and by whose gentleness and sweetness of behaviour, and justice, and virtue, and example, he formed his manners, subdued that pride, and suppressed that heat and passion he was naturally inclined to be transported with.[13]

Mr More has spent his life with "the most excellent men in their several kinds" who have lived in ancient and modern times, has been formed by that real companionship won through study, as we are all formed by the company we keep, and has himself become one of that small number by whose learning, and justice, and virtue, and example we can profit most.

"After all," Mr More has written, "the truth for most of us is like a spark faintly glimmering in some dark corner of the breast until it is kindled into flame by another's fire." Mr More has the rare power of kindling the spark of self-knowledge within us because critical inquiry has been the very substance of his life; and because his life has been, not superficial, not peripheral, not devoted to casual pleasure or to self-advancement or to self-expression, but a life formed by an unescapable, deep inner division, reaching into and opening the central, fundamental problem of all human existence, age-old, perennial, still new in every troubled generation. Thus from his profound, sane distrust of his own unsupported yet unconquerable sense of spiritual reality arose all his wide-ranging study of the masters of human knowledge, and his empirical inquisitions, which led to the formation of comprehensive critical standards solidly based on the constant aspects of human nature, and serving well, not some ephemeral or sectarian purpose, born of problems peculiar to one age or place, but the great purpose of making intelligible and significant the whole body of diverse experience recorded in the literature of all ages and places.

To undertake this task and to carry it out, not perfectly indeed, but faithfully and well, is an unmistakable mark of greatness. And I am impressed anew by Mr More's success, by the *catholicity* of his criticism, when I turn to the produc-

[13] *Life of Edward Earl of Clarendon,* by Himself (Oxford, 1857), Vol. I, p. 27.

tions of our latest school of critics and observe what reason the student of literature and of life now has for feeling ungrateful to Karl Marx. I cannot help thinking of those stern destroyers of "the opposition" who ushered in the New Deal for Russia as I see the havoc wrought in the ranks of American men of letters by Comrade Calverton and Comrade Hicks. Mr Calverton's *Liberation of American Literature* I have already mentioned and sufficiently characterized. Mr Granville Hicks himself, though bound to regard Mr Calverton as a brother-in-arms, is uncomfortable in his presence. *"The Liberation of American Literature,"* he politely says, "is a valuable piece of pioneering, though it may well be superseded by subtler and sounder studies." Subtler and, by comparison, sounder *The Great Tradition* certainly is; and Mr Hicks is an engaging, unpretentious writer, wielding lighter weapons than the brave, blundering pioneer's. Yet his intentions are not less deadly. "There are," he roundly says, "no eternal problems." Conditions are always changing, always unique, so that the problems of each age are solely its own. Hence the successive ages of society are quite unrelated to each other, and "the only problems we really know are those that are posed by our own age." This tall piece of dogmatism unfortunately "proves" too much; for it "demonstrates" that history is not only meaningless, because of the discontinuity of human life on earth, but impossible. If the only problems we can really know are those of our own age, obviously we are forced to consign Comrade Calverton's efforts to limbo, and even, I should think, *The Great Tradition*, whose very title becomes an odd anomaly in such a world as Mr Hicks's theory-ridden imagination portrays. But Mr Hicks goes further. Nothing less than a regular knock-out is his aim, and he finds it as easy as can be to establish a proper critical standard for his purpose:

It has become increasingly clear, even to those who do not want to see, that the central fact in American life is the class struggle. The writer has a series of choices. If he ignores the class struggle, he surrenders all hope of arriving at a clear interpretation, out of which a significant formal pattern may be devised, and he commits himself to evasion after evasion. If he assumes the role of impartiality, he merely deceives and confuses himself, since impartiality is impossible. If he accepts the existing order and assumes that it operates for the best interests of mankind, he becomes an apologist, and dishonesty and misrepresentation follow. If he recognizes the existing order for what it is and nevertheless accepts it because he profits by it, he avoids the weakness of evasion, but he cuts himself off from a large part of the human race, and callousness is substituted for the sympathy which is so important an attribute. If, however, the writer allies himself with the proletariat, there is no need of evasion or self-deception. He may be tempted to exaggerate the faults of capitalists or the virtues of workers, but if he is wise he will find in facts his all-sufficient bulwark. Moreover, as this way of looking at life becomes an integral part of his imaginative equipment, he can not only perceive the operation of underlying forces; he can also rejoice in their play because of his confidence in what they will eventually accomplish.

Naturally, with this criterion Mr Hicks mows them down; and when practically all American novelists, poets, and critics since the Civil War are disposed of, and the smoke clears away, whom should we discover, still erect and unharmed, but our old friend, Comrade Dos Passos. In him "and in his like-minded colleagues," Mr Hicks tells us, "we find the modern expression of the spirit that moves in the noblest creations of the past."

It is not necessary to emphasize the crudity, shallowness, and falsehood of such criticism. The Marxians in the field of literature are comparable to Professor Harry Elmer Barnes in the field of religion. Mr Hicks's book is chiefly interesting as an illustration of the absurdities into which the spirit of fanaticism can lead inexperienced and unreflective young people. Mr Hicks in effect martyrs himself to show us what we descend to when we break the chain of historic culture and bound ourselves by our own immediate and one-sided experi-

ence. Limiting himself to the contemporary scene, he remains
simply ignorant and unintelligent, like Arnold's man who,
knowing only his Bible, could not understand even that.

Mr Clifton Fadiman, in a review of Mr Noel Coward's collected plays, has said:

When a playwright stresses the dexterity of his technique, it
is usually because he has lost faith in the soundness of his ideas.
Mr Coward tries to save the show by implying that he has no
ideas at all. But, much as I should like to agree with him, I
cannot accept this conclusion. It is not that Mr Coward has no
ideas. It is that what ideas he has are so youthful, so confused,
so *teeny-weeny*.[14]

No better words could be found to describe the difference between Mr More's criticism and that not only of Mr Hicks but
of, really, the general run of American critics. Compared with
Mr More's, their ideas are youthful, confused, *teeny-weeny*.
And precisely this, rather than the mistakes and failures Mr
More has been guilty of, has been the chief cause of the abuse
which has been hurled at him. Sainte-Beuve wrote of himself:
"I have indeed my vices and weaknesses, but it is for what is
good in me, for my taste for uprightness and truth and for
my independence of judgement that I have irritated so many
and provoked so much anger." Inevitably—and nowhere
more than in the United States—the teeny-weeny fellows
have resented the presence amongst them of a man whose
thought is incisive and profound, whose judgement is incor-
ruptible, whose concern is with the greatest subjects, and
whose style is that of a Christian gentleman.

14 *The New Yorker,* 16 December, 1933, p. 80.

APPENDIX A

I

VERSE from *Helena and Occasional Poems* (G. P. Put-
nam's Sons, New York and London, 1890). The title-
poem fills the first twenty-seven pages, and is comprised
in twenty-five sections varying in length from three to twenty-
three lines. The sections are practically independent, though
there is a slight narrative element which loosely connects them.

HELENA

IV

All the lilacs were purple 'neath the window,
All the air was of gold when Helen bade me
Leave my papers and help her gather flowers:
You are taller, she said, and you can reach them.
Gladly went I, and never sight was fairer
Than my Helena 'mid the purple clusters.
See, she murmured, a nest among the branches,
Hidden there in the tangle. And I told her
Soon the owners would come with merry music
Learned in sunnier climes, the pair of catbirds
Newly mated the year before who built it.
Favoured shrub! when thy odours all forsake thee,
What sweet melodies through thy leaves will tremble!

TO THE GOOD SHIP "LA CHAMPAGNE"

(Which sailed from Havre, December 15, 1888)

1

I saw the vessel leave her port
And sail into the west;
Now heaven behold yon gallant bark,
For she beareth a lady blest.

May peace attend her o'er the sea,
And weather good and fair;
Nor rougher gale smite her amain
Than the breathing of my prayer.

I saw her sink into the waves—
So hope, I thought, departs—
Till only a line of smoke was left,
Like memory in our hearts.

Now heaven forfend that I repine
Or hide me from the day;
Though yonder boat that swims the tide,
Bear many a hope away.

4

In my dream a storm blew out of the north
And smote the shuddering main;
The wind beat on the frantic waves,
Till I almost felt their pain.

Dear Lord, I cried, as Thou art good,
Pity the ships that are tost;
If a love like my love followeth each,
What love were left if they 're lost.

I awoke in my trouble then, and lo!
A light serene in the sky;
'T was only my heart that was beaten and tost
By doubts, I know not why.

7

I follow my boat afar, afar,
I follow her day and night;
Now wherefore yonder fog drops down
To steal her from my sight?

I see her plunge into the mist,
And close my eyes in despair;
And I pray in the darkness of my soul,
For the boat in the darkness there.

O LIMPID POOL

O limpid pool so clear!
Deep in thy silent dream,
The beauties rare of earth and air
Like faery visions gleam.

And would that in my soul,
Such worlds of wonderment
Might mirrored be, and give to me
Thy dream of pure content.

SONG

If I were where my heart is,
I 'd find my dreams, I know;
And find the fairest maiden,
Whom they found long ago.

If I were where my dreams are,
I 'd find my heart, I wis;
And find the dearest maiden,
And greet her with a kiss.

A VISION

A vision of the watches of the night:
The City of our God, set like a jewel
Upon the utmost verge—O kind and cruel!
Bitter and sweet! how mingled by the Might
That made them for what end? Behold the sight
Of that fair City, and the stately rule
And measure of its golden streets, the cool
Sequestered fountains, and the river's flight.
Behold the towering sapphire walls, and round
A stream of music ever flowing sweet,
A rampart strong, invisible, of sound.
And still behold! the hideous throng that beat
Against its unseen bulwark, to rebound
Like flies that swarm the window's glassy cheat.

HIDDEN MUSIC

As one who carries with him through the day
The memory of music heard before,
While snatches of the half-forgotten score
Start on his lips or through his fancy stray;
I wander with the burden of my lay,
Singing at intervals, though hearing more,
The music flowing from such hidden store,
And song that ere I fashion dies away.
    Thus too the toil of men, their idle word,
And the unremitting murmur of the street;
Or melody of leaf-embowered bird,
And rustle of the clover at our feet,
Recall the perfect strains I somewhere heard,
Whose theme in part my broken songs repeat.

II

VERSE—and, in two instances, prose—from *The Great Refusal;*
Being Letters of a Dreamer in Gotham (Boston and New York,
Houghton, Mifflin and Company, 1894). The longest of the
poems in this volume (*The Pedagogue*, pp. 19–36), not here reproduced, is inspired by James Thomson's *City of Dreadful
Night*. The source is instantly evident, and is acknowledged by
a phrase quoted under the title. It is well done, but—aside from
the difficulty caused by its considerable length—I have thought
it best to reprint pieces less obviously derivative.

V

The tremulous sunlight lay
Dreamily on the floor,
Weaving the colours of the dying day
The Persian emblems o'er;
While odours, as of one just gone away,
Hovered about the door.
And on the carpet scattered,
The purple petals lay
Of lilies-of-a-day,

As if in all that house to none it mattered
That these were cast away.
Over their purple lips
The stamens lolled for breath,
As from the pallid mouth of one who sips
The languid draught of death.
And there I dreamed my dream
Of love and lilies, while the last pale beam
With kisses cherished, ere it crept away,
These flowers of but a day.

IX

. . . Istar, you know, was the old Semitic goddess of beauty
and love, very desirable for the eyes, whose breath was so sweet
that beneath it the flowers unfolded, and whose influence was so
strong that the tides rose under her feet. Certain forward
scholars claim that her name is merely another form of the
Persian Esther, which itself means a star, and might well be
given to one whose glory has ever been symbolized to the people
by the white planet of evening. However that may be, fancy a
young man, grown weary of living in the long reveries of the
monks, and dejected by the tumult of ambitions, who unexpectedly becomes acquainted with the legend of this pagan
divinity, with this goddess whose beauty seemed so passionate
and unregretful, that the soul which had but once looked upon
her unveiled brow would bear with it something of her joy and
whiteness even into the darkness of death. Such a man might
have written what you will now peruse.

Istar, at whose sweet-falling breath the flower
    Unfoldeth on the bough its dainty art,
For whom the tides in elemental power
    Heave with the beating of a human heart;

Unveil to me thy brow's whole loveliness,
    And Jesus' bloody sweat and dropping tears,
I will deny, with all that men confess—
    The builded hope of two long thousand years.

But let thy maid unveil to me thine eyes,
   And all the high ambitions of our race,
The proud achievements and the power they prize,
   I will renounce, and bear me in disgrace.

O Istar, lady of the fragrant breath,
Let not my soul go the long way of death,
   Unwhitened by the glory of thy face!

XVII

The fire light glinting on her face
   Made her a fairy thing,
Upon whose forehead I could trace
   All my imagining.

The shadow and the wandering light
   Troubled her open eyes,
Like pools beneath the falling night
   When the red sunset dies.

So in her heart unreal desires
   Unbidden come and go,
Mere shadows of the burning fires
   That in my bosom glow.

XXIV

As on my heart thy form is prest,
O Spouse of Mary! may my quest
Find harbour in thy saintly breast.

What power was over thee to win
The love of her who knew no sin,
The love of her so pure within,

So chaste within, without so fair,
The God himself might not forbear
To reckon thee his rival there?

O Spouse of Mary! in thy bride
Our human hearts have deified
All fairest things that here abide,—

In her, the mother of our Lord,
Who spake in him the Living Word
Of God's sweet comfort, to afford

Unto our heavyladen brain
The knowledge we might not attain,
That Love o'er God himself doth reign.

O Spouse of Mary! thou wast strong
To win her love who did belong
To God alone for right or wrong:—

Yet I, I know not if thy love
With all its might could rise above
My passion and the hope thereof;

I know not if the gathered fears,
The transports and repentant tears
Of all our race through all the years,

Wherewith thy bride is made divine,
Can more than equal love like mine!
Can more than equal love like mine!

Thou Lord of Love! from thy great dower
Spare me the semblance of thy power
To storm this summit of Love's tower.

O Spouse of Mary! may my quest
Find harbour in thy saintly breast,
As on my heart thy form doth rest.

XXXII

A summer noon we loitered by a brook;
    And I, to win her shy lips oftener,
    Whispered, "Oh, but she knew how fair she were
    When kissing—kiss me, dearest, whilst you look!"
She smiled, and, leaning o'er a waveless nook,
    Half turned her mouth.—Ah me, the mirrored stir
    Of lilies round her flower-face lovelier
    Bewildered so, that kiss I never took.

Even then, how frail, I thought, the shadows rest
On troubled streams that wander to the sea,
How fair and still on so untamed a power!
In such a wise her beauty in my breast,
Above the tide of passions as they flee,
Shall brood serenely like a mirrored flower.

XXXIII

. . . What touched me most, however, was the attitude of a
young Jewess sitting desolate on one of the miserable stoops of
Mott Street. She sat quite still, with one arm supporting her
chin and the other hanging listlessly over a basket at her side.
Her face was inexpressibly beautiful, perfectly pure, with just
the faintest shadow of suffering on it to foretell the ruin that
must fall. She remained motionless as a picture, utterly regardless of the noisy altercation of two men, apparently Irish, who
stood on the steps above her. Her mouth was delicate as a
queen's, and the lips, slightly puckered from the pressure of the
hand on which she leaned, seemed to me to express both weari-
ness and disdain. Her eyes were cast down, and she did not
raise them in the slightest although I involuntarily stopped before her. She appeared oblivious of everything about her, as if
brooding on the great mystery of her life. My first thought was
of the Madonnas I have seen portrayed in the galleries of Italy;
and this unknown Jewess stood before me as the embodiment of
all the dreams of the centuries, the living image of the inspiration which those artists wrought upon their canvas. And then I
wondered what she was brooding upon, and whether her beauty
was to her also a delight, or rather troubled her consciousness
with its weight of mysterious responsibility. Did she realize the
value of this possession which, handed down in the world from
one woman to another, has always been to mankind the enduring sign of the incarnation of his God,—this moulding of inert
matter into the spiritual forms of loveliness, which must appeal
to men as the indwelling of the divine puissance, and as the emblem of the eternal love that pervades the world and that has
been fashioned by religious instinct into the legend of an incarnate virgin-born God? Did the vague shadow of such a thought

trouble her, making this beauty of hers a sacred and awful thing to be borne through the shocks of her rude life? I suppose not. Some nearer grief weighed upon her, or some more definite foreboding. And yet, feeling as I do the higher significance of beauty, I often wonder what burden of possession it brings the owner. You could answer me this if only you would. Is this superlative grace also but a shadow, the work of chance, a mere phenomenon of the surface? or does it arise from some interior necessity, and is it the expression of a spiritual indwelling power? And certainly if it be the emblem of such a controlling force, some intimation thereof must abide with the owner, some intuition, vague perhaps, of the god within him who so clothes himself in corporeal grace. . . .

A FAIR JEWESS

In Mott Street, crouching on the ruined stoop,
    She sits and broods her womanhood complete,
With brow leaned forward and tired lids that droop,
    Unmindful of the rabble of the street.

Some new-born wonder makes her more than fair;
    As if reflecting in her virgin bloom
How one, for comeliness, was said to bear
    The Lord of human triumph in her womb.

Ah, might she dream that beauty such as hers
    Bears still the incarnate Christ whom we implore!
Or is it fear, the shadow of a curse,
    To trail this fragile flower from door to door?

Of all the glory of our Empire City,
This image follows yet with tears and pity
    For something lost that will return no more.

APPENDIX B

I

CONSIDER, for example, Mr More, our chief exponent of the intellectualist position. Mr More, referring to the yellow press, delivers himself of the following remarks: "On days when no sensational event has occurred, it will indulge in the prettiest sentimental sermons on the home and on family felicities. . . . But let the popular mind be excited by some crime of lust, and the same journal will forget the sweet obligations of home and wife . . . and will deck out the loathsome debauchery of a murderer and his trull as the spiritual history of two young souls finding themselves in the pure air of passion." . . . Now, really, whatever the provocations of the yellow press, can one imagine a piece of worse literary breeding than this? Yet it can almost be called Mr More's habitual tone whenever, leaving the charmed circle of literary ideas, he deals with modern society. Far from being reasonable, disinterested, and humane, his note is one of nagging, pettish, and one would almost say vulgar exasperation; he betrays a tendency to break out on every occasion into promiscuous abuse. How then can our intellectualists expect to convert us to the music of the classical discipline when some of their own most representative minds—for Mr More is by no means unique as an advocate of "the classic point of view"—are so singularly ill-nurtured? If this is what the classical discipline does—how can we avoid being led, quite unjustly, to conclude?—let us by all means turn to the discipline of science which produced the ever just and ever genial William James.

That is what we mean when we speak of the breakdown of intellectualism; for of course the reason why Mr More's humane attitude cracks and crumbles so at the touch of life is because it is based on a culture of the intellect that is not borne out by a corresponding culture of the feelings. Mr More's emotional life, as his writings exhibit it, is just as crude and untempered as the intellectual life of the younger generation which he attacks. Why is this so? Because Mr More's intellectualism is the converse and counterpart of the materialism that has led to the younger generation's incapacity to accept the discipline he offers it. He has not been able to feel human values finely because to have done so would have been to upset his whole faith in a society based not upon the creative but upon the acquisitive instincts of men, a society ruled over by the "natural aristocracy" of economic power. Mr More is simply a belated pioneer, with all the repressed impulses, the fundamental limitations, the exaggerated antipathies that belong to the pioneer type, extended and subtilized in the sphere of the intellect alone. Turn from his philosophical and literary essays, in which he is able to be humane at large, to his essays on social and economic themes, and see how quickly he lets the cat out of the bag. "Looking at the larger good of society," he observes, "we may say that the dollar is more than the man and that *the rights of property are more important than the right to life*."[1] . . . Mr Babbitt and Mr Brownell differ from Mr More in being instinctively humane minds.

> Van Wyck Brooks, *Letters and Leadership*, 1918, pp. 70–73 and 81.

II

The professional critic . . . by virtue of his self-appointed office . . . is a guide, a universal guide, through the mazes of art and life. It is no wonder that the average critic, who is either a teacher or a reviewer, shrinks from his true business, and devotes himself to formal studies in literary history, rhetorical trifling, or the expression of the average tribal reaction to new books and plays. . . .

We have critics who conceive more nobly and severely of their calling. Among the older group of them it is necessary to

[1] Mr Brooks makes this sentence up by piecing together parts of two widely separated sentences in Mr More's essay on "Property and Law" in *Aristocracy and Justice* (*Shelburne Essays,* Ninth Series). In so doing Mr Brooks not only omits qualifications attached to each statement by Mr More, but manages to convey an impression radically different from that conveyed by Mr More's essay itself.

point out only Mr Paul Elmer More. He is a scholar of high
and fine accomplishment. He not only knows but with a cool
passion proclaims his knowledge of the oneness of literature
and life and of the deep sources of the critic's aims and works.
Unfortunately for the solidity of his fame and the extent of
his influence, Mr More has an icy and cosmic arrogance which,
by its antecedent assumptions, invalidates his whole critical
thought. Undaunted by history or science, unsubdued by the
surgings of the "cosmic weather," calmly oblivious of the crumbling of every absolute ever invented by man, he continues in
his fierce and growing isolation to assert that he knows what
human life ought to be and what kinds of literature ought to be
permitted to express its character. That a form of art or life
exists and that it engages the whole hearts of men makes little
difference to him. He knows. . . . And what does he know?
Only, at bottom, his own temperamental tastes and impulses
which he seeks to rationalize by an appeal to carefully selected
and isolated tendencies in art and thought. And, having ra-
tionalized them by an artifice so fragile, he seeks to impose them
upon the men and the artists of his own day in the form of laws.
I know his reply so well. It is this, that if you abandon his
method, you sink into universal scepticism and indiscriminate
acceptance. The truth is that I believe far more than he does.
For I love beauty in all its forms and find life tragic and worthy
of my sympathy in every manifestation. I need no hierarchical
moral world for my dwelling-place, because I desire neither to
judge nor to condemn. Fixed standards are useless to him whose
central passion is to have men free. Mr More needs them for the
same inner reason—infinitely rarified and refined, of course—
for which they are necessary to the inquisitor and the militant
patriot. He wants to damn heretics . . . I do not. His last
refuge, like that of every absolutist at bay, would be in the
corporate judgement of mankind. Yes, mankind has let the
authoritarians impose on it only too often. But their day is
nearly over. And I need not stop to show how flimsy a fiction
that corporate judgement is, so soon as any reasonable interpretation is given to the word judgement. . . .

But we are not left, most fortunately, wholly to the mercy of
Mr More's and Professor Irving Babbitt's and Professor Stuart

P. Sherman's vision of a static universe with themselves in the inner shrine determining the eternal fixities that they promulgate. A group of critics, young men or men who do not grow old, are at work upon the creation of a civilized cultural atmosphere in America. Their circle of readers is still small and their influence limited. Every man's hand is against theirs. Like a troup of shivering young Davids—slim and frail but with a glint of morning sunshine on their foreheads—they face an army of Goliaths.

> Ludwig Lewisohn, Introduction to *A Modern Book of Criticism*, 1919, pp. i–iv.

III

How does a critic give the impression that he carries big guns? Some of the younger men, I fancy, believe that the golden rule is to bring in references to little-known authors of the seventeenth century. Paul Elmer More, one of the critical personages of this country, has no such flimsy apparatus. He gives some people the impression that he carries big guns largely because his temperament and habit of mind are the same as a conservative banker's, and this conservative banker-temperament qualifies him to act importantly. He manages, that is to say, to take no chances on the uncertain. He makes it his business to suspect his own nature and the nature of others, and to frown especially on everything in the nature of escapade, experiment or revolution. He invests heavily in the gilt-edge securities of the classics, with a somewhat smaller block of Shakespearean and Miltonian stock. Out of sentiment and with definite reservations he goes in a little for the spirit and poetry of early New England. He snaps up practically anything that bears the name of Oxford. These operations he considers legitimate and he exploits them carefully and thoroughly, avoiding gush and extravagance yet committing himself without question. But when it comes to modernity, whether in the person of romantics, agnostics, socialists, liberals, feminists, or what-not, he buttons up his pockets and tightens his lips. He may be compelled to seem depressed and monotonous, to appear as if he had a slow pulse, low blood pressure and subnormal temperature. He doesn't care.

For the present generation that comes flocking to his credit-department, he has nothing but uncritical rudeness and sneers. The world, as he sees it, is "set free from its moorings." This he deplores. And sitting in his stiff morning-coat style, he reflects on the shabbiness, the ingratitude, the disloyalty of all the younger banking firms that dare to disagree with himself and old Pierpont Morgan on the virtues of conservatism and "the bed-rock of character." . . .

The explanation . . . is, in large measure, nothing more or less than invincible ignorance. Along certain lines Mr More shows himself to be illuminating as well as diligent. He throws light on Jonathan Edwards, Charles Eliot Norton and Henry Adams. But when it comes for example to John Morley and John Morley's version of Burke, Mr More is literally unqualified to deal with the facts. To the discussion of the French Revolution he brings none of John Morley's large political enlightenment. He knows nothing of workingmen, of poverty, of the unprotected struggle and rich development of common men and women. . . . Even a little experience of the actual problems of men and women would have acted on most of his abstractions as fresh air acts on mummies. They'd have crumbled to dust and blown away. His ignorance being preserved, however, and being fortified by egoism, we are treated to the spectacle of this conventual man rapping life on the fingers even in the mild cases of the "romantic" Emerson, the "sentimental" Henry Adams, the brutal Samuel Butler, the feminized Oxford and the faithless John Morley.

Such lapses mean more to me than much high discourse about Jonathan Edwards' theology. They mark Mr More for what he is, an exasperated provincial. . . . Even if he were ten times as formidable as he is in his criticism of the generous emotions and the risks of experiment, even if he were ten times as alive to the falsities and fustian of humanitarianism, I still should discount him because he greets novelty with such trembling fury. The classics, after all, were novel in their time—and it was men like Paul Elmer More who gave Socrates the hemlock.

Francis Hackett, Review of *A New England Group and Others* (*Shelburne Essays*, Eleventh Series), *New Republic*, 6 April, 1921 (Vol. 26, pp. 163–164).

IV

A RECENT historian of American literature accords a high place, amongst contemporary critics, to the author of *Shelburne Essays*, and other works. These volumes are dignified as "our nearest approach to those *Causeries du Lundi* of an earlier age," and may well be taken as representative. Typical of the cold inhumanity which a certain type of "cultured person" deems essential is the circumstance related, by Mr Paul Elmer More himself, in explanation of the genesis of these essays. "In a secluded spot," he writes, "in the peaceful valley of the Androscoggin I took upon myself to live two years as a hermit," and *Shelburne Essays* was the fruit of his solitary meditations. The historian is mightily impressed by this evidence of superiority. "In another and far more unusual way he qualified himself for his high office of critic," says Professor Pattee, "he immured himself for two years in solitude." . . . "The period gave him time to read leisurely, thoughtfully, with no nervous subconsciousness that the product of that reading was to be marketable."

What a revelation of combined timidity and intellectual snobbishness there is in this attitude so fatuously endorsed by a writer for the schools! We can imagine what the effect of such a pose must be upon the minds of the students whom the professor would constrain to respect. Only a young prig could pretend to be favourably impressed by this pseudo-Thoreau in the literary backwoods. The impulse of most healthy young men would be to turn in contempt from an art so unnatural as this conception of criticism implies. How are they to know that the Taines, Sainte-Beuves, Brunetières, and Arnolds of the world are not produced by expedients so primitive as to suggest the *mise en scène* of some latter-day Messiah, a Dowie, or a Mrs Baker Eddy? The heralds of new theologies may find the paraphernalia of asceticism and aloofness a useful part of their stock in trade—neither is associated with the great criticism of literature. The *causeries* of Sainte-Beuve were not written in an ivory tower, yet they show no traces of that "nervous subconsciousness" which our professor finds inseparable from reading that is "marketable."

The suspicion of insincerity in this craving for the wilderness will be strengthened by reference to the first of Mr More's volumes. Whatever may have been the case of its successors, this work was certainly the product of his retirement. What, then, are the subjects of such a delicate nature that they could not be discussed within the sound of "the noisy jargon of the market-place"? Of the eleven essays, only four deal with writers whose proximity to the critic's own age might justify a retreat, in order that they be judged impartially, and without reference to popular enthusiasm and the prevalent fashion of the moment. The seven most substantial studies in the book are devoted to flogging horses so dead that no fear of their kicking existed. *A Hermit's Notes on Thoreau, The Solitude of Nathaniel Hawthorne, The Influence of Emerson, The Spirit of Carlyle*—these are a few of the startling topics which Mr More could discuss only with fasting and prayer! Any European schoolmaster could have written these essays in the leisure moments of his Sunday afternoons or Easter vacation.

No more remarkable profundity or originality will be found in the critic's essays in contemporary literature. His strictures upon Lady Gregory's versions of the Irish epic, and his comments upon the Celtic Renaissance in general are the commonplaces of all hostile English criticism. "The shimmering hues of decadence rather than the strong colours of life," is the phrase in which he attempts to estimate the poetry of the Literary Revival in Ireland. In fact, for all his isolation Mr More was obsessed by the critical cant of the hour, as witness his readiness to apply the term "decadent" to all and sundry. The work of Arthur Symons is illuminated by this appellation, as is also that of W. B. Yeats. The jargon of the literary market-place, to vary Mr More's own *cliché*, is all that he seems to have found in that "peaceful valley of the Androscoggin." Even poor Tolstoy is branded as "a decadent with the humanitarian superimposed," an application of the word which renders its previous employment meaningless. As a crowning example of incomprehension may be cited Mr More's opinion that the English poet, Lionel Johnson, is "the one great . . . and genuinely significant poet of the present Gaelic movement." In the circumstances it is not surprising that he should pronounce Irishmen incapable of exploiting adequately the themes of Celtic literature. For this task he considers the Saxon genius more qualified.

With these examples before us it is unnecessary to examine the remaining volumes of *Shelburne Essays*. Having started with a distorted conception of the critical office, the author naturally contributed nothing helpful to the literature of American criticism. His laborious platitudes do not help us to a better appreciation of the dead, his dogmatic hostility nullifies his judgements upon the living. Not once has he a word of discerning censure or encouragement for any rising talent. Like most of his colleagues, Mr More prefers to exercise his faculties at the expense of reputations already established, save when he condescends to repeat the commonplaces of complaint against certain of the better known modern writers. He is so busy with Mrs Gaskell, Charles Lamb, Milton, Plato, and Dickens that he can find time to mention only some fifteen Americans, not one of them living.

> Ernest Boyd, "American Civilization as an Irishman Sees It" (pp. 489–507), in *Civilization in the United States,* An Inquiry by Thirty Americans, edited by Harold E. Stearns, 1922.

V

Nothing new is to be found in the latest volume of Paul Elmer More's *Shelburne Essays.*[2] The learned author, undismayed by the winds of anarchic doctrine that blow down his Princeton stovepipe, continues to hold fast to the notions of his earliest devotion. He is still the gallant champion sent against the Romantic Movement by the forces of discipline and decorum. He is still the eloquent fugleman of the Puritan ethic and aesthetic. In so massive a certainty, so resolute an immovability there is something almost magnificent. These are somewhat sad days for the exponents of that ancient correctness. The Goths and the Huns are at the gate, and as they batter wildly they throw dead cats, perfumed lingerie, tracts against predestination, and the bound files of the *Nation,* the *Freeman* and the *New Republic*

[2] *A New England Group and Others* (*Shelburne Essays,* Eleventh Series).

over the fence. But the din does not flabbergast Dr More. High above the blood-bathed battlements there is a tower, of ivory within and solid ferro-concrete without, and in its austere upper chamber he sits undaunted, solemnly composing an elegy upon Jonathan Edwards, "the greatest theologian and philosopher yet produced in this country." . . .

More has a solid stock of learning in his lockers; he is armed and outfitted as none of the pollyannas who trail after him is armed and outfitted; he is, perhaps, the nearest approach to a genuine scholar that we have in America, God save us all! But there is simply no truculence in him, no flair for debate, no lust to do execution upon his foes. His method is wholly *ex parte*. Year after year he simply iterates and reiterates his misty protests, seldom changing so much as a word. Between his first volume and his last there is not the difference between Gog and Magog. Steadily, ploddingly, vaguely, he continues to preach the gloomy gospel of tightness and restraint. He was against "the electric thrill of freer feeling" when he began, and he will be against it on that last grey day—I hope it long post-dates my own hanging—when the ultimate embalmer sneaks upon him with velvet tread, and they haul down the flag to half-staff at Princeton, and the readers of the New York *Evening Journal* note that an obscure somebody named Paul E. More is dead.

> H. L. Mencken, *Prejudices*, Third Series, 1922, pp. 176, 178–179.[3]

VI

I CANNOT suppose, as a matter of fact, from the inappropriateness of Mr More's remarks about Joyce, that he has ever done

[3] Mr Mencken's books contain frequent incidental references to Mr More, such as the following: "To More or Babbitt only death can atone for the primary offence of the artist. . . . In all the *Shelburne Essays* there is none on Howells, or on Churchill, or on Mrs Wharton; More seems to think of American literature as expiring with Longfellow and Donald G. Mitchell. . . . He is warned, reading More and Babbitt, that the literatus who lets feeling get into his compositions is a psychic fornicator, and under German influences." (*Prejudices*, Second Series, 1920, pp. 22, 23, 26–27.) In Mr Mencken's *Treatise on the Gods* (1930, p. 306), there is a short passage re-

anything more than look into him, and I will venture to say that
the Humanists' high-handed habit of disposing jeeringly of contemporary writers whom they plainly haven't read is an even
more serious scandal to their cause than their misrepresentation
of the ancients, whom they have at least conscientiously studied.
So Mr More, in *The Demon of the Absolute*, has described Dos
Passos's *Manhattan Transfer* as "an explosion in a cesspool"
without apparently the faintest suspicion that Dos Passos intends his novel as an indictment of the same social conditions of
which Mr More himself has always taken such a gloomy view.
But not only is Mr More unable to recognize in *Manhattan
Transfer* the work of a man who, like himself, has, as he once
wrote of his own state of mind, been "deafened by the 'indistinguishable roar' of the streets" and can "make no sense of the
noisy jargon of the market place" and who finally causes his
hero to escape from the modern American city with as much
relief as Mr More ever did when he went into his celebrated retreat at Shelburne; he has not even succeeded in informing himself from any other sources as to Dos Passos's general point of
view. If Dos Passos had been a second-rate eighteenth-century
essayist, Mr More would know everything about him, political
opinions and all—if he had been the humblest New England
poet (of the seventeenth century, that is) Mr More would have
read him through.

. . . I cannot avoid coming to the conclusion that Mr More's
primary objection is to having anyone, either in science or in
art, find out anything new, and I cannot explain this state of

ferring to Mr More's later work: "In the domain of pure ideas one branch
of the church clings to the archaic speculations of Thomas Aquinas and the
other labours under the barbaric nonsense of John Calvin. The recurrent
effort to reconcile Platonism to the Christian system only serves to show
how far the two stand apart. Plato, as a man of science, was surely cautious
enough, but the church has never been able, in any true sense, to take him
in. Turn to the laborious works of Paul Elmer More if you would see how
brilliantly modern a Greek of the Fourth Century before Christ must appear when his ideas are ranged beside those which inform even the most
Modernistic variety of Christianity. More is constantly confronting a painful choice between Christian theology and the elements of rational thinking,
and every time he allows his congenital piety to make any concession to the
former he has to do violence to the latter."

mind except on the hypothesis that Mr More is really an old-fashioned Puritan who has lost the Puritan theology without having lost the Puritan dogmatism. Mr More is more certainly than Professor Babbitt a man of some imagination; he is able to follow the thought of the modern world, as appears from his very intelligent and often sensitive expositions of the ideas of other writers (if they are not absolutely contemporaries)—but some iron inhibition always comes into play in the long run to restrain Mr More from agreeing with anything which he finds in modern philosophy or art. Everything he encounters there seems to terrify him, even when, as in the case of Whitehead, one would think he ought to find it reassuring. One law for man and another law for thing is the whole of philosophy for Mr More, as the will to refrain is the whole of morals. Outside these —anywhere, that is, except among the brave little band of Humanists—he sees only the abyss. It is as if Mr More, on one of his sides, were capable of meeting on his own ground the great modern philosopher or poet, but as if some other element in his nature—which he tries to foist upon us, too, as the universal and eternal moral law of the "inner check"—had operated to make him afraid of philosophy and poetry, so that, in spite of his vigorous intellect and his esthetic sensibility, he is unable to allow himself to profit by any book not written sufficiently long ago to have acquired an academic sanction almost equivalent to a religious one.

A certain passage from Whitehead's *Science and the Modern World* is quoted by Mr More as follows: "When Darwin or Einstein proclaim[s] theories which modify our ideas, it is a triumph for science." Mr More is going on to criticize this passage, but in the meantime he has observed that Whitehead has been so indiscreet as to write "proclaim" as a plural verb after two subjects connected by "or," and where any ordinary critic would either have left Whitehead's sentence as he wrote it or have made him a present of the singular ending without calling the reader's attention to it, Mr More has put it in brackets, as who should comment scornfully "[sic]!" Mr More may not be able, or may not dare, to imagine, as Whitehead has done, a metaphysical explanation of the relations between the organic and the inorganic worlds, but he can, and, by Heaven, he will, correct Whitehead's grammar!

> Edmund Wilson, "Notes on Babbitt and More," in *The Critique of Humanism*, edited by C. Hartley Grattan, 1930, pp. 56–57, 59–60.[4]

VII

PAUL ELMER MORE, student of Socrates, Plato, the Indians, the Poets, and comparative religions, at the beginning of his career, displayed few of the Socratic virtues. Though he has been critic, scholar, preacher, and sage, he has been these almost accidentally, and not as a result of a definite purpose. His criticism has not been directed to any particular end, nor addressed to any particular public; yet, as he is chiefly a moralist, he cannot have been writing for his own edification. He is a prophet without a people, and his message, lacking any practical intent, is vague and diffuse. He considers himself a follower of Socrates; but though he may agree with many of Socrates' conclusions, in his life and writings he has ignored the methods which Socrates employed and the medium in which he worked. . . .

The *Shelburne Essays* add nothing to our knowledge of More.[5] His ideas are not developed; they are freed from many of their emotional overtones . . . ; they are repeated, and are

---

[4] Elsewhere in his "Notes" Mr Wilson speaks of Mr More's "usual intellectual arrogance," and accuses him of failing to understand how the doctrine of art for art's sake "has been inevitably produced by a particular situation." "From this point of view," Mr Wilson also says, "Mr More's attitude is open to the same sort of criticism as that of the imaginative but rather unintelligent socialist of the type of Upton Sinclair: Upton Sinclair disapproves of works of art which do not point explicitly a socialist moral, as Paul Elmer More disapproves of works of art which do not point explicitly the moral of self-control. Each insists upon denouncing as irresponsible and futile all the writers in whom it is impossible for him to find his own particular moral stated in his own particular terms."

[5] The author's contention is that *The Great Refusal* "contains the key to More's attitude towards life and the essential doctrines of his philosophy." He explains that Mr More's writings were "baffling" to him until he came to *The Great Refusal*, which enabled him to understand practically everything in the *Shelburne Essays* and in *The Greek Tradition*.

often introduced as mechanically as song cues in a musical comedy; and they are stated more authoritatively. . . .

The antipathy to metaphysics, theology, and exact think-ing, in favour of some incommunicable personal experience and private beliefs becomes increasingly pronounced. More does not bother to refute philosophers and theologians any more than did a dreamer in Gotham;[6] he dismisses them and on the strength of his authority assures us that "those questions that touch man's deepest moral experience are not capable of logi-cal solution; indeed, they lose all reality as soon as subjected to dogmatic definition." While for most of us religion without content and without an object, without beliefs, dogmas, and in-stitutions, is meaningless, there is "one man here and there, who can rise to the clear vision of faith unsupported by belief in God." . . .

Of *The Greek Tradition* one can repeat what a dreamer in Gotham said of Albertus Magnus: he "seemed to bring the hard intellectual faculties of the brain into the service of the imagin-ings of the heart, justifying the wildest vagaries of passion." More there concludes that without acceptance of the dogma of the Incarnation mankind is in peril of sinking back into bar-barism. Such a statement seems a long way from the early es-says; but, in reality, it is More's last effort to fortify his "iso-lated life with the virtue and dignity of experience." . . . His Anglicanism, far from representing a new development, is al-ready fully stated in the sixth volume of the *Shelburne Essays*. . . . In fact the thesis and theory of the Greek tradition is expounded in 1905 in the same manner and with the same cogency as it is expounded to-day.[7] . . .

More's ideas have not changed, but only his emotional reac-tions. Some attitudes that he once maintained now seem cold and harsh, and need the support of authority; some supersti-tions that he once condemned now seem desirable; but always he has held to "the inviolable individuality in which lie the pain and glory of our human estate," and he has never demeaned it by an explanation or a defence. At times he seems to confuse

6 The "hero" of *The Great Refusal*.

7 In Mr More's essay on J. Henry Shorthouse, *Shelburne Essays*, Third Series.

the salvation of his soul with the salvation of mankind, but that
is only incidental, for he is scarcely interested in mankind. At
times he seems concerned with literature, but if we recall his
dictum that "the hardest test of the critic, in the exercise of his
special functions, is his tact and sureness in valuing the productions of his own day," and recall his neglect of contemporary
literature and his occasional wrathful utterances about it, we
realize that he has not attempted to be a critic. The best of his
essays are on men like Crabbe, Pope, Lamb, Hazlitt and the
wits, when More forgets his moralizing and chats in the inti-
macy of his library.

The pity of his life is that though he has set out to be a moral
teacher one can learn no lesson from him. He has said too much
and conveyed too little; he has fortified his garden and failed
to cultivate it. He has not been an eclectic; the principles of
assimilation, either a personal moving centre, or an accepted
tradition, he lacks. He has not explored the possibilities of the
American scene, like Hawthorne, or retired from it, like Emily
Dickinson, or remained aloof while within it, like Santayana, or
left it, like Henry James. His purpose from the beginning was
vague; he has followed no line to the end; and one lays down
his work with the feeling that his great erudition was wasted
because it was not directed, because it was not disciplined to
any definite problems or dignified by any consuming interests.

> Bernard Bandler, II, "Paul Elmer More and the External
> World" (pp. 281–297), in *The Critique of Humanism,*
> edited by C. Hartley Grattan, 1930.[8]

VIII[9]

APPARENTLY there has sprung up in the United States a large
reading public with tastes similar to those obtaining among the
English middle classes in 1820 or thereabouts. Children of suc-

---

[8] It is perhaps best to mention that Mr Bandler has explicitly stated that
he wrote the essay from which the above passages are taken on the understanding that "the discussion [of humanism] is about ideas, not words, per-
sonalities, or parties." (*The Critique of Humanism*, p. 281.)

[9] I add to the above excerpts two passages from reviews written in England. Criticism produced for the commercial market, it will be seen, is of
much the same quality on both sides of the Atlantic.

cessful business men, they have inherited the means of leisure
without the traditions of culture necessary for its fine enjoyment, and, conscious at last of this, they are now setting out in
pursuit of the refinements of life with the same strenuous application of mind as their fathers set out in the pursuit of wealth.
Naturally, they have as yet little delicacy or depth of taste:
they are out in search of general information, and what they
really appreciate in literature is its instructive qualities. A
literary critic who intends to inform the minds of a public of
this order must naturally refrain from writing for amateurs of
the finer delicacies of literature, in the manner of Hazlitt, Lamb,
Arnold, or Pater. He must adopt the methods elaborated by
English reviewers of an older school, and not unknown in some
of our modern journals. He must make a display of erudition
about the commonplaces of literary discussion; he must draw
comparisons between different writers, instead of trying to distinguish and define the idiosyncrasy of their genius; and, in
general, he must subordinate matters of fine taste to the com-
moner interest in the biographical side of literature.

This is what Mr More has mainly done in the five volumes of
his *Shelburne Essays,* and on the whole, it seems to us, he has
done it fairly well. . . .

When Mr More . . . turns away from his proper field of
criticism, his work loses much of its interest. In his studies on
English writers, where his personal feelings are not brought
into play, his judgements are often either timid or conventional.
He gets up his subjects industriously, it is true, but he is seldom
able to define vividly the character of the man whose life he
sketches, or to give a clear, personal impression of the quality
of his genius. He is too fond of basing his opinions on the authority of other men. . . . His authentic tastes and sympathies,
as distinct from the tastes and sympathies which he occasionally picks up in his learned excursions, are, we fancy, rather
narrow. In violent reaction against the garish, noisy, whirling
life around him, he has apparently adopted the literary and
political conventions of English society in the eighteenth century. That, we are afraid, is the direction in which the minds of
the public for whom Mr More writes are turning. They are in-

effectual dilettanti in the making, and Mr More, instead of purifying, enlarging, and training their taste, reflects it.

Anonymous review of the first five volumes of the *Shelburne
Essays*, in the *Athenaeum*, 16 January, 1909 (No. 4238,
pp. 67–68).

IX

THE years this American author[10] has spent in England have
inflicted damage on our literature from which it will probably
not recover for a generation. . . .

The case against Mr Eliot is strong. He came over here
about the time of the war, when English criticism was at its low
ebb, when—perhaps because politics exercised such a compelling force on many able minds—it was purely arbitrary and im-
pressionist; and he came over with a defined position.

He had been born in the Middle West where all things are
new. He had been to Harvard and fallen under the influence of
Professor Irving Babbitt and Professor Paul Elmer More, who
have developed a movement known as Humanism, which attempts to correct the intellectual faults likely to arise in a community where all things are new.

This movement very properly attempts to create as lively a
respect as possible for the tradition and achievements of the
past, and it is unfortunate that the limitations of its founders,
which are so considerable as to counterbalance their undoubted
learning, have reduced it to propaganda for a provincial conception of metropolitan gentility.

Its character can be deduced from the fact that Professor
Irving Babbitt considers it a sign of naughty modernity to admire the pictures of Cézanne; and that Professor Paul Elmer
More once counted the references to women's hair in the poetry
of Mr W. B. Yeats and came to the conclusion that they were so
numerous as to be unwholesome. Reading their works, one feels
those who like to call trousers unmentionables have turned their
attention to higher things.

10 Mr T. S. Eliot. The above passage comes from a review of his *Selected
Essays* and of certain other books.

But from these teachers Mr Eliot learned certain facts; that no artist can be isolated, and none can hope to comprehend the present save in the light of the past, and that violence, confusion, and the presentation of unanalysed emotion are poor artistic technique. He was, throughout a period lasting some years, a most useful influence in English criticism.

He put forward certain fundamental truths which had been overlooked, and by his appearance of deliberation and trenchancy he encouraged others to cultivate these virtues in reality.

In recent years, however, Mr Eliot's influence on English letters has been pernicious, for several reasons, which are manifest in this volume. He has made his sense of the need for authority and tradition an excuse for refraining from any work likely to establish where authority truly lies, or to hand on tradition by continuing it in vital creation. . . .

There are people in the Middle West (though mercifully not many, and in diminishing numbers) who . . . honestly believe that Mr Galsworthy must write better than Chaucer because he was born to enjoy the benefits of electric light and the automobile. To them, and not to us, Mr Eliot should address his repetitions of formulae, which have, indeed, no value whatsoever save for these localized heretics.

Rebecca West, "What is Mr T. S. Eliot's Authority as a Critic?" in *The Daily Telegraph*, 30 September, 1932.

INDEX OF NAMES